The Macroeconomics of East Asian Growth

The Macroeconomics of East Asian Growth

Yanrui Wu

University of Western Australia

With contributions from Joanne Boo, Adeline Tan, Alvin W. Tan, Robin Wong and Christopher Heng Boon Yeo

Edward Elgar
Cheltenham, UK • Northampton, MA, USA

Published by
Edward Elgar Publishing Limited
Glensanda House
Montpellier Parade
Cheltenham
Glos GL50 1UA
UK

Edward Elgar Publishing, Inc.
136 West Street
Suite 202
Northampton
Massachusetts 01060
USA

A catalogue record for this book is available from the British Library

Library of Congress Cataloging in Publication Data

Wu, Yanrui.
    The macroeconomics of East Asian growth / Yanrui Wu ;
    with contributions from Joanne Boo ... [et al.].
        p.cm.
    Includes bibliographical references and index.
    1. East Asia–Economic conditions–Case studies. 2. Macroeconomics.
    I. Boo, Joanne. II. Title.

HC460.5.W8 2002
338.95–dc21   2002022845

ISBN 1-84064-638-1

Printed and bound in Great Britain by Bookcraft, Bath

Contents

Figures

Tables

Preface

This volume presents recently completed research outcomes. Some chapters are based on former students' theses submitted to the Department of Economics, University of Western Australia. The authors' names are listed on the title page. The material in this book is original and being published here for the first time. I hope that it will contribute to the understanding of East Asian growth and that it will stimulate more debates. At the completion of the final draft, the world economy is overshadowed by the potential recessions in the United States and Japan. All East Asian economies have to some extent been affected. However, I am optimistic about the economies in the region. The current challenges faced by East Asia will generate more interest in and research on the regional economies.

Work on this volume has benefited from the help of many individuals and institutions. My colleagues in the Department of Economics, University of Western Australia, have always been encouraging and inspiring to me. I benefited a lot from discussions in the seminar rooms and conversations in the corridors. I would also like to thank Joanne Boo, Adeline Tan, Alvin W. Tan, Robin Wong and Christopher Heng Boon Yeo. They all graduated from the Department of Economics at the University of Western Australia, and completed their final-year dissertations under my supervision. They made teaching and supervision very enjoyable. In addition, I thank Kathleen Chindarsi, Paula Madsen, Patricia Wang and Gina Yoon for their assistance with the editorial work at various stages.

Yanrui Wu
University of Western Australia
Perth

1. Introduction

Since the 1980s, economic growth in East Asia has become one of the most important topics that are investigated and debated by economists, policy makers and business advisers. Earlier literature focused on the understanding of sustained high growth in Japan in the 1950s and 1960s and in the four 'Asian Tigers' (Hong Kong, Singapore, South Korea and Taiwan) in the 1970s and 1980s.[1] In the 1990s, the literature was expanded greatly to cover four ASEAN (the Association of South East Asian Nations) economies (Indonesia, Thailand, Malaysia and the Philippines) as those economies achieved impressive performance during that period.[2] More recently, literature on the Chinese economy mushroomed as mainland China maintained robust growth for two decades.[3] Though growth was interrupted temporarily by the dramatic financial crisis in 1997, East Asian economies continue to attract the attention of economists and other researchers. This volume aims to make a substantial contribution to the ongoing debate and hence to the understanding of economic growth in East Asia. In particular, this book addresses some key macroeconomic issues underlying East Asian growth in the past decades. The objective of this introductory chapter is twofold: (a) to shed some light on the broad issues associated with East Asian growth (Section 1.1) and (b) to present an overview of the topics covered in each chapter (Section 1.2).

1.1 STYLIZED FACTS OF EAST ASIAN GROWTH

The economies of East and Southeast Asia grew extremely fast during the past few decades. The eight best performers, i.e. Hong Kong, Singapore, Taiwan, Korea, mainland China, Malaysia, Thailand and Indonesia (henceforth the Asia-8), grew annually at an average rate of about 7.4 per cent during 1970–1999 (Table 1.1). This growth significantly outpaced the industrial countries and every economy in Latin America and Sub-Saharan Africa.[4] Due to robust growth, East Asian developing economies have shown rapid catch-up with advanced countries (see Table 1.1). As a result, a large proportion of humanity has been relieved from poverty in a short period of time. This phenomenon is unprecedented in world history and partly explains the significance and implications of understanding East Asian growth.

Table 1.1   GDP per capita and average growth rates in selected economies

	Average growth rates (%)				GDP per capita (current US$)			
	1970–1979	1980–1989	1990–1999	1970–1999	1970	1980	1990	1999
Hong Kong	9.4	7.3	3.7	6.8	981	5635	13110	26534
Singapore	9.6	7.2	7.7	8.1	896	5010	13556	28970
Taiwan	10.2	8.1	6.4	8.2	426	2326	7881	13344
Korea	8.7	7.6	6.2	7.5	275	1643	5891	10603
Mainland China	7.1	9.8	9.7	8.9	102	307	342	730
Malaysia	7.8	5.9	7.2	7.0	405	1780	2465	740
Thailand	7.0	7.4	5.2	6.5	177	696	1521	483
Indonesia	7.7	5.3	4.8	5.9	91	587	638	1090
Mean of Asia-8	8.4	7.3	6.4	7.4	n.a.	n.a.	n.a.	n.a.
Advanced economies	3.7	3.1	2.6	3.2	n.a.	n.a.	n.a.	n.a.
Japan	5.2	4.6	1.7	3.8	1967	9165	24103	35672
United Kingdom	2.4	2.4	2.0	2.3	2216	9481	14665	24568
United States	3.3	3.0	3.0	3.1	5067	12282	22197	34034
Africa	4.1	2.6	2.1	2.9	n.a.	n.a.	n.a.	n.a.
World	4.5	3.4	3.0	3.6	n.a.	n.a.	n.a.	n.a.

Source: Estimated from the World Economic Outlook 2001 database (IMF 2001).

Many factors have so far been identified as the potential determinants of growth in East Asia. A short list of those factors would include high rates of domestic savings, investment in human capital, economic openness and public policy. Cross-country studies have attempted to examine the interrelationship between growth and its determinants. For example, Sala-i-Martin (1997) identified over 60 economic, social and political factors that might be associated with growth. Though literature in this field has boomed, the issues of debate remain unresolved. This section briefly revisits some of the key issues by presenting some stylized facts.

Increasing Savings and Capital Accumulation Increasing savings and investment have traditionally been viewed as one of the engines of growth. Savings and investment in East Asia increased dramatically during the period of economic take-off. Figure 1.1 shows that the average ratio of savings over GDP has grown steadily since the early 1960s. East Asia's high savings and hence investment were accompanied by large inflows of foreign capital. Table 1.2 clearly shows that the volume of foreign direct investment increased rapidly over the past few decades. Openness to foreign direct investment not only boosted East Asia's access to foreign capital savings but also speeded technology acquisition in the hosting economies.

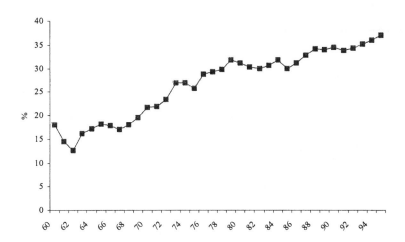

Source: Calculated from the on-line World Savings Database (World Bank 2001).

Figure 1.1 Average savings ratios in eight Asian economies, 1960–95

Human Capital Development East Asian economic growth was accompanied by dramatic change and transformation in the system of education and training. Several indicators have shown that East Asian fast–growing economies made impressive progress in terms of human capital development. Table 1.2 shows that the average rate of secondary school enrolment has increased steadily among the eight Asian economies. Another popular indicator of human capital, i.e. life expectancy, has also shown an upward trend during 1960–1995, according to Table 1.2.

Table 1.2 Human capital and foreign direct investment in eight Asian economies

Year	FDI (US$ billion)	Secondary school enrolment rates (%)	Life expectancy (years)
1960	n.a.	21	57
1965	n.a.	29	60
1970	n.a.	34	63
1975	1.0	45	66
1980	3.4	51	68
1985	4.8	56	70
1990	19.7	60	71
1995	60.0	71	72

Notes: All statistics are calculated from the Global Development Network Growth Database compiled by Easterly and Yu (2000). The figures for life expectancy are the ones every five years beginning with 1962.

Economic Openness and Trade East Asian growth has also been characterized by economic openness to foreign trade. As a result, trade has played an important role in propelling economic growth in the Asian region. Figure 1.2 shows that trade density in East Asia has been rising over time. This upward trend coincides with East Asia's rapid growth during the same period.

Productivity Growth and Technological Progress The role of productivity and hence technological progress in East Asian growth has been controversial, in particular after the publication of the provocative article by Krugman (1994). While more detailed investigation is to be presented later in this volume, a glimpse at Figure 1.3 reveals that labour productivity in East Asian economies has been rising continuously over recent decades.

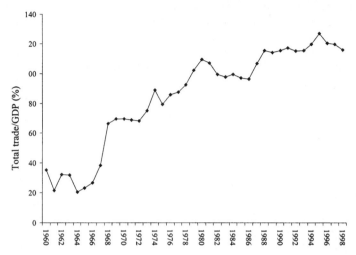

Source: Easterly and Yu (2000).

Figure 1.2 Openness indicator in eight Asian economies, 1960–1998

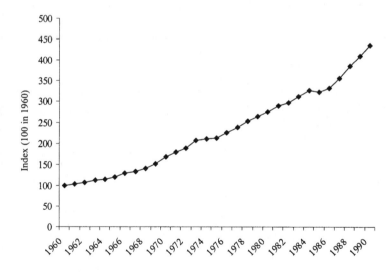

Source: Easterly and Yu (2000).

Figure 1.3 Labour productivity index in eight Asian economies, 1960–1990

Public Policies An analysis of East Asian growth without mentioning public policies is inadequate. Though diverse in culture, political systems and resource endowment, East Asian governments have pursued very similar public policies. Economists have so far identified the following commonalities: small governments, small fiscal deficits, investing in people, infrastructure development and economic openness (Krueger 1995 and Hughes 1995). In those areas, East Asian governments have all played important roles.

1.2 OUTLINE OF THE CHAPTERS

The determinants of East Asian growth are multi-faceted and controversial. Empirical work on the determinants of growth has mushroomed over the past decade.[5] The findings in the existing literature differ from each other as the samples used and objectives of the studies vary. The aim of this study is not to be exhaustive but to focus on several thematic topics with a thorough examination. The chapters in this volume are based on research which is original and appears here for the first time. In dealing with each topic, an analytical framework is proposed and applied to empirical data. Summary information about the core chapters is presented in Table 1.3.

The 1980s and 1990s have witnessed the emergence of many Asian economies as important traders in the world. How has openness to trade and investment affected growth performance in those economies? This question is often tackled with the traditional growth regression method. However, the findings in the existing literature are still inconclusive. Chapter 2 proposes an alternative approach which is employed to examine the impact of openness on the sources of growth in selected Asia Pacific Economic Cooperation (APEC) members. It is found that openness affects not only efficiency changes but also the structure of production technology. While APEC developed members have on the average performed better than their developing counterparts, the latter have shown rapid catch-up with their rich neighbors according to this study.

Advocates of stock market development argue that stock markets boost economic growth through risk diversification, the creation of liquidity thereby facilitating investments in the long run, a reduction in information asymmetry, and changes in incentives for corporate control. Chapter 3 attempts to shed some light on the effects of stock market development on economic growth in Asia. The economies covered include Hong Kong, India, Japan, Korea, Malaysia, Pakistan, the Philippines, Singapore, Taiwan and Thailand. Cross-country regression results show some connection between stock market development and economic growth. But the relationship is sensitive to the choice of samples and indicators.

Table 1.3 Summary of the chapters

Chapter	Topic	Method	Sample
2	Openness and growth	Frontier production function	Cross-section/16 APEC economies
3	Impact of stock markets	Regression approach	Up to 14 economies
4	Intra-industry trade	Index approach	ASEAN-5
5	Role of productivity growth	Production function	Taiwan
6	Engines of growth	Growth equation	Singapore
7	Asian financial crisis	Descriptive analysis	Asian economies

Chapter 4 investigates the structure of ASEAN trade flows over the period of 1986–95. Methodological and empirical issues associated with intra-industry trade (IIT) are reviewed and analysed. Data for Indonesia, Malaysia, Singapore, Thailand and the Philippines are examined using measures of both static and dynamic intra-industry trade. It is found that both the static and the dynamic marginal intra-industry trade values have grown steadily over the period of study. However, trade liberalization does not occur without costs. Adjustment costs resulting from the formation of the ASEAN Free Trade Area (AFTA) were comparatively higher for Indonesia and the Philippines.

The growth performance of the East Asian economy has attracted a very intense and lively debate on the possibilities of sustained growth. On one hand, traditional growth theories dismiss the notion of sustained growth because of the assumption of diminishing returns to capital. On the other hand, new growth theories believe sustained growth can be achieved by promoting technology. Chapter 5 presents a critical examination of the recent literature and raises questions about the sources of growth in East Asian countries. To emphasise the importance of total factor productivity (TFP) in East Asian growth, a case study is conducted to analyse the sources of rapid growth in Taiwan. A further analysis is performed to examine the factors that drive TFP growth. It is found that TFP growth is strongly correlated with the growth of the manufacturing sector in Taiwan. It is also found that trade and government expenditure are important factors affecting TFP growth.

Several models of economic growth have been put forward to explain the East Asian "miracle" but those based on new growth theory may not necessarily be useful in empirical studies. Chapter 6 identifies the macroeconomic determinants of growth for Singapore. Three alternative engines of growth are considered. The results show that compulsory savings and government expenditures on economic services are not conducive to growth. However, trade as an engine of growth is favoured in the case of Singapore.

Finally, Chapter 7 examines the causes of the Asian financial crisis in 1997. The main goal is to provide an assessment of the different explanations advocated so far by different authors. This chapter also discusses the impact of the crisis and analyses the recovery process. It also sheds light on the prospect of growth in Asia.

NOTES

1. Examples include Galenson (1979), Kuo, Ranis and Fee (1981) on Taiwan, Corden (1984) on Singapore and Morishima (1982) on Japan.
2. Representative work includes Hill (1989) on Indonesia, Warr (1993) on Thailand and the World Bank (1993) on East Asia.
3. The World Bank (1997a), Maddison (1998), Woo (1998) and Young (2000) all focused on the Chinese economy, to cite a few.

4. With the exception of diamond-rich Botswana according to the World Bank (1993).
5. See Barro and Sala-i-Martin (1995), and Barro (1997).

2. Openness and Growth

The new growth theory postulates that openness to trade and investment provides access to new technology, enhances efficiency and encourages innovation (Harrison 1996). Thus, an economy that is more open will benefit from greater spillover effect and, therefore, grow faster than a less open economy. However, empirical studies on the relationship between openness and growth are still inconclusive and leave themselves open to criticism by trade-sceptics (Edwards 1998).

Most existing studies applied growth equations to investigate the impact of openness on productivity and growth performance across countries or in individual economies. The literature can be roughly divided into two categories. The first category consists of papers that focus on the impact of international trade on productivity and growth (for example, Edwards 1992, Levine and Renelt 1992). The second group develops indicators of openness and examines the relationship between openness, productivity and growth (for example, Sachs and Warner 1995, Barro and Sala-i-Martin 1995). For example, Harrison (1996) investigated the impact of a wide range of openness measures on economic growth in selected groups of countries. Though the findings are inconclusive, greater openness is found to be associated with higher growth when openness is statistically significant. More recently, Edwards (1998) presented a study of the relationship between openness and total factor productivity growth in 93 countries. The author concluded that productivity growth is faster in more open economies. Coe, Helpman and Hoffmaister (1997) also provided evidence that developing countries with limited investment in R&D can boost productivity by trading with more developed countries that have accumulated a large stock of knowledge from their R&D activities.

In those studies cited, the openness variable is either included in the production function as an intercept or introduced into the productivity equation as a regressor. Both approaches suffer from some drawbacks. On the one hand, the production function approach assumes that 'openness' has a shift effect on technology but has no impact on the structure of the technology. On the other hand, the productivity approach follows a two-stage method, ie. the production function and productivity regression are estimated separately. Thus, there is no interaction between 'openness' and other factor inputs. To overcome those problems, this chapter proposes a stochastic frontier approach and applies it to analyse the relationship between openness, productivity and growth among the Asia Pacific Economic Cooperation (APEC) economies. The next section presents the analytical framework and discusses the main hypotheses to be tested (Section 2.1). This is followed by descriptions of empirical models and data issues (Sections 2.2 and 2.3). Then, the interpretation of the results is presented, with the final section summarising the main findings.

2.1 ANALYTICAL FRAMEWORK

The econometric model used in this study is related to the concept of output-oriented technical efficiency proposed by Farrell (1957) and popularised by Aigner, Lovell and Schmidt (1977), and Meeusen and van den Broeck (1977). The panel data version of this model can be presented as follows

$$y_{it}^F = f(x_{it}, t) \quad , t=1,\ldots, T \text{ and } i = 1,\ldots,N \tag{2.1}$$

where y_{it}^F represents the frontier production level or best practice output for the ith economy at time t, given technology $f(\bullet)$. Then, any observed output, y_{it} given inputs x_{it} , may be expressed as

$$y_{it} = y_{it}^F TE_{it} = f(x_{it}, t) TE_{it} \tag{2.2}$$

where TE_{it} indicates technical efficiency, defined as the ratio of the observed output over the best practice output. Equation (2.2) can be transformed into

$$\dot{y}_{it} = f_x \dot{x}_{it} + f_t + \dot{TE}_{it} \tag{2.3}$$

where dotted variables denote percentage changes, and f_x and f_t represent the derivatives of $f(\bullet)$ with respect to x and t. Under constant returns to scale assumption, Equation (2.3) is identical to the model developed by Nishimuzu and Page (1982). Without the assumption of constant returns to scale, Equation (2.3) implies

$$\dot{TFP}_{it} = f_t + (\Sigma e_{ijt} - 1) \Sigma (e_{ijt} \dot{x}_{ijt}) / \Sigma e_{ijt} + \dot{TE}_{it} \tag{2.4}$$

where $e_{ijt} = \partial \log f / \partial \log x_{ijt}$ is the output elasticity of the jth input x_{ijt}. Equation (2.4) decomposes total factor productivity (TFP) growth into three components: technological progress, scale economies and technical efficiency change. This decomposition extends the work by Solow (1957).

A popular empirical version of Equation (2.2) is the following logarithmic model

$$\log y_{it} = \log f(x_{it}, t) + v_{it} - u_{it} \qquad (2.5)$$

where v_{it} is a random error term and u_{it} is a non-negative random variable which is assumed to capture technical inefficiency in production and to be independent of v_{it}. The above frontier framework has been widely applied to the measurement of performance at both the macro and micro level.[1] Recently, it has been further extended to analyse the influence of firm- or country-specific conditions on productive performance. For example, Huang and Liu (1994) developed a model in which the environmental variables (z_{it}'s) affect technical inefficiency in the following form, ie. $u_{it} = u_{it}(x_{it}, z_{it}, t)$. Battese and Coelli (1995) also proposed a similar model in which $u_{it} = u_{it}(z_{it}, t)$.

This study employs a hybrid of the models by Huang and Liu (1994) and Battese and Coelli (1995) to examine the impact of openness on productivity and growth in APEC economies. Symbolically, the proposed model can be expressed as

$$\log y_{it} = \log f(x_{it}, o_{it}, t) + v_{it} - u_{it}(x_{it}, o_{it}, t) \qquad (2.6)$$

This model implies that openness affects not only technical inefficiency, u_{it}, but also the structure of technology, $f(\bullet)$. The estimation of model (2.6) is however complicated and controversial.[2] The empirical investigation in this paper considers the following five optional models:

- Model A assumes the absence of the influences of openness. This is a standard stochastic frontier model as proposed by Aigner, Lovell and Schmidt (1977), and Meeusen and van den Broeck (1977).

- Model B assumes the presence of the influences of openness on technical efficiency but their effects are neutral. This is the efficiency effect model considered by Battese and Coelli (1995), Huang and Liu (1994), Reifschneider and Stevenson (1991) and Kumbhakar et al. (1991).

- Model C assumes that openness affects not only technical efficiency but also the technology of production. This model is an extension of model B. Openness does not affect the 'slope' of the production frontier but has a 'shift' effect on the structure of technology.

- Model D assumes non-neutral effects of openness on technology. This model is an extension of model C. In this model, openness has not only a 'shift' effect on the production frontier but also affects the 'shape' of the frontier curve.

- Model E assumes non-neutral effects of openness on both technology and technical efficiency. This model combines models C and D.

Models A and B can be estimated by the maximum likelihood approach as proposed by Aigner, Lovell and Schmidt (1977), and Meeusen and van den Broeck (1977). The estimation of models C, D and E is however controversial.[3] For the purpose of comparison, a common approach, ie. the maximum likelihood approach, is employed to estimate all five models. The statistical package is FRONTIER (Coelli 1992).

2.2 EMPIRICAL MODELS AND DATA ISSUES

Empirical Models

The empirical version of model (2.6) can be expressed as follows

$$log\,Y_{it} = \alpha_0 + \alpha_{0d}D + (\beta_0 + \beta_{0d}D)t + \frac{1}{2}\beta_1 t^2 + (\beta_2 + \beta_3 t)\,log\,K_{it}$$

$$+ (\beta_4 + \beta_5 t)logL_{it} + \frac{1}{2}[\beta_6 (logK_{it})^2 + \beta_7\,logK_{it}\,logL_{it} + \beta_8 (logL_{it})^2]$$

$$+ (\beta_9 + \beta_{10}t + \beta_{11}\,logK_{it} + \beta_{12}\,logL_{it})O_{it} + v_{it} - u_{it} \qquad (2.7)$$

where Y_{it} represents output, K_{it} and L_{it} are inputs (ie. capital and labour), O_{it} is the indicator of openness, D is a dummy variable distinguishing the United States from other APEC members, v_{it} and u_{it} are defined in Equation (2.5) with u_{it} being the non-negative truncation of the following normal distribution $N(\mu_{it}, \sigma_u^2)$ where

$$\mu_{it} = \varsigma_0 + \varsigma_1 t + (\varsigma_2 + \varsigma_3\,log\,K_{it} + \varsigma_4\,log\,L_{it})O_{it} \qquad (2.8)$$

Given equations (2.7) and (2.8), the percentage changes in technological progress, scale economics, technical efficiency and total factor productivity can be computed as follows

$$TP_{it} = d \log Y_{it} / dt$$
$$= \beta_0 + \beta_{0d}D + \beta_1 t + \beta_3 \log K_{it} + \beta_5 \log L_{it} + \beta_{10}O_{it} \qquad (2.9)$$

$$\dot{SE}_{it} = (e_{itL} + e_{itK} - 1)(e_{itL} \dot{L}_{it} + e_{itK} \dot{K}_{it})/(e_{itL} + e_{itK}) \qquad (2.10)$$

$$\dot{TE}_{it} = TE_{it} / TE_{it-1} - 1 \qquad (2.11)$$

$$\dot{TFP}_{it} = \dot{TP}_{it} + \dot{SE}_{it} + \dot{TE}_{it} \qquad (2.12)$$

Data Issues

The analytical framework described in the preceding section is applied to a data set of sixteen Asia Pacific Economic Cooperation (APEC) economies for the period 1980–1997. Output takes the value of GDP. It is expressed in 1985 international dollars. The conversion rates of local currencies against the international dollar are derived from the Global Development Network Growth Database.[4] The employment statistics are from the International Labour Organisation online database supplemented by other sources.[5] The value of capital stock is derived from data on capital formation and stock changes reported by the International Monetary Fund (IMF 2000). The following formula is employed to estimate capital stock:

$$K(t) = \Delta K(t) + (1 - \delta)K(t-1) \qquad (2.13)$$

where K(t) is the capital stock at time t for each economy, δ a given rate of depreciation and $\Delta K(t)$ the incremental capital at time t. $\Delta K(t)$ is available for the period 1970–1997 for all economies. The data series for $\Delta K(t)$ are estimated back to the year 1900. Accordingly, equation (2.13) is expanded to

$$K(t) = \Sigma_0^{t-1901}(1 - \delta)^k \Delta K(t-k) + (1 - \delta)^{t-1900} K(1900) \qquad (2.14)$$

Equation (2.14) implies that, given the value of capital stock in 1900 and an appropriate rate of depreciation, a capital stock series for each economy can be derived. In this study, it is assumed that the rate of depreciation is 7 per cent and K(1900) equals zero.

The openness indicator is the most controversial.[6] Given the limitations of data, three variables, i.e. the ratios of exports, imports and foreign direct investment over GDP, are used to derive a 'grand' composite index of openness. The principal component approach is employed to estimate the weights for the 1980s and 1990s, respectively.[7] Summary statistics of the sample are presented in Table 2.1. According to this table, the East Asian economies with the exception of Japan and the Philippines have indeed achieved high growth in the past two decades. It is noted that high growth was matched by the rapid expansion of capital stock in those economies. The openness indicators in Table 2.1 have shown that all but four economies (Japan, Korea, Taiwan and Singapore) have become more open over time. It is also noted that the openness indicators for large economies eg. US, Japan and mainland China are relatively small. This is a technicality problem which has also been raised by other authors. However, the most important information one can get from Table 2.1 is the trend of openness among the economies considered.

2.3 ESTIMATION RESULTS

Models A to E are estimated and tested against each other. The test results in Table 2.2 show that model E is the preferred one. As a result, the estimation results of model E are reported in Table 2.3 and the analyses followed are hence based on this model. Table 2.3 shows that most coefficient estimates are statistically significant and of correct sign. In particular, openness is found to have a positive impact on both technological progress and technical efficiency. Given the estimates in Table 2.3, the rates of technological progress, technical efficiency and productivity growth can be computed following Equations (2.9) to (2.12). A summary of the results is presented in Table 2.4. Several interesting observations are summarised as follows:

First, on the average, total factor productivity growth has been positive during the period considered. In general, APEC developed economies have performed better than their developing counterparts. While TFP performance in APEC developing economies has fluctuated considerably over time, it has been relatively stable among the developed members (Figures 2.1 and 2.2). However, productivity growth has declined in the 1990s. In particular, the largest decline has occurred in Japan, Korea and the Philippines. The impact of the 1997 Asian financial crisis on productivity performance is also evident in Figure 2.2.

Second, according to Table 2.4, technological progress has been the dominant contributor to TFP growth. Countries leading the 'innovation' race include the US, Singapore and Hong Kong among the developed members,

Table 2.1 Summary statistics of the sample

Economies	1980s			1990s			Openness		
	GDP	Capital	Labour	GDP	Capital	Labour	1980s	1990s	Changes
Australia	3.508	2.926	2.388	2.604	2.088	1.076	0.201	0.241	0.040
Canada	3.468	2.446	2.033	1.362	1.440	0.802	0.310	0.397	0.086
Hong Kong	7.510	8.746	2.744	5.276	8.025	1.829	1.303	1.710	0.408
Japan	4.093	2.782	1.127	2.274	3.222	0.852	0.140	0.114	−0.026
New Zealand	2.012	0.296	1.575	2.544	0.267	1.817	0.367	0.379	0.012
Singapore	7.163	7.544	3.240	8.085	6.659	3.470	1.865	1.771	−0.094
USA	2.446	2.365	1.740	2.335	1.823	1.250	0.118	0.146	0.028
Sub-mean	4.314	3.872	2.121	3.497	3.360	1.585	0.615	0.680	0.065

Chile	3.581	6.061	3.342	6.880	8.533	2.493	0.319	0.388	0.069
Mainland China	6.015	6.465	3.038	8.700	7.522	1.817	0.119	0.237	0.118
Indonesia	6.412	11.983	3.763	6.985	8.223	2.157	0.282	0.337	0.055
Korea	7.668	8.593	2.556	7.675	11.071	2.293	0.404	0.388	−0.016
Malaysia	6.040	8.979	3.128	9.206	11.488	3.767	0.685	1.094	0.409
Mexico	2.233	4.105	2.792	3.766	3.720	3.315	0.179	0.290	0.111
Philippines	2.022	1.176	2.697	3.370	2.686	3.109	0.302	0.477	0.175
Taiwan	7.746	5.609	2.536	6.425	7.037	1.329	0.514	0.480	−0.033
Thailand	6.132	7.914	4.478	7.077	10.664	0.995	0.326	0.514	0.188
Sub-mean	5.317	6.765	3.148	6.676	7.883	2.364	0.348	0.467	0.119
Mean	4.878	5.499	2.699	5.285	5.904	2.023	0.465	0.560	0.095

Notes: Statistics in the 'GDP', 'Capital' and 'Labour' columns are mean percentage rates of growth and those in the 'Openness' columns are the indicators of openness. The changes in openness are simply the differences between the indicators for the 1980s and 1990s, respectively.

Table 2.2   Selected tests and test results

Models	LL	χ^2 statistics	Tests	df.	Decisions
A	158.6	240.4 (18.5)	E vs A	7	reject model A
B	164.8	228.0 (16.8)	E vs B	6	reject model B
C	181.4	194.8 (15.1)	E vs C	5	reject model C
D	194.6	168.4 (9.2)	E vs D	2	reject model D

Notes: LL stands for log likelihood function and df the degrees of freedom. The numbers in parentheses are the corresponding values from the χ^2-table at the 1% level of significance.

and Malaysia, Korea and Taiwan among the developing members. In general, APEC developed members are more 'innovative' than their poorer counterparts. However, Japan is an outlier. It has lagged behind other developed economies in terms of technological progress.

Third, technical efficiency change has generally made a positive contribution to productivity growth in the 1980s but its role has diminished in the 1990s. On the one hand, among the developed group, Japan appeared to be a good learner in the 1980s. On the other hand, among the developing members, Korea, Taiwan and Mainland China have been the best learners. In particular, in the 1990s, Mainland China outperformed all other APEC economies by showing rapid catch-up. In the mean time, the Philippines has been the main loser among the developing members.

Finally, it seems there is little gain from scale economies among the APEC economies. This finding is alarming as it implies that countries relying on scale expansion to stimulate growth (i.e. the extensive growth model) may fail to achieve their growth targets.

2.4   CONCLUDING REMARKS

In summary, this chapter employs an alternative approach to examine the impact of openness on productivity and growth performance among APEC economies. Five optional models are discussed and tested in the empirical analyses. It is found that, according to this study, openness affects not only efficiency changes but also the structure of production technology (i.e. technological progress). This study thus extends the conventional research on the relationship between productivity growth and economic openness.

In general, the empirical analyses have shown that, in terms of productivity growth, APEC developed members have performed better than their developing counterparts. In particular, APEC developed economies, led by

Table 2.3   Estimation results

Variables	Coefficients	Standard errors
Constant	−3.431	0.398
Dummy	0.337	0.064
Time	0.048	0.012
Time*Dummy	0.012	0.005
$\frac{1}{2}$ Time*Time	0.001	0.000
log(Capital)	0.701	0.133
Time*log(Capital)	0.012	0.002
log(Labour)	0.704	0.138
Time*log(Labour)	−0.015	0.002
$\frac{1}{2}$ log(Capital)*log(Capital)	0.053	0.042
$\frac{1}{2}$ log(Capital)*log(Labour)	−0.071	0.076
$\frac{1}{2}$ log(Labour)*log(Labour)	−0.023	0.035
Openness	−4.106	0.396
Openness*Time	0.011	0.003
Openness*log(Capital)	−0.444	0.096
Openness*log(Labour)	0.815	0.107
σ^2	0.029	0.004
λ	0.986	0.010
Intercept	−0.136	0.061
Openness	−7.740	0.588
Time	−0.041	0.007
Openness*log(Capital)	−0.788	0.117
Openness*log(Labour)	1.518	0.111
log likelihood function	278.805	

Notes: $\sigma^2 = \sigma_v^2 + \sigma_u^2$ and $\lambda = \sigma_u^2 \,/\, \sigma^2$ where σ_v^2 and σ_u^2 are the variances of v_{it} and u_{it}, respectively, as defined in Equation (2.5).

Table 2.4   Average growth rates of total factor productivity (TFP), technological progress (TP), technical efficiency (TE) and scale economies (SE)

Economies	TFP		TE		TP		SE	
	1980s	1990s	1980s	1990s	1980s	1990s	1980s	1990s
APEC developed economies								
Australia	0.0377	0.0350	0.0093	0.0014	0.0292	0.0348	-0.0008	-0.0012
Canada	0.0417	0.0232	0.0136	-0.0111	0.0293	0.0355	-0.0013	-0.0011
Hong Kong	0.0568	0.0449	0.0158	-0.0054	0.0394	0.0511	0.0016	-0.0007
Japan	0.0594	0.0246	0.0374	-0.0014	0.0250	0.0307	-0.0030	-0.0047
New Zealand	0.0397	0.0437	0.0058	0.0059	0.0335	0.0378	0.0005	0.0000
Singapore	0.0508	0.0522	0.0007	-0.0007	0.0466	0.0519	0.0035	0.0010
USA	0.0423	0.0364	0.0104	-0.0009	0.0354	0.0408	-0.0035	-0.0035
Sub-mean	0.0469	0.0372	0.0133	-0.0018	0.0340	0.0404	-0.0004	-0.0014

APEC developing economies

Chile	0.0140	0.0424	-0.0101	0.0136	0.0236	0.0308	0.0005	-0.0020
Mainland China	0.0261	0.0330	0.0281	0.0334	0.0098	0.0176	-0.0118	-0.0179
Indonesia	0.0221	0.0305	0.0181	0.0188	0.0145	0.0227	-0.0105	-0.0110
Korea	0.0765	0.0099	0.0564	-0.0126	0.0239	0.0316	-0.0038	-0.0091
Malaysia	0.0188	0.0113	-0.0096	-0.0233	0.0286	0.0397	-0.0002	-0.0051
Mexico	0.0105	0.0142	-0.0098	-0.0102	0.0228	0.0288	-0.0025	-0.0045
Philippines	0.0389	-0.0221	0.0204	-0.0447	0.0194	0.0254	-0.0008	-0.0029
Taiwan	0.0810	0.0427	0.0550	0.0127	0.0269	0.0334	-0.0010	-0.0034
Thailand	0.0208	0.0124	0.0073	-0.0059	0.0185	0.0282	-0.0050	-0.0098
Sub-mean	0.0343	0.0194	0.0173	-0.0020	0.0209	0.0287	-0.0039	-0.0073
Mean	0.0398	0.0271	0.0156	-0.0019	0.0266	0.0338	-0.0024	-0.0047

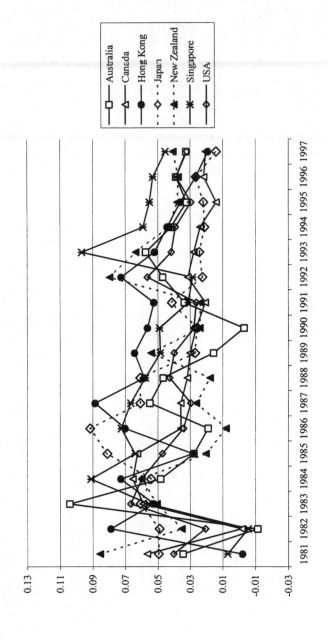

Figure 2.1 TFP growth rates of APEC developed members, 1981–1997

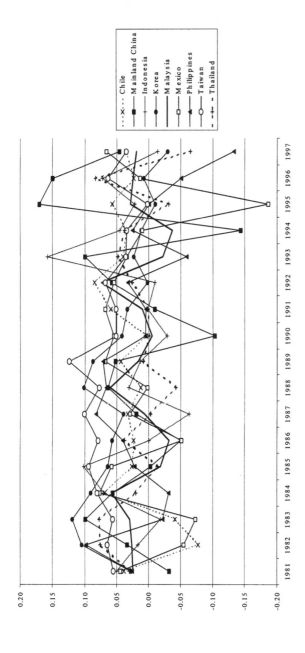

Figure 2.2   TFP growth rates of APEC developing members, 1981–1997

the US, are found to be more innovative than APEC developing members. However, Japan appears to lag behind other developed economies in terms of technological progress.

According to this study, APEC developing members have shown rapid catch–up with their rich neighbours. Korea and Taiwan were the lead performers in the 1980s. Mainland China took over to become the leader in the 1990s. The only exception among the developing members is the Philippines which has lagged behind in terms of catching up with its neighbours.

NOTES

1. See Lovell (1996) and Greene (1997a) for reviews of the literature.
2. See Greene (1997a) for a comprehensive review.
3. Issues concerning the efficiency and consistency of the estimators in the error components models are partly or marginally covered by Hausman and Taylor (1981), Caudill and Ford (1993) and Park et al. (1998).
4. It is available at http://www.worldbank.org/html/prdmg/grthweb/GDNdata.htm.
5. Such as the United Nations (various issues) and the International Monetary Fund (IMF 2000).
6. See Edwards (1998) and Cameron et al. (1999) for detailed discussions.
7. The weights are 0.5948 (imports-GDP ratio), 0.5783 (exports-GDP ratio) and 0.5584 (FDI-GDP ratio) for the 1980s and 0.6173, 0.6114 and 0.4951 for the 1990s.

3. The Impact of Stock Markets

The dramatic collapse of the Asian currencies and stock markets in late 1997 not only interrupted the region's miraculous growth but reinforced the 'casino mentality' shown by many investors, which had a tendency to give stock markets a special character in this region (Dufey 1999). Financial market weaknesses are now widely blamed for the demise of the Asian miracle. Hence policy makers are now taking a hard look at their financial systems.

A review of existing literature shows that economists hold startlingly different opinions about the effect of stock markets on economic growth. Stock market proponents suggest that such markets can boost economic development by raising the level of investment through the mechanisms of reduced information asymmetry, increased diversification opportunities, or liquidity creation. Also, the development of a stock market will attract foreign capital inflows, which in turn will strengthen linkages between domestic and international capital markets. Stock market critics argue that such markets may do more harm than good as their speculative nature makes them highly volatile and inefficient, thus undermining investor confidence.

This chapter attempts to investigate the effect of stock market development on economic growth in the Asian region. Most previous studies have used cross-section approaches (for example, Levine and Zervos 1998a). However, Arestis and Demetriades (1997) argued that a time-series approach is more fruitful than cross-country regressions, which average the effect of a variable across countries and do not account for the possibility of differences in country effects, which can be detected by time-series regressions. To improve on the existing literature, this chapter uses panel data regressions.

Section 3.1 reviews the evolution and growth of stock markets. Section 3.2 examines the major debates on the role of stock markets in economic growth. Section 3.3 describes the analytical framework and applies it to investigate the relationship between stock market development and economic growth. The results are interpreted in Sections 3.4 and 3.5. Section 3.6 concludes the chapter.

3.1 STOCK MARKETS IN ASIA

Observations by Goldsmith (1969) indicate that as economies develop, self-financed capital investments are likely to give way to bank-mediated debt finance. Then equity markets emerge as an additional instrument for raising external funds. In the 1970s, the low-income economies had virtually no stock market activity or non-bank financial institutions. But in the 1990s both non-bank institutions and stock markets began to develop. The financial systems in the middle and high-income economies evolved in a similar pattern.

The pattern of evolution is similar to that of economic growth. Rostow (1960) described economic development as an evolutionary process consisting of five distinct stages. The theory postulates that the development of the financial sector is necessary and a vital catalyst for economic growth. Specifically, the theory posits that the stock market is necessary for the economy to progress into the fourth and fifth stages of economic growth. Since stock markets are a common feature of financial and economic development, global institutions such as the International Finance Corporation (IFC) and governments of various countries acknowledge that stock markets play an important role in economic growth.

According to Hale (1994), one of the most striking developments in the world financial system since the end of the cold war is the dramatic expansion of stock markets in the developing countries. The collapse of communism and the spread of liberal economic ideas to former mercantilist countries in the Third World have altered the perception of and attitudes towards the role of securities markets. The global banking crisis of the early 1980s and the subsequent expansion of securities in the industrial countries are further factors that have encouraged the boom in emerging markets.

In Asia most of stock markets are emerging and hence relatively young (Table 3.1). According to the IFC (various issues), the emerging market group in Asia comprises Malaysia, Korea, Taiwan, China, Sri Lanka, Thailand, Pakistan, India, Indonesia, and the Philippines. Bangladesh is classified under the frontier markets. The developed markets comprise Japan, Hong Kong and Singapore. However, other analysts and financial institutions may classify Hong Kong and Singapore as more mature emerging markets (Hale 1994, Feldman and Kumar 1995).

In the 1980s, Asian stock markets experienced a significant rise in capitalisation. This growth trend continued until the onset of the Asian crisis in July 1997. Possible factors responsible for this growth include the privatisation of state-owned enterprises, the dynamic growth of private corporations in a healthy economic environment, and the capital appreciation that followed strong investor interest (Clemente 1994).

Variations in size are considerable (Table 3.2). Japan's stock market with a market capitalisation of US$2.5 trillion is the largest in Asia and ranks second in the world behind the US. Of the emerging markets, Taiwan comes first, with capitalisation of US$260 billion, ahead of the more established market in Singapore. Bangladesh, with a market capitalisation of US$1 billion, is smaller than some individual companies in mature markets.

Table 3.1   Asian stock markets: year incorporated

Stock exchange	Year	Remarks
Tokyo Stock Exchange	1878	Osaka Securities Stock Exchange was incorporated in the same year.
Taiwan Stock Exchange	1961	
Korea Stock Exchange (KSE)	1956	
Hong Kong Stock Exchange (HKSE)	1891	HKSE was officially formed in 1947 in a merger of two exchanges, ie. the Association of Stock Brokers and the Hong Kong Sharebrokers' Association.
Stock Exchange of Singapore (SES)	1973	In the 1930s, a stock association was organised in Singapore but the SES was officially incorporated in 1973.
Kuala Lumpur Stock Exchange (KLSE)	1976	The stock markets of Singapore and Malaysia started as one entity until the withdrawal of Singapore from Malaysia in 1965.
Securities Exchange of Thailand (SET)	1974	The Bangkok Stock Exchange was established in 1962, but was disbanded soon after.
Philippine Stock Exchange (PSE)	1991	PSE is a joint merger between the Manila Stock Exchange established in August 1927 and the Makati Stock Exchange established in 1964.
The Stock Exchange, Mumbai (BSE)	1875	BSE was initially established as The Native Share and Stockbrokers' Association.
Karachi Stock Exchange (KSE)	1947	
Dhaka Stock Exchange (DSE)	1954	DSE was originally incorporated as the East Pakistan Stock Exchange Association Limited before it was renamed in 1964.
Stock Exchange of Nepal	1976	

Source: George (1989).

Table 3.2 *World stock markets: market capitalisation, number of listed companies and value traded (billions of US$)*

	Market capitalisation			Number of listed companies			Value traded		
	1989	1996	1998	1989	1996	1998	1989	1996	1998
Asian emerging markets									
China	–	113.8	231.3	–	540	853	0.0	256.0	284.8
Korea	141	138.8	114.6	626	760	748	121.3	177.3	137.9
Philippines	12	80.6	35.3	144	216	221	2.4	25.5	10.0
Taiwan	237	237.6	260.0	181	382	437	956.8	470.2	884.7
India	27	122.6	105.2	2,407	8,800	5,860	17.4	109.4	64.5
Indonesia	2	91.0	22.1	57	253	287	0.5	32.1	9.1
Malaysia	40	307.2	98.6	251	621	736	6.9	173.6	28.8
Pakistan	2	10.6	114.6	440	379	773	0.2	6.1	9.1
Sri Lanka	0.4	1.8	1.7	176	235	233	0.0	0.1	0.3
Thailand	25.6	99.8	34.9	175	454	418	13.5	44.4	20.7
Bangladesh	0.5	4.6	1.0	116	186	208	0.0	0.7	0.8
Asian total markets	448	1,095	1,019	4,573	12,826	10,774	1,128	1,295	1,451
World total	745	2,272	1,908	8,709	19,949	26,354	1,169	1,511	1,957

Asian developed markets

Japan	4,393	3,089	2,496	2,019	2,334	2,416	2,801	2,047	1,167
Hong Kong	77	499	343	284	561	658	35	166	206
Singapore	36	150	94	136	233	321	14	43	51
Asian total	4,506	3,688	2,934	2,439	3,128	3,395	2,849	2,256	1,424
Totals									
Developed markets	10,967	20,412	25,554	17,216	20,242	21,111	6,299	12,106	20,917
All Asian markets	4,995	4,783	3,953	7,012	15,954	14,169	3,977	3,552	2,875
World grand total	11,713	22,684	27,462	25,925	40,191	47,191	7,468	13,616	22,874

Source: IFC (various issues).

Individual market size relative to GDP varies as well. The importance of equity financing is more pronounced in Hong Kong and Singapore, while the underdeveloped state of equity markets is readily apparent in Indonesia, Pakistan and Sri Lanka (Clemente 1994). Being relatively young, Asian stock markets have the potential to grow further. For instance, China, whose market capitalisation was less than 1 per cent of GDP, has grown 44 fold in the past seven years. China's market run on capitalisation is now 22 per cent of GDP. India has the largest number of listed companies and is home to 54 per cent of all listed companies in Asia. The average company size in India is approximately US$18 million while two Asian Tigers – Taiwan and Hong Kong – have an average company size of over US$500 million. Korea's industrial structure consisting of a handful of giant companies and a large number of small firms has a low average company size of US$153 million.

Liquidity

According to Clemente (1994), high turnover implies immature markets or speculative market conditions. A monthly turnover of less than 5 per cent of market capitalisation implies low liquidity and high volatility. In a failing market, low turnover may signal an end to selling pressures and an opportunity to buy. Factors underlying such conditions include a heavy presence of retail investors, a shortage of available shares, and minimal attention paid to fundamental company data. Markets with turnover rates above 9 to 10 per cent may reflect the presence of short-term speculators or buying conditions often found in the emerging markets during the bullish period. A turnover rate of less than 5 per cent in markets such as Singapore, Hong Kong and Japan signals their recovery from the Asian crisis. Taiwan is one of the few Asian stock markets relatively unscathed by the crisis.

In general, it can be agreed that the growth path of the Asian market was crippled when the Asian crisis erupted. Between 1989 and 1996, market capitalisation of emerging markets in the region grew more than 100 per cent while value traded rose by 15 per cent. However, in 1998, market capitalisation and value traded declined by 6.9 and 16 per cent respectively. As a result of the economic situation, the number of listed companies fell, with India losing the most. This fall can be attributed to bankruptcies, mergers, or acquisitions. Indonesia, Malaysia and Thailand were the hardest hit by the currency crisis with market capitalisation and value traded falling by an average of approximately 69.6 and 68 per cent respectively. Even the developed Asian markets were unable to escape the injury inflicted on the region's emerging markets and the world in general. Singapore's market capitalisation fell by one third, while the trading value of the Japanese market fell to 40 per cent of its 1996 value. Overall, the number of listed companies, market capitalisation, and value traded shrank during 1997–98 as a result of the Asian crisis.

3.2   STOCK MARKETS AND ECONOMIC GROWTH

Critics often view stock markets as casinos that do more harm than good to economic growth, while supporters of stock markets suggest that they can boost economic development. This section reviews the major issues in the ongoing debate.[1]

Creation of Liquidity

Levine (1991a) and Bencivenga, Smith and Starr (1996) showed that stock markets might affect economic activity through the creation of liquidity. Profitable investments often require a long-term commitment of capital, but many investors are reluctant to relinquish control of their savings for long periods. Liquid stock markets reduce the risks (productivity risk and liquidity risk) and cost of an investment that does not pay off for a long time. Hence investors do not lose access to their savings for the duration of the project because liquid markets enable them to buy and sell equity quickly. In turn, such investments are made more attractive and companies are able to raise capital permanently through equity issues.

In facilitating long-term profitable investment, liquid markets improve the allocation of resources by eliminating premature capital liquidation, thus enhancing the prospects of long-term economic growth. As well as making investments less risky and more profitable, liquid stock markets increase savings and investments because of the relative ease with which investors can enter and exit.

However there are alternative views about the effect of liquidity on long-term economic growth. Some liquidity models have shown that very liquid markets encourage investor myopia. Due to the relative ease and speed with which an investor can enter and exit the market by buying or selling equities, liquid markets may weaken investor commitment. Also, liquid markets may discourage internal monitoring by reducing incentives to exert corporate control in overseeing managers and monitoring firm performance and potential. According to this view, enhanced stock market liquidity may actually hurt economic growth (Bhide 1993, Levine 1996).

Risk Diversification

Investments with high returns tend to be comparatively more risky and hence investors often shun them. However, with the development of the stock markets, agents are able to diversify their portfolios (Levine 1991a). Similarly, facilitating risk sharing can fill this gap of insufficient investors. Greater international risk sharing (portfolio diversification) through internationally integrated stock markets induces a portfolio shift from safe, low-return investments to high-risk return investments, thereby accelerating growth (Obstfeld 1994a). However, Devereux and Smith (1994) argue that higher returns and better risk sharing with internationally integrated stock markets might induce saving rates to fall enough to slow overall growth.

Information Acquisition

Stock markets promote the acquisition of information about firms. According to Grossman and Stiglitz (1980) and Kyle (1984), the price system reflects information of informed individuals for large and liquid stock markets. An investor with exclusive information will be able to trade at posted prices and make a profit before the information becomes widely available and the price changes. The ability to profit from such information will stimulate investors to research and monitor firms. Better information about firms in turn improves resource allocation and accelerates economic growth. Stiglitz (1993) counter-argued that information is the heart of capital markets. If trading is dependent on differences in information, well-functioning stock markets will reveal information quickly through price changes. Consequently, this reduces the incentive to acquire information because investors are able to obtain information by observing price changes.

Corporate Control

Holmstrom and Tirole (1993) demonstrated that the value of stock markets could serve to monitor managerial performance. The conflict of interest between shareholders of a publicly owned corporation and the corporation's chief executive officer (CEO) is a classic example of the principal-agent problem. Jensen and Murphy (1990) found that the main performance incentive of CEOs comes from ownership of their firm's stock. As performance information is incorporated in stock prices, it is easier to link in manager compensation with stock performance. Possible take-over threats as a form of managerial discipline further induce managers to perform well and maximise share prices as they are often replaced following a successful take-over (Laffont and Tirole, 1988). Hence, well-developed stock markets can help align the interest of owners and managers, thereby promoting efficient resource allocation and thus boosting economic growth.

However, opinions differ on this issue. Stiglitz (1985) argued that take-over threats are not effective as a form of corporate control. This is because insiders are likely to be more informed than outsiders. The stock markets become ineffective and fail to mitigate the principal-agent problems, as firms will not seek to maximise stock market value. As mentioned above, with liquid stock markets, a corporation consisting of too many small investors can generate investor myopia. As a result, the high opportunity cost involved reduces the incentives for investors to monitor firms closely (Shleifer and Vishny 1986). Stock market development can also hurt economic growth by facilitating counter-productive corporate takeovers (Levine and Zervos 1996).

Stock Markets and Developing Countries

Historically the view has long prevailed among economists that security markets are of little economic benefit in less developed countries. Drake (1977) suggests that it was Goldsmith's pioneering work that prompted a surge of interest in financial development and capital market operations pertaining to less developed countries. Drake argues that 'the inherent obstacles to securities market development seem to have been overplayed and the prospects for beneficial community response to positive policies correspondingly understated'.

Today many global institutions and government authorities seem to agree with Drake's comment and view stock market development as beneficial to economic development.[2] The rapid growth of emerging stock markets is attributed to such markets playing an increasingly important role in the financial sectors of developing countries. According to Isimbabi (1997), stock market development is now considered an essential aspect of any developing economy. The establishment of stock markets in many developing countries is often encouraged by the World Bank and the International Finance Corporation (IFC). This is because these institutions view stock markets as an important tool for economic development, liquidity creation and lowering firms' cost of capital.[3] For instance, the IFC – leader of the private sector development efforts in Africa – believes that stock markets have a positive impact on economic growth. As a result, its stated priorities for sub-Saharan Africa are to stimulate the development and growth of stock markets there (Isimbabi 1997).

However, critics of stock market development argue that the cost of stock market development outweighs the benefit of economic growth.[4] Singh (1993, 1997) and Singh and Weisse (1998) argue that stock market development is unlikely to help developing countries to achieve faster long-term economic growth. This is due to the high volatility of share markets that make them more like gambling casinos than fully developed markets. The highly volatile share market renders prices inefficient as signals for resource allocation and encourages short-term profits, which leads to management myopia. It is also suggested that stock markets may seriously jeopardise the growth and stability of a country's financial structure by introducing factors that tend to aggravate or cause economic fluctuation, thus adversely affecting the allocation of savings, the reallocation of existing wealth, the redistribution of income, and the conduct of monetary policy (Sudweeks 1989). Proponents of stock market development admit that although the above arguments are plausible, lack of concrete evidence makes them less persuasive than the opposite view that stock markets are beneficial to economic development and growth (Sudweeks 1989).

Empirical Evidence

The growing theoretical debate persists over the links between economic growth and the functioning of stock markets. The little empirical support on this issue is fraught with problems as well. By using a forecasting model, Harvey (1989) showed that stock market development and economic growth are interrelated. Atje and Jovanovic (1993) (henceforth AJ) found that stock markets enhance economic growth. They conducted an empirical study to investigate stock market development as a function of the level/growth rate of economic activity in a sample of 39 countries over the period 1980–1988. The model proposed by Greenwood and Jovanovic (1990) (henceforth GJ) was used to search for growth effects while an amended version of the Mankiw, Romer and Weil (1992) structure was used to investigate level effects. For instance, the GJ model has an AJ structure, with no diminishing returns to the reproducible factor. On the basis of this model, a permanent, exogenous improvement in the financial structure would cause a permanent increase in the rate of growth.

In their study, AJ assumed that both investment and stock market activity are endogenous and thus, lagged or initial investment was used. Their results showed that lagged investment is not significant, but the product of investment with initial stock market activity is. Hence they concluded that there is a large effect of stock markets on subsequent economic development. Their evidence also suggests that the relative size of a country's stock market does not help to explain subsequent growth in per capita GDP. They remarked further that it was surprising that countries were not developing their stock markets as quickly as they could to speed up their economic development.

Harris (1997) re-examined the empirical relationship between stock markets and economic growth using the model proposed by AJ. Harris criticised the use of lagged investment as an inadequate solution to the issue of endogeneity. This was because lagged investment is not highly correlated with current investment and therefore not a good proxy for this variable. In turn, omitted-variable bias in the remaining variables will occur, in particular for the coefficient of the level of stock market activity. The level will be biased upward as it is correlated with subsequent investment. Also, as current investment and GDP per capita are jointly determined, OLS estimates of the stock market effect may be biased. In light of these limitations, Harris modified the AJ model using two-stage least squares regression and current investment. In contrast to AJ's finding, Harris found weak evidence to support the hypothesis that the stock market enhances economic growth, especially in the whole sample and in the sub-sample of less developed countries. However, in the sub-sample of developed countries, although the level of stock market activity does help to explain GDP per capita, the statistical significance is weak.

Levine and Zervos (1996) provided further evidence supporting the argument that stock market development has a positive impact on economic growth. To assess the association between stock markets and growth, they constructed aggregate indices of overall stock market development that combined information on market size, liquidity, and international integration by averaging the means-removed values of the aforementioned stock market development indicators. To empirically evaluate whether the index of stock market development is strongly linked to long run economic growth, regressions were run for a sample of 41 countries for the period 1976–1993. The aim of the analysis was to estimate the strength of the independent partial correlation between stock market development and economic growth. A large set of variables was used to control a variety of factors that may be associated with economic growth. The results suggest that stock market development is positively associated with economic growth.

Another study conducted by Levine and Zervos (1998a) used the standard cross-country regression framework of Barro (1991) to facilitate comparisons with other work. The data sample was the same as in their 1996 study. Besides the direct link with growth, they studied in greater detail the empirical associations between stock market development and physical capital accumulation, productivity improvements, and private saving rates. They also added volatility as the extra indicator for stock market development. They found evidence that stock market liquidity positively predicts growth, even after controlling for economic and political factors, while stock market size, volatility and international integration are not robustly linked with growth.

Arestis and Demetriades (1997) analysed the relationship between stock market development and economic growth using a time-series approach. They argued that a time-series approach yields deeper insights into the relationship between stock market development and economic growth as compared to cross-country regressions. Moreover, the causality link between stock market development and economic growth cannot be implied in a cross-sectional framework. Within the context of causality testing, the 'average effect' of a variable across countries does not account for the possibility of differences in causality patterns across countries, which can be detected by time-series data.

Arestis and Demetriades investigated the relationship between stock market development and economic growth in the United States and Germany using quarterly data for the period 1970(1) – 1991(4). The variables used were the logarithm of real GDP per capita, stock market capitalisation ratio, and an index of stock market volatility. The fourth variable differed: the logarithm of the ratio of M2 to nominal GDP was used for Germany while the logarithm of the ratio of domestic bank credit to nominal GDP was used for the USA. Unit root tests were carried out by the estimation of vector autoregressions (VAR) and tests for co-integration using the trace statistic were performed. The results suggest that long run causality may vary across countries or long run relationships themselves exhibit substantial variation. For instance, they found that in Germany, stock market capitalisation promoted economic growth, while stock market volatility had a negative effect on GDP per capita. In contrast, there was insufficient evidence to suggest that stock market development contributed to economic growth in the USA. Hence this study highlights the possibility of differences between countries.

Stock markets in Asia, particularly in the developing Asian countries, are growing rapidly. However, the lack of empirical studies makes it difficult to identify the impact of stock market development on economic growth. The remainder of this chapter attempts to fill that gap in the literature.

3.3   ANALYTICAL FRAMEWORK AND DATA ISSUES

A variety of measures have been developed to gauge a country's level of stock market development. Single measures may suffer from conceptual and statistical weaknesses such as inaccurate reporting and different accounting standards (World Bank 1998). Most previous studies have used either cross-country regression analysis or time-series analysis. In this study, panel data regression is used to investigate the relationship between economic growth and stock market development. Liquidity, size, volatility and integration with world capital markets are used as the measures of stock market development. The same indicators are employed by Levine and Zervos (1998a). Although each of these indicators has its own shortcomings, the use of a variety of measures may help provide more robust results than that of a single indicator as in previous studies. In this section, five stock market development indicators are discussed. This is followed by a description of the empirical models and data.

Measures of Stock Market Development

Size
Market capitalisation measured in US dollars gives the overall size of the stock market compared to GDP. It is defined as the ratio of the value of shares listed on domestic exchanges to GDP. Atje and Jovanovic (1993) argue that the relative size of a country's stock market can help explain economic growth. Despite the fact that large markets may not function effectively and that taxes may distort incentives to list on the stock exchange, many observers still use capitalisation as an indicator of market development (Levine and Zervos 1998a). According to the World Bank (1998), market size is positively correlated with the ability to mobilise capital and diversify risk.

Liquidity

Market liquidity is the ability to buy and sell securities. It is an important attribute of stock market development because liquid markets improve the allocation of capital and enhance prospects for long-term economic growth (World Bank 1998). Liquidity consists of two measures – value traded and turnover ratio.

Value traded measures trading volume relative to the size of the economy and is defined as the ratio of the value of shares traded on domestic exchanges to GDP. It reflects liquidity on an economy-wide basis. This indicator complements the market-capitalisation ratio by indicating whether market size is matched by trading (World Bank 1998).

Turnover ratio measures the volume of domestic equities traded on domestic exchanges relative to the size of the market. That is, it measures trading relative to the size of the stock market and is defined as the ratio of the value of shares traded on domestic exchanges to the value of listed domestic shares. Turnover ratio reflects the liquidity and transactions costs of a market. (High turnover ratio indicates low transactions costs.) Turnover ratio further complements the ratio of value traded to GDP because the turnover ratio is related to the size of the market (World Bank 1998). According to Levine and Zervos (1996, 1998a), the turnover ratio complements the measure of stock market size because large stock markets do not imply liquid markets. That is, a large but inactive market may have high market capitalisation but a small turnover ratio. A small liquid market may have a high turnover ratio but a small value-traded ratio.

Integration

In asset pricing models, perfectly integrated financial markets imply that the market price of risk is the same across world markets. Countries with integrated financial markets are likely to be free from investment controls and be easily accessible to international investors. If capital controls or other barriers impede capital flows, the price of risk will differ according to the risks of the financial market in each country. As noted by Korajczyk (1996), the drawback of using asset-pricing models to measure integration is the reliance on a particular specification of the model. If the asset–pricing model is incorrect, pricing errors will result. Furthermore, international pricing models lack generality and can be difficult to apply in practice (Akdogan 1996). In this study, the integration measure proposed by Akdogan (1996) is used. This method investigates the degree of integration or ranking of the countries by examining how integrated they are with the global market or a particular market. The integration measure is obtained following a three-stage procedure:

1. Stock market return of country i, R_i, is computed as follows:

$$R_{i,t} = INP_{i,t} - INP_{i,t-1} \qquad (3.1)$$

2.   Regress stock market return for each country on return derived from the Morgan Stanley World Price Index. The single index regression model is as follows:

$$R_{it} = \alpha_I + \beta_i R_{wt} + \varepsilon_i \qquad (3.2)$$

where R_{it} is the rate of return on the market index of country i at period t, α_i is the intercept, β_i is the coefficient of R_w or the measure of systematic risk of the ith country *vis-à-vis* the world index, R_{wt} is the rate of return of the world index at time t, and ε_i is the residual component.

3.   The measure of integration is:

$$I_i = \frac{\beta_i^2 \, Var \, (R_w)}{Var \, (R_i)} \qquad (3.3)$$

where I_i represents systematic risk in country i *vis-à-vis* the world index and measures the contribution of a particular market to the global risk market. I_i thus gives an indication of the degree of integration of country i in the world markets. An increasing (decreasing) fraction I_i of systematic risk suggests that country i has become more (less) integrated into the world market.

Volatility
Many observers have noted the highly speculative and bubble-like nature of the East Asian stock markets (Hargis and Maloney 1997). Empirical studies have given conflicting results on the relationship between volatility and economic growth. Levine and Zervos (1998a) did not find a correlation between stock market volatility and economic growth but Arestis and Demetriades (1997) and Singh (1997) found that stock market volatility retards growth. In this study, volatility is measured using the method proposed by Geyer (1994) and estimated as follows:

1.   Monthly return is defined as the difference of logged prices, which is available for each week:

$$R_{it} = \log P_{it} - \log P_{i,t-1} \qquad (3.4)$$

2.   A yearly time series $S_{t,c}$ of observed volatility in country c is constructed as follows:

$$S_t = \left[\sum_{i=1}^{N_t} (r_{it} - y_t) + 2 \sum_{i=1}^{N_{t-1}} (r_{it} - y_t)(r_{i+1,t} - y_t) \right]^{0.5} \qquad (3.5)$$

where r_{it} denotes the ith weekly return in year t, N_t the number of trading days in year t, and Y_t the average return of year t. [5]

Modelling and Data Issues

Previous studies of the relationship between stock market development and economic growth have used both time-series and cross-section regressions. Some scholars have argued that because variables in development models often have a reciprocal relationship, longitudinal research designs may be more appropriate. They recommend the use of panel data regression analysis (Burrowes 1970, Chase-Dunn 1975, Bradshaw and Tshandu 1990, and Mbaku 1994).[6] The fundamental advantage of a panel data set over a cross-section is that it allows the researcher far greater flexibility in modelling behavioural differences across individuals (Greene 1997b). The basic regression for panel analysis takes the form:

$$\text{Growth}_{it} = \alpha_i + \beta \text{ Stock Market Indicators }_{it} + \varepsilon_{it} \qquad (3.6)$$

where Growth_{it} represents the growth rate of per capita GDP for country i at time t, Stock Market Indicators measures stock market development, and α_i is the constant term which reflects the individual effect and is assumed to be constant over t and specific to the individual cross-sectional unit i.

Two basic frameworks are used to generalise the aforementioned model, i.e. the fixed-effect and random-effect models. The fixed-effect approach takes α_i to be a group-specific constant term in the regression model. The random-effect approach specifies α_i as a group-specific disturbance. Given that there are two general models, the specification test developed by Hausman, otherwise known as the Hausman test, is used to distinguish which model is used (Greene 1997b).

Data are available for only 14 Asian economies, i.e. Bangladesh, China, Hong Kong, India, Indonesia, Japan, Korea, Malaysia, Pakistan, Philippines, Sri Lanka, Singapore, Taiwan and Thailand. Following IFC classification, all the economies except Hong Kong, Japan and Singapore are emerging markets. According to the IFC (various issues), an emerging market can imply that a process of change is under way, with stock markets growing in size and sophistication. The term can also refer to any market in a developing economy. Thus, a stock market is said to be 'emerging' if it meets at least one of the two general criteria, i.e. (i) an emerging economy criterion and (ii) a developing stock market criterion. As many of the Asian markets are emerging markets and hence relatively young, the length of the sample period varies for each country and is relatively short (see Table 3.3). For instance, the IFC only added Indonesia and China to the IFC Indexes in 1990 and 1993 respectively.

As has been done by other researchers, real GDP per capita is used to measure economic growth. In this study, GDP and population data are from the IMF's International Financial Statistics, which are expressed in local currency and converted to US dollars using the exchange rates from the same source. However, for Taiwan, the values of GDP per capita and exchange rates are collected from the Statistical Yearbook of the Republic of China (DGBAS 1998). For all countries, data for market capitalisation and value traded were obtained from the Emerging Market Database Factbook (IFC various issues). For integration and volatility, weekly data from the IFC Global Index (price index) were collected for the emerging markets, while data for Hong Kong, Japan and Singapore were obtained from Morgan & Stanley Capital International (MSCI) Price Index.[7] Table 3.3 summarises the period of data available for each country.

Table 3.3   Summary of data

Country	Market capitalisation	Value traded	Volatility and integration
Bangladesh	1980 – 1998	1985 – 1998	Jan. 1996 – Dec. 1998
China	1991 – 1998	1991 – 1998	Nov. 1993 – Dec. 1998
Hong Kong	1980 – 1998	1980 – 1998	Jan. 1980 – Dec. 1998
India	1980 – 1998	1980 – 1998	Jan. 1980 – Dec. 1998
Indonesia	1987 – 1998	1980 – 1998	Jan. 1990 – Dec. 1998
Japan	1980 – 1988	1980 – 1998	Jan. 1980 – Dec. 1998
Korea	1980 – 1998	1980 – 1998	Jan. 1980 – Dec. 1998
Malaysia	1980 – 1998	1980 – 1998	Jan. 1985 – Dec. 1998
Pakistan	1980 – 1998	1984 – 1988	Jan. 1985 – Dec. 1998
Philippines	1980 – 1998	1980 – 1998	Jan. 1985 – Dec. 1998
Sri Lanka	1980 – 1998	1980 – 1998	Oct. 1993 – Dec. 1998
Singapore	1980 – 1998	1985 – 1998	Jan. 1980 – Dec. 1998
Taiwan	1980 – 1998	1980 – 1998	Jan. 1985 – Dec. 1998
Thailand	1980 – 1998	1980 – 1998	Jan. 1980 – Dec. 1998

A panel data set covering the period 1985–1997 is constructed for ten economies: Singapore, Hong Kong, Japan, India, Malaysia, Thailand, Taiwan, Pakistan, the Philippines and Korea. To capture possible variations associated with structural change, the sample is divided into the periods 1985–1990 and 1991–1997. In the 1980s, many Asian markets were liberalised while the 1990s reflects the period of the Asian miracle and the onset of the Asian meltdown.

The countries included in the sample range from Singapore with GDP per capita of US$33,370 in 1997 to Pakistan with GDP per capita of US$424 in the same year. Lumping these countries together could introduce an aggregation bias into the results (Mbaku 1994). To avoid this problem, the sample is divided into more homogenous sub-groups following the World Bank:

(i)   Low-income economies are those with GDP per capita of US$785 or less.
(ii)   Middle-income economies are those with GDP per capita of US$786–$9,665.
(iii) High-income economies are those with GDP per capita of US$9,666 or more.

According to the above classification Singapore, Hong Kong, Japan and Taiwan are high-income economies. Korea, Thailand, Malaysia and the Philippines are middle-income economies, while Pakistan and India are low-income economies. The drawback of this method is the insufficient number of observations (26) needed to run a panel regression for the low-income group. Panel-data regressions are run for the middle- and high-income groups over the period 1985–1997.

Another panel data set is constructed for the period 1980–1997 covering six economies, i.e. Hong Kong, Japan, Singapore, Thailand, Korea and India. The sample is divided into two nine-year intervals, 1980–1988 and 1989–1997, to capture structural changes. To avoid introducing aggregation bias, the sample of six countries is then divided into two homogenous groups based on GDP per capita.

The final panel-data set is based on the level of development of the stock market in each country proposed by Feldman and Kumar (1995). India, Pakistan and the Philippines are in one group. Korea, Malaysia and Thailand are in another group. Overall, 13 regressions are run and the estimated results are discussed in the following two sections.

3.4   STOCK MARKET INDICATORS

This section presents the estimates of the stock market indicators. First, a brief overview of the correlation coefficient of integration is provided. Then with the help of a chart the volatile nature of the Asian stock markets is illustrated. Using the integration and volatility statistics, inferences are drawn about the relationship between integration and volatility.

Integration

Correlation coefficients
Correlation coefficients for monthly returns during the period 1985–1997 are provided in Table 3.4.[8] Japan, Singapore and Hong Kong (in that order) have the highest positive correlation coefficients with the world index. Malaysia,

Thailand, the Philippines and Korea have a medium positive correlation with the world. Taiwan and Pakistan have the lowest positive correlation. India is the only country negatively correlated with the world markets. All the other countries have low to medium, positive correlation coefficients with Japan, except for India and Pakistan. Among all the countries, Korea has the largest correlation coefficient with Japan.

Comparison of the correlation coefficients of the ASEAN countries of Singapore, Malaysia, Thailand and the Philippines shows that these four countries are highly correlated with one another. Singapore and Malaysia have the highest correlation coefficient among the ASEAN countries. This is not surprising as historically Singapore and Malaysia shared a common stock exchange. Despite the separation of the stock exchange in 1973, the majority of the listed companies incorporated in either Singapore or Malaysia were listed on both stock exchanges in their respective currencies (George 1989). Finally, the results also indicate that the ASEAN markets are highly correlated with Hong Kong's stock market.

Integration

Table 3.5 illustrates the regression results for each country, for 1985–1997. The monthly return series is created from the Morgan & Stanley Capital International World Index and reports the systematic risk fraction I_i in equation (3.3). As discussed in the preceding section, this fraction gives the share of systematic risk in total risk compared to the market model. Higher values of I imply greater degrees of integration with the benchmark world market. This measure of I equals R-squared of the single index regression, that is, equation (3.2).

The calculated I value for Japan is the highest. Surprisingly, the I value for Singapore is higher than that for Hong Kong, implying that Singapore is more integrated with world markets. This is followed by the ASEAN countries Malaysia, Thailand and the Philippines (in that order). The I values for these three ASEAN countries are relatively close, suggesting that their markets are similarly responsive to the world trends and show the same tendency towards integration. In a study conducted by Low and Mitra (1998), during 1994–1996 the I value for Japan was the largest of all the Asian markets. This implies that among the Asian markets Japan is the most integrated with world markets. The results for Japan in this study are consistent with Low and Mitra. However, they found that Hong Kong was the second most integrated Asian market while Singapore was the third.

The beta coefficient also gives some insight into how returns of country i are affected by world markets. In the sample of ten countries during 1985–1997, all but India are positively correlated with returns of the world index. This implies that if returns of the world's benchmark portfolio were to rise, returns of country i would rise as well.

Table 3.4 Correlation coefficient for monthly returns (1985–1997)

Country	Hong Kong	Singapore	Thailand	India	Korea	Malaysia	Pakistan	Philippines	Taiwan	Japan	World Index
Hong Kong	1.000										
Singapore	0.668	1.000									
Thailand	0.616	0.618	1.000								
India	0.028	-0.000	0.131	1.000							
Korea	0.218	0.188	0.211	0.049	1.000						
Malaysia	0.597	0.815	0.643	0.088	0.264	1.000					
Pakistan	0.237	0.108	0.273	0.150	0.082	0.151	1.000				
Philippines	0.427	0.446	0.443	-0.000	0.202	0.494	0.163	1.000			
Taiwan	0.306	0.383	0.378	-0.014	0.144	0.298	0.084	0.211	1.000		
Japan	0.174	0.247	0.164	-0.110	0.336	0.188	-0.059	0.199	0.175	1.000	
World Index	0.529	0.552	0.346	-0.061	0.281	0.406	0.056	0.321	0.261	0.761	1.000

Table 3.5   Regression results and I values (1985–1997)

Country	α	t-ratio	β	t-ratio	I_i	F-statistic
Hong Kong	0.0007	0.2563	1.1642	7.7388	0.2800	59.8886
India	0.0036	1.0703	−0.0139	−0.7588	0.0037	0.1538
Japan	−0.0030	−1.7631	1.3587	14.5354	0.5784	211.2772
Korea	−0.0014	−0.4574	0.6027	3.6414	0.0793	13.2596
Malaysia	−0.0036	−1.2643	0.8573	5.4940	0.1648	30.1845
Pakistan	0.0021	0.0808	0.0987	0.6967	0.0032	0.4854
Philippines	0.0042	1.2055	0.7762	4.0676	0.0976	16.5450
Singapore	−0.0018	−0.7844	1.0014	8.2098	0.3044	67.4012
Taiwan	0.0022	0.4682	0.8504	3.3384	0.0679	11.1447
Thailand	−0.0025	−0.7295	0.8480	4.5806	0.1199	20.9816

Note: The dependent variable is the logarithm of country monthly return. The independent
variable is the Morgan & Stanley Capital World Price Index.

The size of the beta coefficient also gives an indication as to how world trends affect each country's stock market. Generally, the larger the size of the beta coefficient, the greater the impact of world markets on the individual country markets. Taking Japan as an example, if returns on world stock markets rise by 10 per cent, *ceteris paribus*, returns on Japanese markets will rise by about 12 per cent. In the whole sample, Japan has the largest beta value followed by Hong Kong and Singapore. This is expected as these three countries are the most integrated countries in Asia and hence would be most affected by world trends.

Table 3.6 reports the single regression results of monthly returns for each country during the periods 1985–1990 and 1991–1997 respectively. The beta coefficients reflect the relationship between an individual country's monthly returns and returns from the world index. As illustrated in Table 3.6, the beta coefficients for all countries are positively related to the returns of each individual country in both periods except for India. However, in terms of statistical significance, stock market returns in all countries except India and Pakistan are robustly linked with returns from the world index. The results indirectly imply that India and Pakistan are segmented from world markets and are not very much affected by the world trends.

During 1991–1997 the most integrated markets were Japan, Singapore and Hong Kong (in that order). During the two periods, the degree of integration of Asian markets with the exception of Pakistan did not change. These results do not necessarily suggest that these markets are absolutely segmented from the benchmark world portfolio. Rather, they indicate that these markets were

Table 3.6   Regression results and I values

Country	α	t-ratio	β	t-ratio	I_i	F-statistic
1985–1990						
Hong Kong	0.0001	0.0333	1.1315	5.986	0.339	35.83
India	0.0072	1.5639	−0.1977	−0.944	0.013	0.89
Japan	0.0005	0.1969	1.2749	10.500	0.612	110.24
Korea	0.0066	1.5787	0.5877	3.093	0.120	9.56
Malaysia	−0.0036	−0.9003	0.9102	5.127	0.276	26.28
Pakistan	0.0017	1.1499	0.0083	0.122	0.000	0.01
Philippines	0.0087	1.5146	0.8182	3.171	0.127	10.06
Singapore	−0.0030	−0.7170	1.0850	5.786	0.324	33.47
Taiwan	0.0062	0.7223	0.8770	2.271	0.070	5.16
Thailand	0.0027	0.6249	0.8701	4.485	0.223	20.12
1991–1997						
Hong Kong	0.0011	0.2872	1.2382	4.757	0.216	22.63
India	0.0004	0.0758	−0.0418	−0.123	0.001	0.15
Japan	−0.0624	−2.8857	1.5110	9.946	0.547	98.91
Korea	−0.0081	−1.9099	0.5741	1.931	0.044	3.73
Malaysia	−0.0035	−0.8399	0.7442	2.552	0.074	6.51
Pakistan	0.0021	0.4471	0.2942	0.899	0.010	0.81
Philippines	0.0007	0.1647	0.6540	2.170	0.054	4.71
Singapore	−0.0005	−0.2086	0.8321	5.466	0.267	29.88
Taiwan	−0.0010	−0.2122	0.7665	2.296	0.060	5.27
Thailand	−0.0067	−1.3024	0.7621	2.119	0.052	4.49

Notes: The dependent variable is the logarithm of country monthly return. The independent
variable is the Morgan & Stanley Capital World Price Index.

less responsive to world trends. For instance, the data of the second period
covers the boom and bust period for the Asian markets. During the boom
period, the markets in Asia were relatively unaffected by the world trends as
investor confidence was high. Thus the *I* values were smaller for the period
1991–1997 as the region became less responsive to world trends.

Volatility

Figure 3.1 presents the annual volatility series of the IFC Global Index and
MSCI Price Index of various countries. The highest peaks of volatility for
Singapore, Hong Kong, Malaysia and the Philippines were observed in the
years 1987 and 1997/98. The high volatility in these two periods could be
attributed to shocks which affected the world markets, such as the stock

market crash in October 1987 and the onset of the Asian currency crisis in July 1997. The other countries that experienced high volatility during the latter crisis were Taiwan, Korea, China, Indonesia and Thailand. Another shock which affected Asian stock market volatility to a much lesser extent was the Gulf War in 1990. Such a contemporaneous relationship of volatility is consistent with the study by So, Lam and Li (1997). They found simultaneous causality of volatility among Hong Kong, Malaysia, the Philippines, Singapore, Thailand and Taiwan. The exception was Korea, which seemed to have an independent market in which market volatility was not contemporaneously correlated with other stock exchanges. As depicted in Figure 3.1, volatility shocks in India, Pakistan and Sri Lanka seemed to be caused by localised events in each country rather than global or regional shocks. For example, the upsurge of volatility in 1992 for India was attributed to the liberalisation policy which allowed foreigners to trade on the Indian stock exchange. However, the effect was only temporary. According to Levine and Zervos (1998b) liberalisation tends to increase stock return volatility, but the effect is 'short-lived'.

Relationship between Integration and Volatility

Examining the relationship between integration and volatility, Korajczyk (1996) and Bekaert and Harvey (1997) found that the greater global integration of emerging markets reduces volatility in these markets. In contrast, Levine and Zervos (1998b) found that stock markets tend to become larger, more liquid, more volatile and more integrated following the liberalisation of stock markets. For instance, volatility peaked in India in 1992 when the Indian stock market was liberalised. Furthermore, countries with stock markets that are integrated with the world markets tend to be more vulnerable to global shocks and capital flows. As Pakistan, India and Sri Lanka only recently opened their markets to foreigners, they are least integrated with the world markets and are also comparatively less volatile and less responsive to world trends.

Table 3.7 presents a summary for each of the five stock market development indicators for the 10 countries that are considered, following the IFC classification. The five indicators exhibit considerable variability both across countries and over time within the same country. Among the emerging markets, Malaysia has the highest capitalisation but its turnover ratio is below average. Korea has a capitalisation value that is below average but ranks second in turnover ratio.

Taiwan appears to be the most volatile market. It is twice as volatile as the Singapore market, which is the least volatile market of the ten countries. Comparing the volatility means of the developed and emerging markets, less developed stock markets appear to be more volatile. For integration, Pakistan

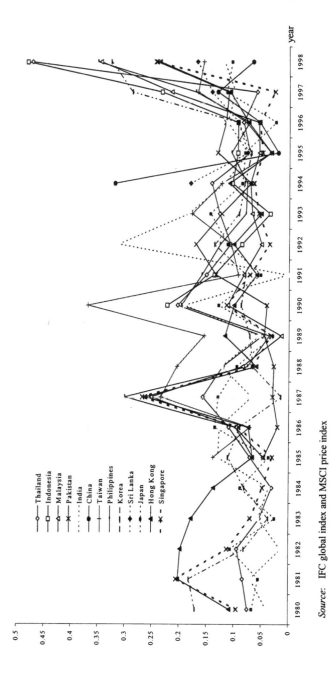

Source: IFC global index and MSCI price index

Figure 3.1   Annual volatility

Table 3.7   Summary of stock market development indicators (mean values)

Country	Capitalisation	Value traded	Turnover ratio	Volatility	Integration
Developed markets					
Hong Kong	1.7663	0.8587	0.4762	0.0939	0.2800
Japan	0.8902	0.4473	0.4698	0.0903	0.5784
Singapore	1.2435	0.5234	0.3852	0.0741	0.3044
Mean	1.3000	0.6098	0.4437	0.0861	0.3876
Emerging markets					
Philippines	0.3806	0.1044	0.2741	0.1204	0.0976
Taiwan	0.7584	2.2918	2.7024	0.1503	0.0679
India	0.1988	0.0635	0.4049	0.1233	0.0037
Korea	0.3396	0.3707	1.2175	0.0989	0.0793
Pakistan	0.1308	0.0399	0.2434	0.0822	0.0032
Thailand	0.4131	0.2774	0.6804	0.1121	0.1199
Malaysia	1.5474	0.7391	0.3972	0.0928	0.1648
Mean	0.5384	0.5553	0.8457	0.1114	0.0766

is the least integrated with an integration indicator 183 times smaller than that of Japan. The three most integrated markets are Japan, Hong Kong and Singapore. Furthermore, the values of the integration indicators of the ASEAN countries are relatively close. The mean of the integration value of the developed countries is 30 per cent larger than that of the emerging markets.

Table 3.8 presents the correlation matrix of the five stock market development indicators. Capitalisation is positively related to value traded, turnover ratio and integration but negatively related to volatility. In addition, volatility is negatively related to integration suggesting that more integrated markets are more volatile. The value traded is significantly correlated with turnover ratio, with a correlation coefficient of 0.78.

According to Levine and Zervos (1998a), correlation between value traded and liquidity is a result of the forward-looking nature of financial markets. For instance, if investors anticipate large corporate profits, prices will rise and in turn be reflected in the value traded due to the increase in the number of transactions. Moreover, the liquidity indicator will rise without an increase in the number of transactions or a fall in transaction cost. Capitalisation is affected by this price effect as well. However, when capitalisation and value traded are included in the regression analysis, the influence of the price effect can be gauged. The price effect does not affect the turnover ratio because stock prices enter both the numerator and denominator. If the turnover ratio is positively and robustly linked with economic growth, this implies that the price effect does not influence the relationship between liquidity and growth (Levine and Zervos 1998a).

Table 3.8   Correlation coefficients of stock market development indicators

Development indicators	Capitalisation	Value traded	Turnover ratio	Volatility	Integration
Capitalisation	1.000				
Value traded	0.473	1.000			
Turnover ratio	0.023	0.776	1.000		
Volatility	−0.195	0.223	0.453	1.000	
Integration	0.207	0.111	0.056	0.194	1.000

3.5   ESTIMATION RESULTS AND ANALYSIS

This section discusses the results of the 13 regression equations that were run. The aim of subdividing the sample periods is to observe structural changes in stock markets. For instance, the period 1980–1997 captured the liberalisation of many markets in Asia that began in the 1980s. The Philippines and Thailand liberalised capital and dividend repatriation in 1988. Malaysia completed liberalisation of direct foreign investment and portfolio inflow restrictions in 1986. Liberalisation within the Asian markets intensified in the 1990s. Taiwan opened its stock market to foreign investment in 1991. Korea liberalised portfolio inflows and outflows in 1992. Table 3.9 presents the estimation results of the 13 regression models.

For the period 1985–1997 for ten countries, all the indicators are positive except the liquidity indicators, which are both negative (Model 1). Only capitalisation is significant at the 5 per cent level. Furthermore, the size of the estimated coefficient implies that the links between capitalisation and growth may be economically important.

The period 1985–1997 is further divided into two sub-samples: 1985–1990 and 1991–1997. Capitalisation once again is significantly positively correlated with growth at the 1 per cent and 5 per cent levels for the periods 1985–1990 and 1991–1997, respectively. Moreover, the regression coefficients in both periods are, on average, three times larger than the coefficient in the full sample period (Models 2 and 3).

The results here support the hypothesis that larger stock markets are better able to mobilise capital and diversify risk (World Bank 1998). This indirectly

Table 3.9 *Summary estimates of stock market development indicators*

	Capitalisation	Value Traded	Turnover Ratio	Volatility	Integration	Constant	R–Squared	Hausman Test	Model Used	Number of Observations
1	0.0156** (2.097)	−0.0007 (−0.099)	−0.0034 (−0.511)	0.0516 (1.018)	0.0149 (1.048)	0.0264 (2.415)	0.050	6.63	Random Effects	130
2	0.0943* (2.807)	−0.0238 (−1.651)	0.0022 (0.183)	0.1187 (1.429)	0.0204 (0.427)	−	0.527	11.14**	Fixed Effects	60
3	0.0369** (2.013)	0.0079 (0.908)	−0.0024 (−0.318)	0.1784 (0.290)	0.0045 (0.571)	0.0388 (−2.964)	0.128	1.95	Random Effects	70
4	0.0656 (0.694)	0.0030 (0.206)	−0.0021 (−0.220)	0.0556 (0.974)	0.0143 (0.3974)	0.0345 (2.634)	−0.047	2.57	Random Effects	108
5	0.0247 (1.386)	0.0400 (0.096)	0.07494** (2.086)	0.6734 (−0.762)	0.2897 (0.275)	0.0311 (0.880)	0.131	2.02	Random Effects	54
6	0.0008 (0.072)	0.01056 (0.738)	0.0081 (−0.880)	0.0280 (0.383)	−0.0192 (−1.000)	0.493 (3.067)	0.022	3.34	Random Effects	54
7	0.00589 (0.613)	0.000 (0.016)	−0.00101 (−0.122)	0.1152 (1.438)	0.0026 (0.144)	0.0248 (1.631)	0.075	0.00	Random Effects	52
8	0.0237 (1.417)	−0.010 (−0.439)	−0.0022 (−0.184)	0.0362 (0.364)	0.2092 (0.751)	0.2801 (1.300)	−0.070	0.00	Random Effects	52
9	0.0363* (2.775)	−0.7549* (−2.602)	0.1471* (2.813)	0.1062 (1.482)	0.0081 (0.471)	0.0380 (−1.609)	0.157	0.00	Random Effects	54

10	0.0579 (1.204)	-0.036 (-0.556)	0.0118 (0.764)	-0.1707 (-1.198)	0.0271 (0.728)	0.0580 (4.009)	0.131	0.00	Random Effects	36
11	-0.0230 (-0.341)	0.2138 (0.899)	-0.0408 (-0.851)	0.0234 (0.289)	0.0036 (0.088)	0.0236 (1.032)	-0.0497	0.00	Random Effects	39
12	0.0043 (0.267)	0.0045 (0.196)	-0.0023 (-0.190)	-0.0018 (-0.190)	0.0060 (0.014)	0.0554 (0.200)	-0.0522 (3.451)	0.00	Random Effects	39
13	-0.0027 (-0.267)	0.0025 (0.280)	-0.0030 (-0.318)	0.1476 (1.592)	0.0047 (0.202)	0.0357 (2.203)	0.1302	0.00	Random Effects	39

Notes:

1 based on a sample of 10 countries for the period 1985–1997.
2 based on a sample of 10 countries for the period 1985–1990.
3 based on a sample of 10 countries for the period 1991–1997.
4 based on a sample of six countries for the period 1980–1997.
5 based on a sample of six countries for the period 1980–1988.
6 based on a sample of six countries for the period 1989–1997.
7 estimated for high-income countries (1985–1997): Japan, Hong Kong, Singapore and Taiwan.
8 estimated for middle-income countries (1985–1997): Thailand, Korea, Malaysia and the Philippines.
9 estimated for high-income countries (1980–1997): Japan, Hong Kong and Singapore.
10 estimated for middle-income countries (1980–1997): Thailand and Korea.
11 estimated for India, Pakistan and Philippines.
12 estimated for Korea, Malaysia and Thailand.
13 estimated for Hong Kong, Singapore, Taiwan.

t-ratio in parentheses.

* and ** indicate statistical significance at the 1 per cent and 5 per cent levels, respectively.
Random effects model was used due to the presence of time-invariant regressors, which cannot compute the fixed-effects estimator. (The fixed-effects estimator requires that there be within-group variation in all variables for at least some groups.)

implies that the liberalisation of stock markets may be a useful policy tool for countries seeking to boost stock market development. Increased foreign investment as a result of liberalisation will encourage stock markets to grow. Thus, the expansion of stock markets is likely to assist an economy to develop and grow.

The above exercises are repeated for a subgroup of six countries. A regression using the full sample 1980–1997 is estimated first (Model 4). Then the sample is divided into two sub-samples of nine-year intervals: 1980–1988 and 1989–1997. Model 4 indicates that the turnover ratio is negatively related to growth while other indicators are positive. In the first period, 1980–1988, all the indicators except volatility have a positive link with growth (Model 5). The negative relation of volatility with growth implies that volatile stock markets render share prices inefficient as signals for resource allocation. Such markets also encourage short-term profits, which can lead to management myopia. Apart from the turnover ratio, none of the other indicators are robustly linked with growth in this model. In particular, the estimated coefficient for the turnover ratio is significantly large. The findings for the sample period 1980–1988 are consistent with the view that stock market liquidity facilitates long run economic growth (Levine and Zervos 1998a). The results are not supportive of liquidity models that emphasise the negative implications of stock market liquidity (Bhide 1993, Shleifer and Vishny 1986). The regression coefficients for the second period, 1989–1997 (Model 6), are similar to that of the full sample period but with integration being negatively related to growth in the former. However, none of the indicators in models 4 or 6 is significant.

Analysis of Estimation Results by Country Groups

Given the heterogeneous nature of the countries in the 10-country sample and the six-country sample, the results reported above could suffer from aggregation biases. To deal with this possibility, the two samples are divided into subgroups based on the United Nations' classification.

High-income economies
The summary results for the high-income economies are presented in models 7 and 9. Capitalisation, volatility and integration are positively correlated with growth. For the liquidity indicators, an opposing effect occurs, i.e. the regression coefficient for turnover ratio in Model 7 is negative while in Model 9, turnover ratio is positive and vice versa for value traded. None of the stock market development indicators in Model 7 is closely linked with growth. However, in Model 9, only capitalisation and the liquidity indicators are significant at the 1 per cent level. The estimated coefficients of the three indicators are large as well. In terms of the liquidity indicators, suppose turnover ratio and value traded increase by 5 per cent, *ceteris paribus*. Isolating the effects of each individual indicator, the rise in turnover ratio

increases the growth rate by approximately 0.75 per cent per annum. In contrast, value traded has a nullifying effect on turnover ratio, i.e. growth decreases by 3.7 per cent. The overall effect of both indicators is a decrease of 2.95 per cent per annum in the growth rate. The results here support the view that liquid markets encourage investor myopia. Furthermore, the results also contradict the theory that mature stock markets are liquid and efficient and have low transaction costs.

Middle-income economies

Models 8 and 10 report the results for the middle-income economies. For both models, capitalisation and integration are positively related to growth. This suggests that large and internationally integrated markets are able to facilitate risk sharing, thereby affecting growth through increased investment. The relation of the other indicators to growth varies in both models. In Model 8, both liquidity indicators retard growth, while only value traded is negatively related to growth in Model 10. Volatility in this model retards growth as well. However, in Model 8, volatility is positively related to growth. Nonetheless, none of the economic indicators is robustly linked to growth.

The magnitudes of the coefficients for capitalisation and integration in both models for the middle-income economies are larger than those for the high-income economies. This suggests that as an economy develops, stock markets begin to play a more important role in the financial sector. Though large, the initial impact levels off as the markets mature over time. Further, the theory postulates that large and internationally integrated markets are better able to diversify risk. However, the results are unable to support this hypothesis, as neither indicator is statistically significant. The impact of the liquidity and volatility indicators on economic growth varies. According to the estimates in models 9 and 10, value traded is negatively related to growth while turnover ratio has a positive relationship with growth.

The impact of liquidity on economic growth is greater for the high-income economies than for the middle-income economies. The conflicting effect that liquidity has on economic growth in models 9 and 10 contradicts the two differing views of liquidity models. Levine and Zervos (1998a) vindicated the theory that stock market liquidity facilitates long run economic growth. In contrast, other liquidity models support the negative implications of stock market liquidity (Bhide 1993, Shleifer and Vishny 1986). Here, the liquidity coefficient in Model 8 is relatively large, suggesting that less developed stock markets are inefficient. The higher transaction costs associated with less mature markets in turn impede the efficient functioning of stock markets.

Level of Development

Given the heterogeneous nature of the level of development of stock markets in the sample, the countries were subdivided into three homogenous groups based on Feldman and Kumar's (1995) classification. The estimation results are reported in models 11, 12 and 13.

The two liquidity indicators show an offsetting effect on growth in all three groups. The turnover ratio enters the regression in all groups negatively with the estimated coefficient in Model 12 being the largest. In the case of Pakistan, when the mean value of turnover ratio is increased to the mean of the emerging markets, growth rate of per capita income will fall by approximately 2.4 per cent per annum. This can be economically detrimental, especially for low-income economies. In contrast, value traded is positively related to growth. Furthermore, the magnitude of the coefficients decreases down the group as illustrated in models 11, 12 and 13. This indicates that the impact stock markets have on economic growth levels off as they mature. Whether liquidity will have an overall positive or negative impact will depend on the growth of the two liquidity indicators.

Integration is positively correlated with growth in all three groups. This suggests that greater capital market integration is positively related to economic performance. The point estimates do not imply potentially large effects. For instance, if Korea's mean integration value rises to the mean of the developed countries, GDP per capita will rise by approximately 0.17 percentage points.

Among all the stock market development indicators, the effect of capitalisation and volatility varies between each group. Capitalisation is negatively correlated with growth, suggesting that larger stock markets are not beneficial to growth, while in Model 13 the reverse is true. Likewise, volatility retards growth in Model 13, but in models 11 and 12 volatility is positively related to growth.

However, none of the five stock market development indicators is statistically significant or robustly linked to economic growth in any of these three models. Further, when an F-test for the overall significance of the model is conducted for this group of sub-samples, the null hypothesis is not rejected. This implies that the regression model is not valid. In comparison, the other 10 regression models are valid.

To sum up, on the basis of the 13 regressions that were run, volatility and integration are not robustly linked with economic growth. The findings here are similar to those of Levine and Zervos (1998a). The results do not support the hypothesis that internationally integrated markets promote growth in an economy through risk diversification and increased investment.

Capitalisation and liquidity indicators are found to be linked with economic growth in various subgroups. In particular, capitalisation is found to be robustly linked with growth during 1985–1997 and the subsequent subgroups in that period. It was noticed that in models 1, 2 and 3, as stock markets become well developed over the years, the magnitude of the estimated coefficient falls. The findings in this study suggest that larger stock markets are able to boost economic growth by increasing overall investment in an economy through the mobilisation of savings, risk diversification and finally, the issuance of equity to finance corporate investment.

Turnover ratio is positively and robustly linked with growth as well. These results have the following policy implications. By lowering international investment barriers, stock markets become larger and more liquid. With larger, more liquid and internationally integrated stock markets, growth can be accelerated through risk diversification and increased investment. Demirguc and Levine (1996) argue that liquid stock markets can deter growth through the following channels. First, by increasing returns to investment, liquid stock markets can reduce saving rates through income and substitution effects. Second, by decreasing the uncertainty associated with an investment, saving rates can be reduced because of the ambiguous effect of uncertainty on savings. Finally, liquid markets may adversely affect corporate governance.

Considering the two opposing views of the effect liquidity has on economic growth, policy makers have to be cautious when liberalising stock markets. As mentioned above, stock markets tend to become more liquid following liberalisation. If the overall effect of liquidity retards growth, the effect of liberalising capital controls may have a detrimental impact on an economy's development.

3.6 CONCLUSION

A stock market is a mature form of financial intermediary. It serves to 'marry' the interests of wealth owners and investors. The role of stock markets in economic growth is debatable. Critics contend that stock market development is unlikely to help economies, especially in developing countries, achieve faster industrialisation and long-term economic growth. The high volatility of share prices has been used to liken the stock market to a gambling casino. Keynes (1936) warned that it would be foolish to leave the capital development of a country to such casinos. The speculative nature of stock markets renders prices inefficient as signals for resource allocation. Furthermore, stock markets encourage short-term profits resulting in management myopia, which has important implications for efficient investment. On the other hand, a developed stock market can accommodate foreign investment and play a useful role in economic growth. Stock markets can boost economic growth by (1) diversifying risk, (2) facilitating investment in the long run through the creation of liquidity, (3) improving resource allocation by reducing information asymmetry and (4) bringing about changes in incentives for corporate control.

This study investigated the effect of stock market development on economic growth in Asia. The stock market development indicators consist of market capitalisation, turnover ratio, value traded, volatility, and integration. The use of panel regressions in this study allows the modelling of different behaviours across countries. Two sets of panel data were constructed and further divided into eleven different sub-samples. The results and analyses were based on the 13 regression exercises.

Generally, variations in the results are observed in the sub-samples. In all of the 13 models, integration and volatility are not robustly linked with economic growth and these results confirm the findings by Levine and Zervos (1998a). The other three stock market development indicators (market capitalisation, turnover ratio and value traded) are found to be robustly linked with growth, but these relationships are sensitive to the sample considered.

This study has attempted to estimate the effects of structural change on stock markets over time and across different countries. For instance, government policies such as the liberalisation of the financial markets or trading policies affect the development of stock markets. Such changes would have been detected by the differences in the coefficient magnitude of the indicators when comparisons are made between the different groups of sub-samples. However, as the indicators in most of the sub-groups are not robustly correlated with growth, the structural changes that may have occurred over time as a result of changing economic and financial environments and the impact on growth were not detected.

This study finds that large and liquid stock markets seem to aid growth. Hence, policy makers should consider removing impediments to stock market development. By lowering international investment barriers and easing restrictions on international capital flows, stock market development can be boosted, which in turn aids growth. However, the results are sensitive to the sample considered. Policy makers need to examine the macroeconomic and political environment before a decision is made to promote the development of stock markets. Moreover, given that stock markets only start to play a crucial role in the later stages of financial development, policy makers should consider fostering bank-based financial systems before encouraging the development of stock markets.

NOTES

1. For a detailed discussion on the role of stock markets and economic growth see Levine (1991b).
2. For a review of stock market benefits in developing countries see Drake (1977), Feldman and Kumar (1995), Jefferis (1995) and Sudweeks (1989).
3. The IFC is the private sector arm to the World Bank Group and the world's largest source of financing for private enterprises in emerging economies. Specifically, the IFC is actively involved in fostering stock market development in the developing countries. The IFC encourages these countries to open up to foreign portfolio investment by providing technical

assistance to a large number of countries on the legal, regulatory and fiscal issues as well as other aspects of the institutional framework for the development of these markets.

4. For a review of stock market costs in developing countries see Drake (1977), Sudweeks (1989), Feldman and Kumar (1995) and Jefferis (1995).

5. For other models estimating volatility see Bollerslev (1986), Nelson (1991), Engel (1982), Pagan and Schwert (1990), Schwert (1989), Taylor (1994), and Kritzman (1991a, 1991b). According to Geyer (1994), the second term in the definition of $S_{t,c}$ accounts for the auto-correlation that may be observed in the return series.

6. For detailed discussion of the merits and flaws of panel data, see Hsiao (1986) and Klevmarken (1989).

7. Data obtained from the IFC Global Index and MSCI Price Index were retrieved from Datastream International.

8. Monthly returns are calculated in US dollars. Hence the results here take into account the combined effects of local currency returns as well as the exchange rate movements via US dollars for each country.

4.   Intra-Industry Trade

The growth of intra-industry trade (IIT) between developing countries in recent decades has attracted much attention in the economic literature. Since its emergence in the late 1960s, the concept of IIT has had an enormous impact on the empirical and theoretical analysis of international trade and on ensuing policy recommendations. The existing literature on IIT covers: (i) measurement, (ii) theoretical explanation and (iii) empirical determinants. This study belongs to the first group. One set of questions with important economic implications revolves around the impact of trade liberalisation on the amount of IIT within an economy, especially where factor-market adjustment issues and costs are concerned.

The theoretical literature on imperfect competition and IIT expanded rapidly in the late 1970s and early 1980s. However, since the mid-1980s development of the core models has been limited. The major innovation has been in the new field of 'geography and trade' proposed in Krugman (1991a) and summarised in Krugman (1991b). More recent models of geography and trade have added agglomeration forces (through input-output links and factor price changes) to the study of trade liberalisation and location. The developments in geography and trade by Greenaway and Milner (1987) and Markusen and Venables (1996) have also made it possible to advance the theory of multinational firms and IIT. Another important development during the last decade has been the construction of dynamic endogenous growth models by Rivera-Batiz and Romer (1991) and Grossman and Helpman (1990), for instance. These models are built upon earlier static models of IIT.

On the measurement of IIT, the key accomplishment has been the insights gained into the properties and deficiencies of the main 'workhorse' indices, in particular the G-L index (Grubel and Lloyd 1975). The principal weakness identified in the 1970s pertains to the issue of categorical aggregation and its impact on the interpretation of the G-L index, which remains widely disputed. The two issues that have dominated the discussion of measurement in recent years are refining the G-L index and adjusting IIT measures to effectively disentangle inter-industry trade (IT) from vertical intra-industry trade (VIIT) *vis-a-vis* horizontal intra-industry trade (HIIT). Hamilton and Kniest (1991) introduced a measure of marginal intra-industry trade (MIIT) that was instrumental in analysing adjustment costs and consequences following trade liberalisation. Brulhart (1994) took the analysis somewhat further by developing a wider and sharper menu of indices and measures. The introduction of the industry trade box by Azhar, Khalifah and Elliott (1998, 1999) has further expanded the scope for examining the trade and adjustment relationship for the various IIT measures.

Given the apparent dearth of empirical literature on the Association of South East Asian Nations (ASEAN) following the range of new developments and refinements in IIT measures, this study hopes to fill the void by exploring and reviewing ASEAN's IIT measures more definitively. This will give further insights into the adjustment problems and costs associated with ASEAN Free Trade Areas (AFTA) implementation. Furthermore, by focussing on ASEAN's individual commodity sectors, this study will aid in the identification of sectors least or most affected by ASEAN's trade liberalisation and will predict which industries may be susceptible to adjustment problems in the future, assuming existing trends continue.

Section 4.2 applies the measurement techniques discussed in Section 4.1 in the context of ASEAN. Section 4.3 concludes the chapter and presents policy implications for ASEAN.

4.1 MEASUREMENT OF INTRA–INDUSTRY TRADE

Empirical research in international trade is confounded by the phenomenon of countries simultaneously importing and exporting similar products. This phenomenon, known as 'intra-industry trade', is inconsistent with the standard theories of international trade derived from Ricardo, Heckscher and Ohlin. Traditional Heckscher-Ohlin theory based on factor endowments postulates trade of the inter-industry type although IIT is an undeniable fact of modern industrial economies with similar factor endowments.

The empirical work by Grubel and Lloyd (1975), though not the first application of the concept of IIT, is perhaps the most extensive study on the implications of IIT for trade theory. While some authors have expressed doubt that IIT is trade in commodities with similar factor characteristics, most trade theorists have argued that there is some truth in the Grubel and Lloyd contention (Finger 1975, Lipsey 1976, and Finger and De Roosa 1979).

Two competing views about the basic causes of IIT were discussed in Ray (1991). The causes of IIT are usually divided into two general categories. The first category describes trade in 'functionally homogeneous' products, where differentiated consumer goods are produced using identical technologies and relative factor intensities to satisfy consumer tastes for variety. The second category describes trade in slightly differentiated intermediate products where the goods are close but imperfect substitutes in consumption. These goods are produced using identical technologies and relative factor intensities to satisfy finished goods producers' demands for diverse production components and to keep costs down.

According to the dissenting views, trade under the 3-digit Standard International Trade Classification (SITC) or overlapping trade as Finger (1975) prefers to label it, can still be Heckscher-Ohlin trade because there is as much, if not more variation in factor characteristics within these industry groups as between them. In effect, this suggests that the high IIT values may be only a statistical artifact resulting from inadequate disaggregation to capture industries with unique capital-labour ratios.

While some IIT would disappear if industries are defined in more disaggregated statistics, some two-way trade in statistically different categories may be in goods with the same capital intensity, and in principle, non-Heckscher-Ohlin trade. After all, as Havrylyshyn and Civan (1983) point out, the fundamental point of factor endowment theory pertains neither to arbitrarily defined categories of statistics nor to specific end-use characteristics of products, but rather to factor characteristics of goods. Though the value of IIT diminishes when one calculates IIT using more disaggregated data, disaggregation, as noted by Gray (1983), does not cause the IIT phenomenon to disappear.

Hence, the principal difficulty with computing a meaningful statistic of IIT lies in the unambiguous definition of the term 'industry'. Invariably, IIT is measured at a particular level for some activities but not others. Although there is no *a priori* reason why one particular level of aggregation should necessarily be more appropriate than others, many researchers have used the three-digit level of the SITC as a suitable level for empirical analysis. But it was recommended by Oliveras and Terra (1997) that IIT be measured at different levels of aggregation to avoid the risk of incorrectly interpolating the characterisation of one sector to all its sub-industries. However, in this study, the three-digit level of SITC is used owing to the paucity of more disaggregated data.

4.1.1   Grubel and Lloyd's (G-L) IIT Measure

Following Grubel and Lloyd (1975), trade in similar products is given by the residual of trade after subtraction of inter-industry trade, that is,

$$IIT_i = (X_i + M_i) - |X_i - M_i| \qquad (4.1)$$

where X_i is the value of exports of industry i and M_i the value of imports of industry i.

For purposes of presenting data at a more aggregated level in order to measure the extent of IIT at its elementary industry form, the use of an aggregation formula is required. The aggregated IIT index is:

$$B = \frac{\sum\limits_{i=1}^{n}(X_i + M_i) - \sum\limits_{i=1}^{n}|X_i - M_i|}{\sum\limits_{i=1}^{n}(X_i + M_i)} \tag{4.2}$$

where n is the number of industries (activities) at a chosen level of aggregation, and $0 \leq B \leq 1$.

The weighted average G-L index can then be defined as follows:

$$B_w = \sum\limits_{i=1}^{n} w_i \frac{|X_i - M_i|}{(X_i + M_i)} \tag{4.3}$$

where: $\qquad w_i = \dfrac{X_i + M_i}{\sum\limits_{j=1}^{n} X_j + \sum\limits_{j=1}^{n} M_j}$

However, Grubel and Lloyd (1975) and Aquino (1978) observed that a simple mean of three-digit IIT values will be a downward-biased measure of IIT if a country's total commodity trade is imbalanced, as exports cannot match imports in every industry. Given the perceived undesirability of the trade imbalance, Grubel and Lloyd proposed to deal with the problem by subtracting the global trade imbalance from the total amount of trade in the denominator of B, that is,

$$C = \frac{\sum\limits_{i=1}^{n}(X_i + M_i) - \sum\limits_{i=1}^{n}|X_i - M_i|}{\sum\limits_{i=1}^{n}(X_i + M_i) - \left|\sum\limits_{i=1}^{n}X_i - \sum\limits_{i=1}^{n}M_i\right|} \tag{4.4}$$

In words, equation (4.4) implies that IIT is now measured with respect to total balanced trade rather than total trade. Thus, it is claimed that C can correct the downward bias of the B measure in equation (4.2).

Arguably, the correction of the B index in equation (4.2) for the total trade imbalance was justified by the need to allow it to reach its maximum value (100) even though total trade is often not balanced. This argument does not appear convincing or justifiable for the following reasons. One can understand that the B index will correctly attain its maximum value (100) when trade is balanced at its elementary level, but it makes no sense for G-L to account for this trade imbalance in equation (4.4) when trade is not balanced. These imbalances are precisely why an aggregate imbalance does exist. Although the value of $\sum_{i=1}^{n}|X_i - M_i|$ is greater than that of $\left|\sum_{i=1}^{n}X_i - \sum_{i=1}^{n}M_i\right|$, this is because in trade overlap measures, the signs of the elementary imbalances are not relevant. In fact, many of the empirical works on IIT, for example Aquino (1978), Finger (1975), Havrylyshyn and Civan (1983) and Khalifah (1996), refer to the manufacturing sector. There is no theoretical justification for imposing balanced trade on each of the countries considered, because in practice a country may very well run a deficit in its manufacturing sector, while earning surpluses in its other sectors (mining and minerals, agriculture etc.).

In view of the theoretically unsound and unreliable adjustment procedures suggested by Grubel and Lloyd's (1975) 'need for correction argument', the uncorrected B index in equation (4.2) would seem a more appropriate index for empirical studies, as argued by Vona (1991) and Kol and Mennes (1989).

4.1.2 Alternative IIT Measures

The traditional G-L unadjusted index is the most widely used and best known measure of IIT. It is most appropriate for documenting an industry's trade pattern in a single period of time, that is for measuring IIT in a static sense. The G-L index is interpreted as an indicator of the composition of trade flows annually and changes in the G-L index indicate how this structure is changing over time. However, the observation of a high proportion of IIT in one particular time period does not justify _a priori_ any likely predictions of trade flow changes.

The relevant issue in analysing adjustment costs following the formation of a free trade area involves knowing how much of the growth in trade is intra-industry in nature, as opposed to net trade. Movements in the G-L index are incapable of providing this information. Furthermore, changes in the G-L index may be misleading when tabulating the contribution of IIT to the growth in total trade. For example, it is possible for the G-L index to increase from 10 per cent of total trade in 1980 to 80 per cent in 1990 despite IIT contributing less than net trade to the growth in total trade and vice versa. In addition, the increase (decrease) in the G-L index over time could also indicate a decrease (increase) in absolute amount of IIT.

Hence, rather than compare the composition of trade at different points in time, it is necessary to analyse the pattern of change in trade flows in order to draw conclusions on adjustment from IIT measurements. An alternative measure of change in IIT is MIIT (Hamilton and Kniest 1991), which is further expounded upon by Greenaway, Hine, Milner, and Elliot (1994) and Brulhart (1994).

Marginal intra-industry trade (MIIT)

Hamilton and Kniest (1991) proposed the first MIIT index to measure changes in total IIT. Using the Australia-New Zealand Closer Economic Relations Agreement (CER) as the focal point of their argument, they scrutinised the usefulness and reliability of the G-L index for the analysis of adjustment issues. They argued that if adjustment consequences are to be analysed as a result of any perceived trade expansion or contraction, what matters is IIT changes at the margin. To measure this, they considered the following MIIT index:

$$MIIT = \frac{X_t - X_{t-n}}{M_t - M_{t-n}} \quad \text{for } M_t - M_{t-n} > X_t - X_{t-n} > 0 \quad (4.5)$$

or

$$MIIT = \frac{M_t - M_{t-n}}{X_t - X_{t-n}} \quad \text{for } X_t - X_{t-n} > M_t - M_{t-n} > 0 \quad (4.6)$$

where X_t (M_t) and X_{t-n} (M_{t-n}) are exports (imports) in years t and $t-n$ respectively, and n refers to the liberalisation period. The index calculates the proportion of the increase in imports (or exports) relative to changes in the value of exports (or imports).

However, as pointed out by Greenaway et al. (1994), the Hamilton-Kniest measure suffers from several shortcomings. First, only non-negative values of ΔX and ΔM can be used to calculate MIIT values, thus rendering the measure undefined should ΔX and ΔM values be negative. Second, analogous to the G-L index, the measure is unscaled, that is it provides information about IIT in new trade (when both ΔX and ΔM are negative) without reference to either the amount of new trade, the initial level of trade, or the value of production in the sector concerned. Greenaway and Torstensson (1997) argued that this was the main drawback to the Hamilton-Kniest measure.

The above problems were discussed by Brulhart (1994). Brulhart suggested a dynamic index based on the concept of MIIT. This index is defined as the difference between changes in total trade flows and changes in net trade, that is:

$$MIIT_i = |\Delta X_i| + |\Delta M_i| - |\Delta X_i - \Delta M_i| \quad (4.7)$$

where Δ is the first difference operator. Dividing through by the change in total trade flows gives Brulhart's dynamic G-L index or A_i:

$$A_i = 1 - \frac{|\Delta X_i - \Delta M_i|}{|\Delta X_i| + |\Delta M_i|} \quad (4.8)$$

Brulhart's index is always defined and varies between zero and one. An index of zero indicates marginal trade in the particular industry or sector to be completely of the inter-industry type. Relatively high levels of MIIT are indicated by a value close to unity. In contrast to the static G-L index, Brulhart's measure provides information on the direction and structure of changes in exports and imports between different time periods.

In addition, Thom and McDowell (1999) point out that whereas the static G-L index measures the ratio of IIT to total trade in a given period, the dynamic index measures the proportion of change in total trade flows attributable to IIT. On the one hand, positive values of A_i imply converging trends in sectoral exports and imports, and values close to unity indicate a predominance of MIIT in the adjustment process. On the other hand, zero values of A_i imply diverging trends in sectoral trade flows, and *ceteris paribus*, higher transitional adjustment costs.

It should be noted that like the G-L index, A_i can be summed across industries of the same level of statistical disaggregation as suggested by Brulhart (1994), by applying the following formula for a weighted average:

$$A_w = \sum_{i=1}^{N} w_i A_i \qquad (4.9)$$

$$w_i = \frac{|\Delta X_i| + |\Delta M_i|}{\sum_{j=1}^{N} \left(|\Delta X_j| + |\Delta M_j| \right)}$$

and A_w is the weighted average of MIIT over all industries of the economy or over all the sectors of an industry.

Vertical *vs* horizontal intra-industry trade

IIT can be decomposed into two forms – horizontal and vertical intra-industry trade. In recent years, the issue of disentangling HIIT and VIIT has dominated the subject. Abd-el-Rahman (1991) and Greenaway et al. (1995) argue that such a distinction is important as the determinants of each type of IIT differ.

VIIT involves simultaneous export and import of similar goods of varying qualities. The theoretical exposition for this type of IIT was first developed by Falvey (1981), who showed that VIIT might arise in situations where large numbers of firms produce varieties of different qualities but there are no increasing returns in production. The pattern of VIIT follows traditional endowment-based models, with the relatively capital-abundant country exporting higher-quality products and the relatively labour-abundant country exporting lower-quality goods. Shaked and Sutton (1984) demonstrated that VIIT may also arise in a market structure with small numbers of firms and increasing returns.

HIIT arises when there is two-way trade in products of similar quality, but different characteristics or attributes. Models of HIIT explicitly introduce economies of scale and imperfect competition in the analysis. Most of the basic elements of HIIT can be found in the so-called 'neo-Chamberlinian' and 'neo-Hotelling' models (Krugman 1979a, Lancaster 1980, Helpman 1981). In the neo-Hotelling models it is assumed that different consumers have different preferences for alternative varieties of given commodities. In the neo-Chamberlinian models, consumers endeavour to consume as many varieties as possible and more than one firm would produce the same variety. These varieties are distinguished in terms of their actual or perceived characteristics, that is they are horizontally differentiated.

Given the different circumstances and situations in which HIIT and VIIT occur, it is therefore crucial to distinguish between these types of trade flows, as neglecting them carries the risk of imputing an erroneous indication of IIT and obtaining inaccurate economic implications. The next section provides a method of distinguishing VIIT and HIIT in light of the inadequacy of the MIIT index to do so.

Separating VIIT and HIIT

Thom and McDowell (1999) conceded that Brulhart's dynamic index is an adequate indicator of HIIT, but criticised its inability to distinguish between VIIT and IT, thereby underestimating the importance of IIT in the process. The problem lies with the fact that Brulhart's index treats each sub-sector of an industry as a separate industry while an index of VIIT requires industry level measurement.

Consequently, Thom and McDowell (1999) proposed a measure for disentangling VIIT from IT. Letting $X_J = \sum_I^N X_i$ and $M_J = \sum_I^N M_i$, an equivalent industry index can be defined as:

$$A_J = 1 - \frac{\left|\Delta X_J - \Delta M_J\right|}{\sum\limits_{i=1}^{N}\left|\Delta X_i\right| + \sum\limits_{i=1}^{N}\left|\Delta M_i\right|} \tag{4.10}$$

Given that A_J measures the distribution of matched two-way trade at the industry level, it enables the aggregation of both horizontal and vertical IIT. As such, with the proportion of HIIT contributed by equation (4.9), it follows that the proportion of total trade flows attributable to VIIT is given by $(A_J - A_W)$ and the share due to IT is $(1-A_J)$.

4.1.3 The Smooth Adjustment Hypothesis and IIT

Before embracing the often assumed proposition that IIT entails lower costs of factor market adjustment than IT, it is essential to note that this much-quoted conjecture, known as the Smooth Adjustment Hypothesis (SAH) has been subjected to little formal scrutiny in the empirical literature. Thus, the evidence to date is suggestive rather than conclusive.

However, sceptics of the SAH on theoretical grounds have been rare. The monopolistic competition model of IIT is generally put forward as the cornerstone of the SAH. Krugman's model (1981, p.970) argues that IIT 'poses fewer adjustment problems than IT'. But the use of 'adjustment' in the exegesis of such a model is misleading. The welfare effects Krugman implied did not relate to end-state utility distribution before and after trade liberalisation.

The analysis of IIT has been implicitly concerned with adjustment in the labour market. Brulhart and Thorpe (1999) formulated the IIT-adjustment hypothesis in terms of the specific-factors model, expounded concisely by Neary (1985). Thus according to the IIT literature, adjustment is smoother in terms of 'adjustment services' and unemployment if the expanding and contracting activities are contained within the same industry, than if they represent two different industries. This hypothesis assumes one of the following:

(i)   *Ceteris paribus*, labour is more easily adapted within industries than between industries, or

(ii)   *Ceteris paribus*, relative wages are more flexible within industries than between industries.

The first assumption for the expectation of smooth intra-industry adjustment has intuitive appeal because if IIT is defined as the exchange of goods with similar production requirements, it is implied that labour requirements are more similar within than between industries. Consequently, if the skills acquired by the workers of a contracting firm can be re-applied without much re-training in an expanding firm of the same industry, then labour mobility would be higher as workers can be transferred from one department to another.

The second assumption seems less likely given the impediments to wage flexibility following minimum-wage laws and contractual wage agreements between labour-market institutions. If temporary wage inflexibility through industry-wide centralised bargaining is a major cause of adjustment problems, then adjustment costs would be higher when trade shocks are intra-industry as opposed to trade altering the relative positions between industries.

Intuitively, adjustment seems likely to be more disruptive in homogenous industries with a concentrated market structure than in sectors with differentiated products and large firm numbers. But these issues have neither been explored in terms of their implications for real factor rewards nor in terms of transitional adjustment costs. Although a wide array of trade-induced adjustments exists in the literature, these studies emanated from neo-classical trade models with perfect competition in two homogeneous goods with no integrated theory of IIT and adjustment (Neary 1985). The problem is further exacerbated by methodological limitations and difficulty in obtaining sufficient and appropriate data for further empirical tests. However, the current study, along with recent studies on the SAH, presents increasing evidence that adjustment is smoother and costs lower if IIT is understood in the sense of MIIT (Brulhart et al. 1998, Brulhart and Thorpe 1999).

This section has reviewed a multitude of IIT measurement techniques. The strengths and weaknesses of the static and dynamic measures of IIT were assessed. In the following section, the appropriate indices are applied to explain ASEAN's manufacturing trade.

4.2   ASEAN MANUFACTURING IIT (1986–1995)

This section applies the techniques discussed in the preceding section to examine the trade structure and characteristics of ASEAN's manufacturing IIT prior to and after the launch of AFTA. The results in this study are calculated using the Standard International Trade Classification (SITC) Revision 3 data at the three-digit level. Three-digit sectors correspond to the standard definition of an 'industry' in the IIT literature (Greenaway and Milner 1986). There are 149 industries at the three-digit level for the manufacturing sector (Sections 5–8 less Divisions 67 and 68), which can be headed under four specific categories: chemicals (SITC 5), basic manufactures (SITC 6), machinery and transport equipment (SITC 7) and miscellaneous manufactured goods (SITC 8).[1]

4.2.1   Composition of ASEAN Manufacturing Trade

The profile of ASEAN manufacturing trade from 1986 to 1995 is presented in the Appendix to Chapter 4 (Tables A4.2 and A4.3). In order to keep the analysis manageable, the empirical results were aggregated using equation (4.2) and presented at the two-digit level, where the contribution of each industry is tabulated for the individual countries.

According to Tables A4.2 and A4.3, Singapore accounted for about 40–49 per cent of ASEAN manufacturing trade during 1986–91. After AFTA's inception in 1992, Singapore's percentage share of ASEAN manufacturing trade dropped to between 37 and 42 per cent for the years 1992–95.

Prior to the introduction of AFTA, Singapore maintained a relatively tariff-free trade environment, which was substantiated by its high volume of entrepot trade. With the inception of AFTA, other member nations with comparatively higher and more protected tariff markets began a process of reducing and eliminating their trade tariffs, and this could possibly be a reason for the marked rise in their manufacturing trade.

However, Table A4.3 indicates that the value of Singapore's manufacturing trade rose from US$90 billion in 1991 to US$197 billion in 1995, which by no means diminished Singapore's entrepot status. At the same time, total ASEAN manufacturing trade also boomed and the value of some of the other ASEAN members' (such as Malaysia and Thailand) manufacturing trade over this period rose by a larger percentage than that of Singapore.

In 1986 and 1987, Malaysia was the second largest contributor to ASEAN manufacturing trade, contributing 19.68 and 19.51 per cent respectively. In 1988, Thailand attained this second position. But in 1989, Malaysia regained its standing as the second largest contributor to ASEAN manufacturing trade and has since maintained its position. Thailand's share in ASEAN manufacturing trade remained constant at 18 to 19 per cent during 1991–95, while that of the Philippines also remained relatively dormant. Malaysia's share has been on a gradual upward trend from 19.68 per cent in 1986 to 23.91 per cent in 1995. Indonesia's contribution to ASEAN manufacturing trade varied between 10 and 13 per cent during 1991–95.

Where product groups are concerned, the share of SITC 7 in ASEAN manufacturing trade consistently increased during 1986–95, posting the strongest percentage share of 67.24 per cent in 1995. This suggests that the main thrust and strength of ASEAN manufacturing trade lies in that category. For the other categories, (SITC 5, SITC 6, and SITC 8) the respective percentage share of ASEAN manufacturing trade gradually declined over the period 1986–95, again indicating a pattern of gradual shift towards trade in SITC 7 manufacturing products.

Overall, Singapore is the largest contributor to trade in SITC 7 products followed by Malaysia, Thailand, Indonesia and then the Philippines. Sub-division 75 (office machines and automatic data processing equipment), sub-division 76 (telecommunications and sound recording apparatus and equipment) and sub-division 77 (electrical machinery, apparatus and appliances, n.e.s, and electrical parts thereof) have provided the backbone and strength for the volume of trade in SITC 7 products. Over the period 1991–95, sub-divisions 75, 76 and 77 contributed 38 to 47 per cent of ASEAN's manufacturing trade (see Table A4.3).[2] This was largely because the electronics sector had traditionally been the main engine of manufacturing growth for ASEAN, given the dominance of multi-national corporations (MNCs) in this area (Chalmers 1991).

Sub-division 77 remained the strongest contributor to ASEAN manufacturing growth over the period analysed. The growing importance of sub-division 77 is perhaps indicative of the trend towards manufacturing products embodying higher technological content and hence growth in this sector denotes a shift towards high value-added production.

4.2.2 IIT Patterns of ASEAN Nations

The relative contribution of the different ASEAN countries and product groups towards total ASEAN manufacturing IIT is shown in the Appendix to Chapter 4 (Tables A4.4 and A4.5). As noted in the tables, certain IIT percentage shares are zero. This does not mean that there is no IIT within the commodity sector concerned. In most cases, it means that available data on either exports or imports for the relevant commodity group are negligible or unavailable.[3]

Table A4.5 shows that SITC 7 is the most significant contributor to ASEAN IIT and its share accounted for about 67 to 72 per cent of ASEAN IIT during 1991–95, with Singapore's contribution representing the highest percentage at 34 to 39 per cent. Sub-division 77 remains the largest contributor to ASEAN IIT, up from about one-quarter in 1991 to about one-third of all IIT in 1995. The contribution of sub-divisions 75 and 76 to ASEAN's IIT remained relatively constant at 11 to 14 per cent during 1991–95. In the case of sub-divisions 76 and 77, Singapore has always been the largest contributor followed by Malaysia. In sub-division 75, Singapore remained the largest contributor, followed by Thailand.

Sub-divisions 75, 76 and 77 accounted for over 59 per cent of ASEAN IIT while they represented about 50 per cent of ASEAN manufacturing trade in 1995. In comparison, the IIT shares of other commodity sectors showed little change for each of the member nations.

Singapore's contribution to ASEAN IIT remains the highest among the ASEAN nations but this rate has been diminishing over the years. Apart from Singapore, Thailand registered the greatest change in its IIT shares, which is highly indicative of increasing intra-industry specialisation as a result of fast growing per capita income, convergence in income levels and progressing industrialisation (Fukasaku 1992).

4.2.3 ASEAN's G-L Indices

The G-L indices for ASEAN manufacturing trade are shown in the Appendix to Chapter 4 (Table A4.6 for 1986–90 and Table A4.7 for 1991–95). As mentioned, these tables are computed using three-digit level manufacturing data and aggregated using equation (4.2) to derive the figures at the two-digit level.[4] Again it is observed that there are zero G-L indices for some commodity groups due to the round-up as explained.

The results tabulated in Tables A4.6 and A4.7 document the remarkably consistent upward trend in the IIT of each country. Between 1986 and 1995, the aggregate G-L index for manufacturing products (SITC 5–8) grew from 8.68 to 33.22 in Indonesia, 58.15 to 73.30 in Malaysia, 72.40 to 84.29 in Singapore, 38.22 to 43.50 in Thailand, and 31.89 to 56.61 in the Philippines. The sectoral composition of imports and exports has become substantially more similar over time in all these countries. Singapore and Malaysia traditionally displayed higher IIT shares than Indonesia and the Philippines. However, the trade patterns of Indonesia and the Philippines have exhibited a surge in IIT during 1986–95. Though Indonesia produced the largest increase in its G-L index during this period, it remains the only country among the five ASEAN nations with significantly below-average aggregate G-L levels.

In 1995, the G-L index for SITC 7 is the highest with a value of 86.36. Within SITC 7, sub-division 77 has the highest index with a value of 87.49 followed by sub-divisions 76 and 75 with indices of 71.44 and 62.84 respectively. The relative ranking of the divisions is fairly constant across the period studied. The division with the second highest G-L index is SITC 6 followed by SITC 8 and then SITC 5.

The products that contribute to high IIT are dominated by MNCs especially in Malaysia. These MNCs play a crucial role in contributing to the high G-L indices for Malaysia. Trade barriers may be high in some ASEAN countries, but the investment incentives offered to MNCs probably offsets the negative effects of these trade barriers.

The formation of AFTA may lead to trade liberalisation, but the investment decisions of MNCs help shape the pattern and direction of post-AFTA trade. These investment decisions will be determined by fiscal policies such as tax incentives (for example, tax holidays, accelerated depreciation) and export-promotion policies that include tariff rebates or duty drawback schemes.

4.2.4   Commodity Groups of Individual ASEAN Members' IIT

The primary focus of this section is based on individual ASEAN countries' top ranking industries that cumulatively contributed approximately 50 per cent to IIT for the year 1995. The position as well as percentage values of the top contributors to IIT of the ASEAN countries together with their respective G-L indices for the commodities (both manufacturing and non-manufacturing totalling 248 commodities) at the three-digit SITC level is shown in Table 4.1.[5]

A useful categorisation of SITC groups is to classify all goods by production and end-use characteristics. First, a distinction is made between capital-intensive and labour-intensive goods. Second, a mutually exclusive distinction is made between intermediate, investment and consumption goods. This classification is depicted in Table 4.1.

More than one-third of Malaysia's IIT is generated by group 776. The bulk of Malaysia's IIT is in the electronics sub-sector and a majority of these commodities are reflected in Table 4.1. The early dependence of Malaysia on the export of simple resource-based manufactures (including food, wood,

Table 4.1   Rank and value (%) of intra-industry trade and the Grubel-Lloyd index for the ASEAN countries, 1995

SITC	Description of product group	Value IIT(%)	G-L index	Type of good according to end use
	Malaysia			
776	Thermionic, cold and photo-cathode valves, tubes and parts	35.89	92.08	Parts and accessories of capital goods, intermediate goods
764	Telecommunications equipment and parts	9.42	97.18	Capital goods
759	Petroleum products, refined	3.03	61.63	Parts and accessories of capital goods, intermediate goods
334	Parts and accessories suitable for 751, 752	2.89	82.25	Processed fuels and lubricants, intermediate goods
772	Electrical apparatus such as plugs and fuses	2.51	61.97	Parts and accessories of capital goods, intermediate goods
	Total	53.74		
	Indonesia			
333	Petroleum oils, crude, and crude oils obtained from bituminous materials	22.59	40.77	Primary fuels and lubricants, intermediate goods
334	Petroleum products, refined	12.55	88.6	Processed fuels and lubricants, intermediate goods
287	Ores and concentrates of base metals, n.e.s	3.23	12.43	Primary industrial supplies, intermediate goods
653	Fabrics, woven man-made fabrics	2.97	47.61	Processed industrial supplies, intermediate goods
641	Paper and paperboard	2.78	32.82	Processed industrial supplies, intermediate goods
684	Aluminium	2.16	92.14	Processed industrial supplies, intermediate goods
651	Textile yarn	2.01	56.47	Processed industrial supplies, intermediate goods, non-durable

				consumer goods
	Total	48.29		
	The Philippines			
776	Thermionic, cold and photo-cathode valves, tubes and parts	23.26	83.00	Parts and accessories of capital goods, intermediate goods
334	Petroleum products, refined	6.32	67.30	Processed fuels and lubricants, intermediate goods
287	Ores and concentrates of base metals, n.e.s	5.85	59.63	Primary industrial supplies, intermediate goods
562	Fertilizers, manufactured	4.92	68.95	Processed industrial supplies, intermediate goods
081	Food stuff for animals (not including unmilled cereals)	4.68	40.81	Primary and processed industrial supplies, Intermediate goods
764	Telecoms and parts	3.88	66.16	Capital goods
773	Equipment for distributing electricity	2.94	76.94	Processed industrial supplies, intermediate goods
	Total	51.85		
	Thailand			
776	Thermionic, cold and photo-cathode valves, tubes and parts	13.98	83.26	Parts and accessories of Capital goods, Intermediate goods
759	Parts and accessories suitable for 751, 752	12.02	86.52	Parts and accessories of capital goods, intermediate goods
667	Pearls, precious and semi-precious stones	10.89	90.02	Primary and processed industrial supplies, intermediate goods
764	Telecoms and parts	6.13	78.23	Capital goods
749	Non-electric accessories of machinery	2.78	71.56	Capital goods, parts and accessories of capital goods, intermediate goods
651	Textile yarn	2.63	94.23	Processed industrial supplies, intermediate goods
034	Fish, fresh (live or	2.61	40.39	Primary and processed

	dead), chilled or frozen			food and beverages for household consumption
	Total	51.04		

Singapore

776	Thermionic, cold and photo-cathode valves, tubes and parts	11.01	91.25	Parts and accessories of capital goods, intermediate goods
664	Petroleum products, refined	7.63	48.12	Processed fuels and lubricants, intermediate goods
764	Telecoms equipment and parts	6.98	98.68	Capital goods
759	Parts and accessories suitable for 751 and 752	5.93	90.39	Parts and accessories of capital goods, intermediate goods
752	Automatic data processing machines and units thereof	5.02	45.23	Capital goods
763	Gramophones, dictating and sound recorders	3.95	85.79	Durable consumer goods, capital goods
772	Electrical relays such as switches, relays, fuses and plugs	2.58	68.26	Parts and accessories of capital goods, intermediate goods
583	Polymerization and Copolymerization products	2.13	94.83	Processed industrial supplies, intermediate goods
761	Television receivers	2.08	60.29	Durable consumer goods
778	Electrical machinery and apparatus, n.e.s	2.01	74.10	Capital goods, parts and accessories of capital goods, intermediate goods, processed industrial supplies
762	Radio broadcast receivers	1.79	58.29	Durable consumer goods
	Total	51.11		

cork and rubber products) declined from the 1970s to the mid–1980s as labour- and capital-intensive resource-based industries developed in areas such as textiles, clothing, electronics and petroleum products. Following that period, there was an expansion of exports in electrical and mechanical machinery, telecommunications equipment, semiconductors, chemicals and pharmaceuticals. Malaysia's high levels of imports and exports of intermediate goods suggests that many products were re-exported after processing. High levels of imported capital goods as well as parts and components were also necessary because of the lack of a strong local domestic industry in these areas.

Indonesia's top seven commodity groupings contrast with that of Malaysia and Thailand. Indonesia features the prominence of petroleum oils (Group 333) and petroleum products (Group 334) while electronic goods are notably absent. The type of goods involved in Indonesia's IIT mainly encompasses primary fuels and lubricants as well as processed industrial supplies classified as intermediate goods.

Thailand's IIT yields a larger and more diverse range of products in comparison with Malaysia and Indonesia. Except for Indonesia, Group 776 ranks top for Thailand as well as for the other ASEAN countries' IIT.

A salient feature in Singapore's top 11 products is the importance of the SITC 7 product group. The top 11 product groups which represent 51.11 per cent of Singapore's IIT are widely dispersed. This dispersion is mainly contained within the SITC 7 category.

The Philippines has a wide variety of product groupings. Group 776 is ranked as its top product industry, followed by product categories within SITC 0, 2, 3, 5 and 7. This indicates that the Philippines does not have a focused or targeted industry trade but deals mainly in fragmented product commodities. Furthermore, as the profile of its manufacturing trade had remained relatively insignificant at 4 to 6 per cent of total ASEAN manufacturing trade during 1986–95, it seems unlikely that the Philippines' trade structure will be altered materially in the foreseeable future.

4.2.5   ASEAN's Marginal Trade Flows

In the context of ASEAN, adjustment costs associated with the formation of AFTA in 1992 may differ depending upon whether emerging trade can be classified as IT or IIT. As these costs may influence both the gains from trade and the political consensus underpinning the creation of AFTA, it is important that the composition of trade flows be identified and measured correctly. Therefore, if IIT is to be used as an indicator of any perceived changes in import and export flows, it must be measured by an index which is capable of decomposing changes in trade flows between periods, rather than by the level of trade flows in each period. Thus the accuracy of the standard G-L index is undermined.

Tables 4.2 to 4.6 provide estimates of MIIT for ASEAN during 1986–95. The calculations are based on trade data of 149 industries or sectors at the 3-digit classification level for the manufacturing sector (SITC 5–8). The final results are aggregated to the 2-digit level for data handling convenience.[6] Table 4.2 shows that Indonesia's weighted average industry index A_w for SITC 5 (chemicals), measured at the aggregated 2-digit level, is about 40 per cent. This indicates that 40 per cent of the absolute trade flow changes are matched on the export and import sides. But, as it is not possible to segregate VIIT and IT with this index, the weighted average industry index A_w necessarily underestimates the extent of IIT. Hence for all empirical inference and analysis, Brulhart's index (A_w) is sufficient only to reflect the industry's HIIT. Thus, total MIIT can only be reached using equation (4.10) to reflect the aggregation of VIIT and HIIT. Conversely, the interpretation of this figure as a high or relatively low level of MIIT has to be ratified by comparison with the other manufacturing sectors and ASEAN member nations.

For instance, the MIIT index A_J (SITC 5) for Singapore as denoted in Table 4.4 is tabulated at 92.4 per cent. This means that Singapore's emerging trade or marginal trade for SITC 5, composed largely of IIT, would affect an easier transition following the predominance of MIIT in AFTA's adjustment process. At the other extreme, the Philippines' (Table 4.6) A_J index for SITC 5 is tabulated at 5.5 per cent. This means that 94.5 per cent of the Philippines' marginal trade is predominantly inter-industry in nature. For Indonesia, Malaysia and Thailand (Tables 4.2, 4.3 and 4.5) the nature of their SITC 5 marginal trade was, on average, evenly distributed between IIT and IT.

For SITC 6, Tables 4.2 to 4.6 show Malaysia, Singapore and Thailand's high levels of MIIT while Indonesia and the Philippines display comparatively lower levels of MIIT at 49 and 38 per cent respectively. A stark similarity for Malaysia, Singapore and Thailand in this category (SITC 6) is the relatively higher levels of the contribution of sub-divisions 65, 66 and 69 to MIIT. This can mostly be attributed to HIIT reflecting a strong A_w influence. The results for SITC 7 mirror the findings for SITC 6 in that Singapore, Malaysia and Thailand's marginal trade was predominantly intra-industry in nature as compared to Indonesia and the Philippines. Sub-division 77 posted the strongest contribution to MIIT for Singapore, Malaysia and Thailand. This result is consistent with Table 4.1, highlighting Group 776 as the top-ranking contributor towards the IIT and G-L indices for Singapore, Malaysia and Thailand.

On a country-by-country basis, Indonesia and the Philippines were observed to incur markedly higher IT values for their manufacturing sectors compared to Malaysia, Singapore and Thailand. In this context, given the implication of a predominantly inter-industry reallocation, the potential for higher adjustment costs would seem to impact negatively on both Indonesia and the Philippines. On the basis of this measure alone, the Philippines and

Table 4.2 ASEAN trade (Indonesia): 1986–1995

SITC	Description	ΔXi	ΔMI	AI	wi	wiAi	B
51	Organic chemicals	1793365	468567	0.414	0.446	0.185	-0.586
52	Inorganic chemicals	196494	0	0.000	0.039	0.000	-1.000
53	Dyes, tanning, colour products	373979	0	0.000	0.074	0.000	-1.000
54	Medicinal, pharm. products	155815	0	0.000	0.031	0.000	-1.000
55	Perfume, cleaning etc. products	171129	139320	0.898	0.061	0.055	-0.102
56	Fertilizers	110570	148429	0.854	0.051	0.044	0.146
57	Plastics in primary forms	0	0	NA	0.000	NA	NA
58	Plastic materials etc.	876065	305775	0.517	0.233	0.121	-0.483
59	Chemical materials n.e.s	333318	0	0.000	0.066	0.000	-1.000
5	Chemicals, related products n.e.s	4010735	1062091	0.419	1.000	0.419	-0.581

$\Delta MJ=4010735$
$\Delta XJ=1062091$

$\sum|\Delta Mi|=4010735$ $\sum|\Delta Xi|=1062091$ $AW=0.404$ $AJ=0.419$ $AI=0.419$ $(AJ-AW)=0.015$
$(1-AJ)=0.581$

SITC	Description	ΔXi	ΔMI	AI	wi	wiAi	B
61	Leather	439586	-16064	0.000	0.044	0.000	-1.000
62	Rubber manufactures n.e.s	70327	223817	0.478	0.029	0.014	0.522
63	Wood, cork manufactures n.e.s	0	3522790	0.000	0.343	0.000	1.000
64	Paper and paperboard	198373	899861	0.361	0.107	0.039	0.639
65	Textile yarn, fabrics etc.	1134096	2431340	0.636	0.347	0.221	0.364
66	Non-metal mineral n.e.s	325073	283293	0.931	0.059	0.055	-0.069

Code	Item	$\sum\|\Delta Mi\|$	$\sum\|\Delta Xi\|$	AW	AJ	AI	
69	Metal manufactures n.e.s	318035	421147	0.861	0.072	0.062	0.139
6	Basic manufactures	2485490	7766184	0.485	0.997	0.483	0.515
	$\Delta MJ = 2485490$ $\Delta XJ = 7766184$	$\sum\|\Delta Mi\| = 2485490$	$\sum\|\Delta Xi\| = 7798312$	AW=0.390	AJ=0.487	AI=0.485	(AJ − AW) = 0.097 (1−AJ) = 0.513
71	Power-generating equipment	1266645	0	0.000	0.080	0.000	−1.000
72	Machines for special industries	3039134	160807	0.101	0.202	0.020	−0.899
73	Metalworking machinery	510744	0	0.000	0.032	0.000	−1.000
74	General industrial machinery n.e.s	2417686	144498	0.113	0.162	0.018	−0.887
75	Office machines, ADP equip.	129047	501433	0.409	0.040	0.016	0.591
76	Telecoms, sound equip.	894329	1634280	0.707	0.159	0.113	0.293
77	Electric machinery n.e.s	1482215	795250	0.698	0.144	0.100	−0.302
78	Road vehicles	2330316	372173	0.275	0.170	0.047	−0.725
79	Other transport equipment	69552	107911	0.784	0.011	0.009	0.216
7	Machines, transport equip.	12139668	3716352	0.469	1.000	0.469	−0.531
	$\Delta MJ = 12139668$ $\Delta XJ = 3716352$	$\sum\|\Delta Mi\| = 12139668$	$\sum\|\Delta Xi\| = 3716352$	AW=0.324	AJ=0.469	AI=0.469	(AJ − AW) = 0.145 (1−AJ) = 0.531
81	Boilers	0	0	NA	0.000	NA	NA
82	Furniture, parts thereof	0	856573	0.000	0.147	0.000	1.000
83	Travel goods, handbags	0	0	NA	0.000	NA	NA
84	Clothing and accessories	0	2929884	0.000	0.504	0.000	1.000

		ΔX_i	ΔM_i	A_i	w_i	w_iA_i	B
85	Footwear	0		0.000	0.001	0.000	-1.000
87	Precision instruments n.e.s	289973	-7787	0.000	0.050	0.000	-1.000
88	Photo equipment, optical goods etc.	176231	200042	0.937	0.065	0.061	0.063
89	Misc. manufactured goods n.e.s	303784	1043365	0.451	0.232	0.105	0.549
8	Misc. manufactured goods	769988	5022077	0.266	0.997	0.265	0.734
	$\Delta MJ=769988$ $\Delta XJ=5022077$	$\sum\|\Delta M_i\|$ $=769988$	$\sum\|\Delta X_i\|$ $=5037651$	$AW=0.165$	$AJ=0.268$	$AI=0.266$	$(AJ-AW)=0.103$ $(1-AJ)=0.732$

Note: n.e.s. = nowhere else specified.

Source: author's own calculations.

Table 4.3 ASEAN trade (Malaysia): 1986–1995

SITC	Description	ΔX_i	ΔM_i	A_i	w_i	w_iA_i	B
51	Organic chemicals	1045607	439467	0.592	0.248	0.147	-0.408
52	Inorganic chemicals	420417	0	0.000	0.070	0.000	-1.000
53	Dyes, tanning, colour products	310595	0	0.000	0.052	0.000	-1.000
54	Medicinal, pharm. products	203295	0	0.000	0.034	0.000	-1.000
55	Perfume, cleaning etc. products	249818	193431	0.873	0.074	0.065	-0.127

		$\sum|\Delta Mi|$	$\sum|\Delta Xi|$	AW	AJ	AI	
56	Fertilizers	234784	0	0.000	0.039	0.000	-1.000
57	Plastics in primary forms	0	0	NA	0.000	NA	NA
58	Plastic materials etc.	1395550	545260	0.562	0.324	0.182	-0.438
59	Chemical materials n.e.s.	418620	530406	0.882	0.159	0.140	0.118
5	Chemicals, related products n.e.s	4278686	1708564	0.571	1.000	0.571	-0.429
ΔMJ=4278686 ΔXJ=1708564		$\sum|\Delta Mi|$ =4278686	$\sum|\Delta Xi|$ =1708564	AW=0.533	AJ=0.571	AI=0.571	
61	Leather	0	0	NA	0.000	NA	NA
62	Rubber manufactures n.e.s	149847	339352	0.613	0.053	0.033	0.387
63	Wood, cork manufactures n.e.s	0	1697498	0.000	0.184	0.000	1.000
64	Paper and paperboard	1083810	339281	0.477	0.154	0.074	-0.523
65	Textile yarn, fabrics etc.	1181567	969631	0.901	0.233	0.210	-0.099
66	Non-metal mineral n.e.s	1080181	586376	0.704	0.181	0.127	-0.296
69	Metal manufactures n.e.s	1102128	689589	0.770	0.194	0.150	-0.230
6	Basic manufactures	4597533	4621727	0.997	1.000	0.997	0.003
ΔMJ=4597533 ΔXJ=4621727		$\sum|\Delta Mi|$ =4597533	$\sum|\Delta Xi|$ =4621727	AW=0.593	AJ=0.997	AI=0.997	$(AJ - AW)$= 0.404 $(1-AJ)$= 0.003
71	Power-generating equipment	1855477	579627	0.476	0.031	0.015	-0.524
72	Machines for special industries	3983183	340260	0.157	0.055	0.009	-0.843
73	Metalworking machinery	1626562	0	0.000	0.021	0.000	-1.000
74	General industrial machinery n.e.s	2987337	1534643	0.679	0.058	0.039	-0.321

		$\sum\|\Delta Mi\|$	$\sum\|\Delta Xi\|$	AW	AJ	AI	
75	Office machines, ADP equip.	2645275	7167088	0.539	0.125	0.068	0.461
76	Telecoms, sound equip.	3426216	11779677	0.451	0.194	0.087	0.549
77	Electric machinery n.e.s	19168927	13807105	0.837	0.421	0.353	-0.163
78	Road vehicles	2414311	466253	0.324	0.037	0.012	-0.676
79	Other transport equipment	3097668	1452803	0.639	0.058	0.037	-0.361
7	Machines, transport equip.	4204956	37127456	0.948	1.000	0.948	-0.052

$\Delta MJ=4204956$ $\sum\|\Delta Mi\|=4204956$ $AW=0.619$ $AJ=0.948$ $AI=0.948$ $(AJ-AW)=0.329$

$\Delta XJ=37127456$ $\sum\|\Delta Xi\|=37127456$ $(1-AJ)=0.052$

81	Boilers	0	0	NA	0.000	NA	NA
82	Furniture, parts thereof	0	898298	0.000	0.105	0.000	1.000
83	Travel goods, handbags	0	0	NA	0.000	NA	NA
84	Clothing and accessories	114391	1860396	0.116	0.230	0.027	0.884
85	Footwear	0	0	NA	0.000	NA	NA
87	Precision instruments n.e.s	1062190	377183	0.524	0.168	0.088	-0.476
88	Photo equipment, optical goods etc.	679358	669036	0.992	0.157	0.156	-0.008

		ΔXi	ΔMi	Ai	wi	wiAi	B
89	Misc. manufactured goods n.e.s	1138959	1768132	0.784	0.339	0.266	0.216
8	Misc. manufactured goods	2994898	5573045	0.699	1.000	0.699	0.301

ΔMJ=2994898	Σ|ΔMi|=2994898		AW=0.537	AJ=0.699	AI=0.699	(AJ − AW)= 0.162
ΔXJ=5573045	Σ|ΔXi|=5573045					(1−AJ)= 0.301

Source: author's own calculations.

Table 4.4 ASEAN trade (Singapore): 1986–1995

SITC	Description	ΔXi	ΔMi	Ai	wi	wiAi	B
51	Organic chemicals	1349829	1922489	0.825	0.277	0.229	0.175
52	Inorganic chemicals	306672	0	0.000	0.026	0.000	-1.000
53	Dyes, tanning, colour products	388562	478343	0.896	0.073	0.066	0.104
54	Medicinal, pharm. products	531049	466142	0.935	0.084	0.079	-0.065
55	Perfume, cleaning etc. product	605209	542005	0.945	0.097	0.092	-0.055
56	Fertilizers	0	0	NA	0.000	NA	NA
57	Plastics in primary forms	0	0	NA	0.000	NA	NA
58	Plastic materials etc.	1370711	1281509	0.966	0.225	0.217	-0.034
59	Chemical materials n.e.s	1802314	768780	0.598	0.218	0.130	-0.402
5	Chemicals, related products n.e.s	6354346	5459268	0.924	1.000	0.924	-0.076

		$\sum\|\Delta Mi\|$ =6354346	$\sum\|\Delta Xi\|$ =5459268	AW=0.812	AJ=0.924	AI=0.924	(AJ − AW)= 0.112 (1−AJ)= 0.076
	ΔMJ=6354346 ΔXJ=5459268						
61	Leather	0	0	NA	0.000	NA	NA
62	Rubber manufactures n.e.s	451711	282923	0.770	0.081	0.063	−0.230
63	Wood, cork manufactures n.e.s	164508	17594	0.193	0.020	0.004	−0.807
64	Paper and paperboard.	883848	443250	0.668	0.147	0.098	−0.332
65	Textile yarn, fabrics etc.	1079536	1069273	0.995	0.238	0.237	−0.005
66	Non-metal mineral n.e.s	1493721	609158	0.579	0.233	0.135	−0.421
69	Metal manufactures n.e.s	1548682	990101	0.780	0.281	0.219	−0.220
6	Basic manufactures	5622006	3412299	0.755	1.000	0.755	−0.245
		$\sum\|\Delta Mi\|$ =5622006	$\sum\|\Delta Xi\|$ =3412299	AW=0.755	AJ=0.755	AI=0.755	(AJ — AW)= 0.000 (1−AJ)= 0.245
	ΔMJ=5622006 ΔXJ=3412299						
71	Power-generating equipment	2375929	1422800	0.749	0.029	0.022	−0.251
72	Machines for special industries	3205626	1744191	0.705	0.038	0.027	−0.295
73	Metalworking machinery	638928	410398	0.782	0.008	0.006	−0.218
74	General industrial machinery n.e.s	4473467	2940199	0.793	0.056	0.045	−0.207
75	Office machines, ADP equip.	12227464	26937182	0.624	0.298	0.186	0.376
76	Telecoms, sound equip.	7837442	11272312	0.820	0.146	0.119	0.180
77	Electric machinery n.e.s	26906557	22540928	0.912	0.376	0.343	−0.088
78	Road vehicles	2370537	1054207	0.616	0.026	0.016	−0.384

		ΔMi	ΔXi	AW	AJ	AI	$(AJ-AW)$
79	Other transport equipment	2411415	566580	0.381	0.023	0.009	−0.619
7	Machines, transport equip.	62447365	68888797	0.951	1.000	0.951	0.049
	ΔMJ=62447365 ΔXJ=68888797	$\sum \|\Delta Mi\|$ =6244736	$\sum \|\Delta Xi\|$ =68888797	AW=0.773	AJ=0.951	AI=0.951	$(AJ-AW)$= 0.178 $(I-AJ)$= 0.049
81	Boilers	0	0	NA	0.000	NA	NA
82	Furniture, parts thereof	328380	128621	0.563	0.028	0.016	−0.437
83	Travel goods, handbags	239377	0	0.000	0.014	0.000	−1.000
84	Clothing and accessories	1284217	789967	0.762	0.125	0.095	−0.238
85	Footwear	−88566	0	0.000	0.005	0.000	1.000
87	Precision instruments n.e.s	2134836	1402011	0.793	0.213	0.169	−0.207
88	Photo equipment, optical goods etc.	1847123	1572642	0.920	0.206	0.190	−0.080
89	Misc. manufactures goods n.e.s	3968762	2978403	0.857	0.419	0.359	−0.143
8	Misc. manufactured goods	9714129	6871644	0.829	1.000	0.829	−0.171
	ΔMJ=9714129 ΔXJ=6871644	$\sum \|\Delta Mi\|$ =9714129	$\sum \|\Delta Xi\|$ =6871644	AW=0.829	AJ=0.829	AI=0.829	$(AJ-AW)$= 0.000 $(I-AJ)$= 0.171

Source: author's own calculations.

Table 4.5 *ASEAN trade (Thailand): 1986–1995*

SITC	Description	ΔXi	ΔMi	Ai	wi	wiAi	B
51	Organic chemicals	2151338	210523	0.178	0.309	0.055	-0.822
52	Inorganic chemicals	270928	0	0.000	0.035	0.000	-1.000
53	Dyes, tanning, colour products	471046	463991	0.992	0.122	0.121	-0.008
54	Medicinal, pharm. products	358839	126297	0.521	0.063	0.033	-0.479
55	Perfume, cleaning etc. products	243833	0	0.000	0.032	0.000	-1.000
56	Fertilizers	453199	0	0.000	0.059	0.000	-1.000
57	Plastics in primary forms	0	0	NA	0.000	NA	NA
58	Plastic materials etc.	1251271	665362	0.694	0.251	0.174	-0.306
59	Chemical materials n.e.s	628440	347800	0.713	0.128	0.091	-0.287
5	Chemicals, related products n.e.s	5828894	1813973	0.475	1.000	0.475	-0.525

ΔMJ=5828894
ΔXJ=1813973

		∑│ΔMi│ =5828894	∑│ΔXi│ =1813973	AW=0.475	AJ=0.475	AI=0.475	(AJ – AW)= 0.000
							(I –AJ)= 0.525

61	Leather	322400	400887	0.891	0.067	0.059	0.109
62	Rubber manufactures n.e.s	299841	377889	0.885	0.062	0.055	0.115
63	Wood, cork manufactures n.e.s	0	214393	0.000	0.020	0.000	1.000
64	Paper and paperboard	644434	308586	0.648	0.088	0.057	-0.352
65	Textile yarn, fabrics etc.	1232016	1477349	0.909	0.249	0.227	0.091
66	Non-metal mineral n.e.s	1480755	1486505	0.998	0.273	0.272	0.002

		$\sum |\Delta Mi|$	$\sum |\Delta Xi|$	AW	AJ	AI	
69	Metal manufactures n.e.s	1946940	684303	0.520	0.242	0.126	-0.480
6	Basic manufactures	5926386	4949912	0.910	1.000	0.910	-0.090
	ΔMJ=5926386 ΔXJ=4949912	$\sum |\Delta Mi|$ =5926386	$\sum |\Delta Xi|$ =4949912	AW=0.796	AJ=0.910	AI=0.910	$(AJ-AW)$= 0.114 $(1-AJ)$= 0.090
71	Power-generating equipment	1526333	538031	0.521	0.042	0.022	-0.479
72	Machines for special industries	3849390	129500	0.065	0.081	0.005	-0.935
73	Metalworking machinery	1096864	0	0.000	0.022	0.000	-1.000
74	General industrial machinery nes	4414475	1627828	0.539	0.123	0.066	-0.461
75	Office machines, ADP equip.	2742932	5658334	0.653	0.171	0.112	0.347
76	Telecoms, sound equip.	2121023	3035780	0.823	0.105	0.086	0.177
77	Electric machinery n.e.s	8774021	5683568	0.786	0.295	0.232	-0.214
78	Road vehicles	4915063	706521	0.251	0.115	0.029	-0.749
79	Other transport equipment	1616617	636142	0.565	0.046	0.026	-0.435
7	Machines, transport equip.	31056718	18015704	0.734	1.000	0.734	-0.266
	ΔMJ=31056718 ΔXJ=18015704	$\sum |\Delta Mi|$ =31056718	$\sum |\Delta Xi|$ =18015704	AW=0.578	AJ=0.734	AI=0.734	$(AJ-AW)$= 0.156 $(1-AJ)$= 0.266
81	Boilers	0	0	NA	0.000	NA	NA
82	Furniture, parts thereof	0	684485	0.000	0.045	0.000	1.000
83	Travel goods, handbags	0	427112	0.000	0.028	0.000	1.000
84	Clothing and accessories	0	4242258	0.000	0.276	0.000	1.000

SITC	Description	ΔXi	ΔMi	Ai	wi	wiAi	B
85	Footwear	0	1984533	0.000	0.129	0.000	1.000
87	Precision instruments n.e.s	828930	311461	0.546	0.074	0.041	-0.454
88	Photo equipment, optical goods etc.	510158	639921	0.887	0.075	0.066	0.113
89	Misc. manufactured goods n.e,s	2032871	3711494	0.708	0.374	0.264	0.292
8	Misc. manufactured goods	3371959	12001264	0.439	1.000	0.439	0.561

ΔMJ=3371959	$\sum \lvert \Delta Mi \rvert$ =3371959	$\sum \lvert \Delta Xi \rvert$ =12001264	AW=0.371	AJ=0.439	AI=0.439	$(AJ-AW)$= 0.067
ΔXJ=12001264						$(1-AJ)$= 0.561

Source: author's own calculations.

Table 4.6 ASEAN trade (Philippines): 1986–1995

SITC	Description	ΔXi	ΔMi	Ai	wi	wiAi	B
51	Organic chemicals	295880	-15085	0.000	0.166	0.000	-1.000
52	Inorganic chemicals	135502	-15646	0.000	0.081	0.000	-1.000
53	Dyes, tanning, colour products	128308	0	0.000	0.069	0.000	-1.000
54	Medicinal, pharm. products	230193	0	0.000	0.123	0.000	-1.000
55	Perfume, cleaning etc. products	122822	0	0.000	0.066	0.000	-1.000
56	Fertilizers	132507	6468	0.093	0.074	0.007	-0.907
57	Plastics in primary forms	0	0	NA	0.000	NA	NA

No.	Description	$\sum\lvert\Delta Mi\rvert$	$\sum\lvert\Delta Xi\rvert$	AW	AJ	AI	
58	Plastic materials etc.	555422	23015	0.080	0.309	0.025	−0.920
59	Chemical materials n.e.s	186512	22070	0.212	0.112	0.024	−0.788
5	Chemicals, related products n.e.s	1787146	20822	0.023	0.967	0.022	−0.977
	ΔMJ=1787146 ΔXJ=20822	$\sum\lvert\Delta Mi\rvert$ =1787146	$\sum\lvert\Delta Xi\rvert$ =82284	AW=0.055	AJ=0.055	AI=0.023	$(AJ-AW)$= 0.000 $(1-AJ)$= 0.945
61	Leather	81472	0	0.000	0.039	0.000	−1.000
62	Rubber manufactures n.e.s	139289	0	0.000	0.066	0.000	−1.000
63	Wood, cork manufactures n.e.s	0	34613	0.000	0.016	0.000	1.000
64	Paper and paperboard	278565	54689	0.328	0.158	0.052	−0.672
65	Textile yarn, fabrics etc.	729313	168789	0.376	0.425	0.160	−0.624
66	Non-metal mineral n.e.s	223850	90189	0.574	0.148	0.085	−0.426
69	Metal manufactures n.e.s	262854	51952	0.330	0.149	0.049	−0.670
6	Basic manufactures	1715343	400232	0.378	1.000	0.378	−0.622
	ΔMJ=1715343 ΔXJ=400232	$\sum\lvert\Delta Mi\rvert$ =1715343	$\sum\lvert\Delta Xi\rvert$ =400232	AW=0.346	AJ=0.378	AI=0.378	$(AJ-AW)$= 0.033 $(1-AJ)$= 0.622
71	Power-generating equipment	470238	0	0.000	0.040	0.000	−1.000
72	Machines for special industries	1226105	0	0.000	0.104	0.000	−1.000
73	Metalworking machinery	184813	0	0.000	0.016	0.000	−1.000
74	General industrial machinery n.e.s	792025	0	0.000	0.067	0.000	−1.000
75	Office machines, ADP equip.	508251	442613	0.931	0.081	0.075	−0.069

		ΔM_i	ΔX_i	AW	AJ	AI	
76	Telecoms, sound equip.	1279836	794440	0.766	0.176	0.135	−0.234
77	Electric machinery n.e.s	1882416	1945205	0.984	0.325	0.319	0.016
78	Road vehicles	1459116	207295	0.249	0.141	0.035	−0.751
79	Other transport equipment	596625	0	0.000	0.051	0.000	−1.000
7	Machines, transport equip.	8399425	3389553	0.575	1.000	0.575	−0.425
	ΔMJ=8399425 ΔXJ=3389553	$\sum \lvert \Delta Mi \rvert$ =8399425	$\sum \lvert \Delta Xi \rvert$ =3389553	AW=0.564	AJ=0.575	AI=0.575	$(AJ - AW)$= 0.011 $(1-AJ)$=0.425
81	Boilers	0	0	NA	0.000	NA	NA
82	Furniture, parts thereof	0	186848	0.000	0.079	0.000	1.000
83	Travel goods, handbags	0	98583	0.000	0.042	0.000	1.000
84	Clothing and accessories	0	801416	0.000	0.341	0.000	1.000
85	Footwear	0	123018	0.000	0.052	0.000	1.000
87	Precision instruments n.e.s	197910	0	0.000	0.084	0.000	−1.000
88	Photo equipment, optical goods etc.	137680	0	0.000	0.059	0.000	−1.000
89	Misc. manufactured goods n.e.s	427512	379201	0.940	0.343	0.322	−0.060
8	Misc. manufactured goods	763102	1589066	0.649	1.000	0.649	0.351
	ΔMJ=763102 ΔXJ=1589066	$\sum \lvert \Delta Mi \rvert$ =763102	$\sum \lvert \Delta Xi \rvert$ =1589066	AW=0.322	AJ=0.649	AI=0.649	$(AJ - AW)$= 0.326 $(1-AJ)$=0.351

Source: own calculations

Indonesia would potentially incur the greatest adjustment costs with the introduction of AFTA. This is because both countries' exports and imports in their manufacturing sectors show, on average, (SITC 5–8) diverging trends (low A_w). In contrast, Singapore would perhaps benefit most from AFTA given the high level of MIIT, which is concomitant with low adjustment costs as a result of trade-induced factor reallocation within sectors.

The decomposition of ASEAN's manufacturing trade flows is reflected in Table 4.7. The table calculates and segments individual country-weighted IIT, HIIT, VIIT and IT for the manufacturing industry. VIIT accounts for 14 to 36 per cent of total IIT between the ASEAN member nations, while HIIT was responsible for 33 to 78 per cent of total IIT. The variation in the relative importance of HIIT and VIIT across the economies in the sample can be explained in large part by industry- and country-specific factors. Indonesia's and the Philippines' IIT were the lowest among the ASEAN nations and this probably reflects their status as developing nations. The more industrialised countries evidently have more evenly distributed trade growth across sectors than countries at the take-off stage, where export growth tends to be concentrated in a narrow group of industries. These export industries are distinct from the sectors where imports grew most. The high levels of HIIT for Singapore, Malaysia and Thailand are associated with economies of scale and occur when products are differentiated and consumers express preferences for product variety.

Table 4.7   Decomposition of ASEAN marginal trade flows, 1986–1995

	IIT (AJ)	HIIT (AW)	VIIT (AJ-AW)	IT (1-AJ)
Indonesia	0.532	0.328	0.204	0.468
Malaysia	0.960	0.605	0.355	0.040
Singapore	0.997	0.780	0.217	0.003
Thailand	0.887	0.559	0.328	0.113
Philippines	0.599	0.455	0.144	0.401

Source: Own calculations.

On the other hand, the higher levels of inter-industry marginal trade for Indonesia and the Philippines on an overall basis are symptomatic of adjustment difficulties following AFTA. Concerns have also been raised by Indonesia and the Philippines, who are the two most protected countries in ASEAN, that their firms will not be able to compete with the more efficient producers in the other ASEAN nations (DeRosa 1995).

4.3   CONCLUSION

This chapter has looked into the various components of IIT measurements with regard to ASEAN's manufacturing industries. The patterns of IIT and changing structure of ASEAN manufacturing trade were examined over a 10-year period under two distinctly disparate trading structures. The introduction of AFTA in 1992 impacts differently on each member nation's commodity groups. Adjustment issues and transitional costs associated with ASEAN's trade liberalisation were also appraised and examined following the SAH.

Singapore ranks first as an exporter of office and computing machinery and electrical machinery. Its dominant position can be accounted for by domestic production and entrepot trade. The largest categories of domestic exports were disk drives, computers, sub-assemblies, integrated circuits, television receivers and colour TV sets. Re-exports were concentrated in integrated circuits, computers, disk drives, colour TV sets, radios and telecommunications equipment.

Since 1986, Thailand has experienced a rapid increase in merchandise exports, and this growth has in turn proven to be a major source of overall growth for the Thai economy. In recent years, by far the most conspicuous export growth for Thailand has been in office and computing machinery and electrical machinery. On the import side, Thai trade has historically been weighted toward manufacturing, especially chemicals, metals, non-electrical machinery, electrical machinery and transport machinery.

Malaysia is ASEAN's largest exporter of semiconductors and videocassette recorders. Export of electronic products and electrical machinery has grown exponentially over the past two decades and is in line with measures by the Malaysian government to increase the export of higher value-added products. On the import side, manufactured imports grew nearly fourfold during 1986–92. This rapid growth was the result of continued expansion of economic activity, with investment goods being the fastest-growing category.

Indonesia's trade reforms and an export promotion policy in the late 1980s contributed to increased manufacturing exports, initially in textiles and plywood products, but later in clothing, footwear, electronic equipment and chemicals. Exports of petroleum-related products continued to be important. Imports also increased dramatically, mainly in chemicals and machinery (where exports are very low), but remained a relatively small share of output compared with the other ASEAN nations.

In the Philippines before the recent push towards trade liberalisation, industries such as manufacturing and textiles enjoyed significant barriers to entry. Almost all firms in house-appliance manufacturing were either licencees or joint-venture partners of Japanese or American manufacturers (USAID 1992). Even though the Philippines has gradually reduced its protectionist policies, its government must continue to resist domestic lobbying for greater protection. The successful implementation of AFTA hinges on the eventual elimination of protectionist policies within ASEAN but the associated political and financial costs for the government are a potential difficulty for the Philippines.

The proliferation of technological manufacturing trade in ASEAN is attributed to the dominant role of MNCs in ASEAN where the location of higher value-added segments is dependent upon an economy's industrial structure. For instance, the factor-driven economies of Indonesia and the Philippines are characterised by sales and service affiliates and labour-intensive assembly operations. In Thailand, production of low-value added components is increasing. Malaysia is moving towards increasing capital accumulation and sophisticated production techniques as components-production facilities are upgraded. Singapore's industrialisation is characterised by the dominant participation of MNCs from Japan, the United States and Europe and by its high trade orientation. Singapore's move towards the innovation-driven stage has benefited from the highly focused government policies aimed at attracting managerial, design and research segments of the value-added chain, in addition to its high value-added components production.

For ASEAN, one of the benefits of trade liberalisation is that it provides a means of directly lowering the general price level by making imported goods and services less costly. The adjustment costs from trade liberalisation will include the uncomfortable decisions of closing down or restructuring inefficient companies. Inefficient state enterprises in politically sensitive areas are likely to pose a more difficult challenge to free trade. Bailing out these loss-making industries is an expensive proposition and risks the erosion of macroeconomic discipline. The findings of the MIIT indices indicate the relatively high costs of industrial adjustment for the Philippines and to a lesser extent Indonesia. The industrial structure of Indonesia is dominated by large state-owned enterprises in strategic industries such as cement, fertilisers and steel. The rent-seeking interests can be expected to react to the adjustment process by resisting trade and investment liberalisation. The threat these protected industries pose to economic growth can be minimised by transparent adjustment policies and rigorous implementation of trade liberalisation, first under the Common Effective Preferential Tariff, and then on a multilateral basis. Banks must be prepared to accept losses as well, given the excessive unsecured debts.

As tariffs are reduced and non-tariff measures eliminated, it is predicted that new forms of protection such as anti-dumping petitions will increase. These contingent forms of protection can be non-transparent and subject to anti-competitive abuses by the industry. Hence, it will be important to guard against their undisciplined use as import duties are lowered.

With the establishment of anti-dumping regulations in Indonesia in 1996, each of the ASEAN nations would now have a potential mechanism for protecting inefficient industries from import competition as tariff and traditional non-tariff barriers are lowered. A rise in the incidence of anti-dumping complaints within ASEAN would be consistent with the earlier experiences of Europe, North America and Australia. Transparent and GATT-consistent anti-dumping procedures and a sceptical attitude on the part of responsible government officials towards complaints of dumping from industry will help limit the re-emergence of protectionist policies in the guise of anti-dumping.

The slower growth in ASEAN following the financial crises of 1997 presented another hurdle to progress in trade liberalisation and expansion. Protectionism is a common refuge for economies in times of slower growth. At the 31st ASEAN Economic Ministers meeting held in Singapore, concerns about back-tracking on AFTA was raised in light of delays to reduce tariffs on key products by January 2000 (Velloor 1999). Despite rapid recovery in the region, the lack of a wholehearted commitment to trade liberalisation impinges negatively an eventual total free-trade area for ASEAN.

APPENDIX TO CHAPTER 4

Table A4.1   Standard international trade classification, revision 3 (manufacturing: SITC 5–8)

Division Sub-division Group Industry

---

5   CHEMICALS AND RELATED PRODUCTS

     51   Organic chemicals
          511 Hydrocarbons, n.e.s and related products
          512 Alcohols, phenols, phenol-alcohols and related products
          513 Carboxylic acids and related products or derivatives
          514 Nitrogen-function compounds
          515 Organo-inorganic compounds and related salts
          516 Organic chemicals, n.e.s

     52   Inorganic chemicals
          522 Inorganic chemical elements and related salts
          523 Metallic salts and peroxysalts of inorganic acids
          524 Inorganic chemicals, n.e.s
          525 Radioactive and associated materials

Table A4.1 Continued

Division Sub-division Group Industry

53   Dyeing, tanning and colouring materials
   531 Synthetic organic colouring matter based products
   532 Dyeing and tanning extracts and synthetic tanning materials
   533 Pigments, paints, varnishes and related materials

54   Medicinal and pharmaceutical products
   541 Medicinal and pharmaceutical products
   542 Medicaments

55   Essential oils, resinoids and perfume materials
   551 Essential oils, perfume and flavour materials
   553 Perfumery, cosmetics or toilet preparations
   554 Soap, cleansing and polishing preparations

56   Fertilisers
   562 Fertilisers

57   Plastics in primary forms
   571 Polymers of ethylene in primary forms
   572 Polymers of styrene in primary forms
   573 Polymers of vinyl chloride related materials in primary forms
   574 Polyacetals and related materials in primary forms
   575 Plastics, n.e.s. in primary forms
   579 Waste, parings and scrap of plastics

58   Plastics in non-primary form
   581 Tubes, pipes and hoses of plastics
   582 Plates, sheets, film, foil and strip if plastics
   583 Monofilament related plastics, n.e.s.

59   Chemical materials and products, n.e.s.
   591 Insecticides and related products
   592 Starches, glues and related substances
   593 Explosives and pyrotechnic products
   597 Prepared additives for mineral oils etc.
   598 Miscellaneous chemical products, n.e.s.

6   BASIC MANUFACTURES

Table A4.1   Continued

Division Sub-division   Group Industry

61   Leather, leather manufactures, n.e.s
   611 Leather
   612 Manufactures of leather or composition leather
   613 Furskins and related materials

62   Rubber manufactures, n.e.s
   621 Materials of rubber etc.
   625 Rubber tyres and related products
   629 Articles of rubber, n.e.s

63   Cork and wood manufactures other than furniture
   633 Cork manufactures
   634 Veneers, plywood, particle board and other woods
   635 Wood manufactures, n.e.s

64   Paper, paperboard and related articles
   641 Paper and paperboard
   642 Paper and paperboard, cut to size or shape

65   Textile yarn, fabrics, n.e.s and related products
   651 Textile yarn
   652 Cotton fabrics, woven
   653 Woven fabrics of man-made textile materials
   654 Woven fabrics of textile materials other than 653
   655 Knitted or crocheted fabrics, n.e.s
   656 Tulles, lace, embroidery, ribbons, trimmings and other wares
   657 Special yarns, special textile fabrics and related products
   658 Man-made articles of textile materials, n.e.s
   659 Floor coverings, etc.

66   Non-metallic mineral manufactures, n.e.s.
   661 Lime, cement and fabricated construction materials
   662 Clay construction materials etc.
   663 Mineral manufactures, n.e.s.
   664 Glass
   665 Glassware
   666 Pottery
   667 Pearls, precious and semi-precious stones etc.

Table A4.1 Continued

Division Sub-division Group Industry

69   Manufactures of metals, n.e.s.
  691 Metal structures and parts, n.e.s. of iron, steel or aluminium
  692 Metal containers for storage or transport
  693 Wire products and fencing grills
  694 Nails, screws, nuts etc and similar articles of iron, steel, copper or aluminium
  695 Tools for hand-use or in machines
  696 Cutlery
  697 Household equipment of base metal, n.e.s.
  699 Manufactures of base metals, n.e.s.

7   MACHINERY AND TRANSPORT EQUIPMENT

71   Power-generating machinery and equipment
  711 Steam, vapour boilers and plants and related parts
  712 Steam, other vapour turbines and parts, n.e.s.
  713 Internal combustion piston engines and parts
  714 Engines and motors and parts, n.e.s.
  716 Rotating electric plants and parts, n.e.s.
  718 Power-generating machinery and parts, n.e.s.

72   Machinery specialised for particular industries
  721 Agricultural machinery (excluding 722) and parts
  722 Tractors
  723 Civil engineering and contractors' plant and equip.
  724 Textile and leather machinery and parts, n.e.s
  725 Paper mill, pulp mill and paper-cutting machinery for manufacture of paper articles and parts
  726 Printing and book-binding machinery and parts
  727 Food-processing machines
  728 Specialised machinery and equipment and parts, n.e.s

73   Metal-working machinery
  731 Machine tools for removing metals or other materials
  733 Machine tools for working metals and related metals without removing material
  735 Parts and accessories suitable for use with 731 or 733
  737 Metal-working machinery and parts, n.e.s

Table A4.1 Continued

Division Sub-division Group Industry

74 General industrial machinery and equipment or parts, n.e.s
   741 Heating and cooling equipment and parts, n.e.s
   742 Pumps for liquids and related parts
   743 Pumps (excluding 742) and parts
   744 Mechanical handling equipment and parts, n.e.s
   745 Non-electrical machinery and related tools or apparatus and parts, n.e.s
   746 Ball or roller bearings
   747 Taps, cocks, valves and similar appliances etc.
   748 Transmission shafts, cranks and parts etc.
   749 Non-electric parts and accessories of machinery

75 Office machines and automatic data processing machines
   751 Office machines
   752 Automatic data processing machines and related units, n.e.s
   759 Parts and accessories suitable for use with 751 or 752

76 Telecoms and sound-recording apparatus and equipment
   761 TV receivers and apparatus
   762 Radio-broadcast receivers and apparatus
   763 Sound recorders or reproducers
   764 Telecoms equipment and parts or accessories, n.e.s

77 Electrical machinery, apparatus, appliances and parts, n.e.s
   771 Electric power machinery and parts
   772 Electrical apparatus for use with electrical circuits
   773 Equipment for distributing electricity, n.e.s
   774 Electro-diagnostic apparatus for medical usage
   775 Household type electrical and non-electrical equipment, n.e.s
   776 Thermionic, cold cathode or photocathode valves and tubes, n.e.s
   778 Electrical machinery and apparatus, n.e.s

78 Road vehicles
   781 Motor cars and vehicles (excluding public vehicles)
   782 Motor vehicles for transport of goods and special purpose motor vehicles
   783 Road motor vehicles, n.e.s.
   784 Parts and accessories of 781 and 782
   785 Motorcycles etc.
   786 Trailers and semi-trailers etc.

Table A4.1 Continued

Division Sub-division Group Industry

79   Transport equipment, n.e.s
   791 Railway vehicles and associated equipment
   792 Aircraft and associated equipment or parts
   793 Ships, boats and floating structures

8   MISCELLANEOUS MANUFACTURED GOODS

81   Pre-fabricated buildings and associated materials, n.e.s
   811 Pre-fabricated buildings
   812 Sanitary, plumbing and heating fixtures and fittings, n.e.s
   813 Lighting fixtures and fittings, n.e.s

82   Furniture and parts thereof
   821 Furniture and parts thereof

83   Travel goods, handbags and similar containers
   831 Travel goods, handbags, i.e. camera cases, travel sets etc and related products

84   Articles of apparel and clothing materials
   841 Men's or boys' clothing of woven textile fabrics
   842 Women's or girls' clothing of woven textile fabrics
   843 Men's or boys' clothing, knitted or crocheted textile fabric
   844 Women's or girls' clothing, knitted or crocheted textile fabric
   845 Articles of apparel and textile fabrics, n.e.s
   846 Clothing accessories of textile fabrics
   848 Articles of apparel and clothing accessories of headgear of all materials

85   Footwear
   851 Footwear

87   Professional, scientific and controlling instruments and apparatus, n.e.s.
   871 Optical instruments and apparatus, n.e.s
   872 Instruments and appliances, n.e.s for medical, surgical, dental or veterinary purposes
   873 Meters and counters, n.e.s
   874 Measuring, checking, analysing and controlling instruments and apparatus, n.e.s

Table A4.1   Continued

Division Sub-division   Group Industry

  88   Photographic apparatus, equipment and supplies and optical goods
      881   Photographic apparatus and equipment, n.e.s
      882   Photographic and cinematographic supplies
      883   Cinematographic film
      884   Optical goods, n.e.s
      885   Watches and clocks

  89   Miscellaneous manufactured articles, n.e.s
      891   Arms and ammunition
      892   Printed matter
      893   Articles, n.e.s of plastics
      894   Baby carriages, toys, games and sporting goods
      895   Office and stationery supplies, n.e.s
      896   Works of art, collectors' pieces and antiques
      897   Jewellery, goldsmiths' and silversmiths' wares, n.e.s
      898   Musical instruments, parts and accessories
      899   Miscellaneous manufactured articles, n.e.s

Source: Policy Analysis Division, Faculty of Commerce and Business Administration,
       University of British Columbia.

Table A4.2 Profile of ASEAN manufacturing trade, 1986–90 (%)

SITC 1986	Indonesia	Malaysia	Singapore	Thailand	Philippines	ASEAN
51	0.87	0.37	1.12	0.64	0.40	3.40
52	0.56	0.22	0.22	0.15	0.20	1.34
53	0.22	0.08	0.26	0.20	0.07	0.83
54	0.17	0.21	0.42	0.20	0.12	1.12
55	0.19	0.19	0.41	0.12	0.06	0.96
56	0.24	0.20	0.10	0.29	0.33	1.14
57	0.01	0.01	0.03	0.01	0.01	0.07
58	0.81	0.39	1.13	0.49	0.27	3.10
59	0.30	0.32	0.69	0.32	0.14	1.77
5	3.36	1.99	4.36	2.42	1.59	13.72
61	0.03	0.01	0.05	0.14	0.02	0.26
62	0.15	0.15	0.29	0.15	0.05	0.77
63	1.78	0.33	0.46	0.14	0.19	2.90
64	0.25	0.44	0.71	0.25	0.14	1.78
65	0.78	0.88	2.27	1.30	0.40	5.63
66	0.33	0.31	0.77	0.90	0.07	2.38
69	0.46	0.41	1.21	0.36	0.11	2.56
6	3.79	2.53	5.76	3.24	0.97	16.29
71	0.88	0.43	1.42	0.28	0.14	3.15
72	1.34	0.87	1.50	0.64	0.23	4.57
73	0.13	0.11	0.28	0.09	0.04	0.66
74	1.03	0.94	2.49	0.74	0.20	5.39
75	0.18	0.25	4.65	0.50	0.06	5.64
76	0.30	1.49	4.78	0.47	0.08	7.12
77	0.78	7.46	10.23	2.37	1.04	21.89
78	1.02	0.54	0.71	0.60	0.14	3.02
79	0.87	0.97	2.38	0.14	0.04	4.41
7	6.52	13.05	28.43	5.84	1.98	55.83
81	0.02	0.03	0.09	0.02	0.01	0.16
82	0.03	0.05	0.33	0.12	0.14	0.67
83	0.00	0.01	0.14	0.05	0.02	0.22
84	0.82	0.70	1.62	1.30	0.46	4.89
85	0.02	0.05	0.17	0.18	0.05	0.47
87	0.28	0.32	0.97	0.20	0.05	1.82
88	0.15	0.31	0.97	0.24	0.05	1.72
89	0.34	0.64	2.12	0.79	0.33	4.22
8	1.67	2.11	6.40	2.89	1.10	14.17
All manufacturing	15.33	19.68	44.96	14.38	5.65	100.00

Manufacturing trade value 64090145

Table A4.2 Continued

SITC	Indonesia	Malaysia	Singapore	Thailand	ASEAN
1987					
51	0.72	0.36	1.14	0.74	2.95
52	0.57	0.20	0.22	0.16	1.15
53	0.21	0.08	0.26	0.23	0.78
54	0.15	0.18	0.36	0.18	0.87
55	0.15	0.18	0.42	0.13	0.88
56	0.17	0.20	0.09	0.22	0.67
57	0.01	0.01	0.02	0.00	0.04
58	0.78	0.45	1.43	0.54	3.20
59	0.40	0.30	0.64	0.33	1.66
5	3.15	1.95	4.57	2.53	12.20
61	0.06	0.01	0.06	0.20	0.34
62	0.10	0.17	0.31	0.15	0.73
63	2.36	0.42	0.53	0.18	3.49
64	0.30	0.43	0.74	0.29	1.76
65	0.83	0.90	2.45	1.40	5.59
66	0.26	0.30	0.76	1.09	2.41
69	0.41	0.42	1.14	0.42	2.39
6	4.32	2.65	5.99	3.73	16.69
71	0.91	0.56	1.57	0.41	3.43
72	1.39	0.74	1.50	0.76	4.37
73	0.21	0.12	0.36	0.13	0.83
74	0.95	0.88	2.52	0.91	5.26
75	0.12	0.23	5.97	0.70	7.02
76	0.35	1.67	5.83	0.46	8.30
77	0.74	7.39	10.66	2.52	21.31
78	0.87	0.43	0.88	0.83	3.02
79	0.44	0.68	2.06	0.08	3.26
7	5.97	12.69	31.35	6.80	56.80
81	0.03	0.02	0.07	0.02	0.14
82	0.04	0.06	0.28	0.17	0.56
83	0.00	0.01	0.17	0.10	0.29
84	0.74	0.80	1.85	1.85	5.22
85	0.03	0.06	0.16	0.27	0.52
87	0.35	0.31	1.02	0.21	1.90
88	0.10	0.30	0.98	0.23	1.62
89	0.18	0.66	2.23	1.01	4.07
8	1.47	2.22	6.76	3.85	14.31
All Manufacturing	14.92	19.51	48.67	16.90	100.00

Manufacturing trade value   81693495

Table A4.2 Continued

SITC	Indonesia	Malaysia	Singapore	Thailand	Philippines	ASEAN
1988						
51	0.62	0.37	1.11	0.67	0.30	3.07
52	0.37	0.18	0.23	0.14	0.13	1.06
53	0.15	0.09	0.26	0.20	0.06	0.75
54	0.11	0.15	0.30	0.15	0.10	0.80
55	0.11	0.14	0.41	0.11	0.05	0.82
56	0.18	0.22	0.09	0.25	0.17	0.90
57	0.01	0.01	0.03	0.00	0.00	0.05
58	0.63	0.46	1.60	0.51	0.23	3.43
59	0.25	0.28	0.57	0.31	0.12	1.53
5	2.42	1.89	4.59	2.35	1.16	12.41
61	0.07	0.01	0.07	0.18	0.02	0.36
62	0.09	0.15	0.29	0.14	0.05	0.72
63	1.93	0.30	0.48	0.12	0.16	2.98
64	0.25	0.40	0.68	0.22	0.11	1.65
65	0.83	0.75	1.81	1.15	0.34	4.87
66	0.26	0.28	0.67	0.90	0.08	2.18
69	0.24	0.37	1.06	0.45	0.09	2.21
6	3.67	2.25	5.05	3.16	0.84	14.97
71	0.58	0.40	1.51	0.49	0.06	3.05
72	1.09	0.89	1.64	0.99	0.29	4.90
73	0.21	0.11	0.38	0.22	0.04	0.95
74	0.77	0.88	2.68	1.03	0.19	5.55
75	0.12	0.25	6.52	1.22	0.08	8.18
76	0.26	1.71	6.16	0.51	0.15	8.79
77	0.43	6.17	10.21	2.55	0.89	20.25
78	0.67	0.51	0.97	1.16	0.22	3.52
79	0.25	0.36	1.72	0.60	0.11	3.05
7	4.38	11.26	31.77	8.77	2.03	58.22
81	0.02	0.02	0.06	0.02	0.01	0.13
82	0.07	0.07	0.24	0.21	0.16	0.74
83	0.00	0.01	0.18	0.12	0.02	0.33
84	0.67	0.74	1.54	1.63	0.38	4.96
85	0.07	0.05	0.15	0.31	0.04	0.62
87	0.18	0.27	0.97	0.24	0.05	1.71
88	0.10	0.28	1.12	0.24	0.04	1.78
89	0.24	0.59	2.03	1.00	0.28	4.13
8	1.35	2.03	6.30	3.75	0.97	14.41
All manufacturing	11.80	17.44	47.71	18.05	5.00	100.00
Manufacturing trade value			119291469			

Table A4.2 Continued

SITC	Indonesia	Malaysia	Singapore	Thailand	ASEAN
1989					
51	0.65	0.32	1.08	0.61	2.65
52	0.35	0.18	0.22	0.14	0.89
53	0.18	0.10	0.28	0.22	0.78
54	0.09	0.14	0.28	0.15	0.65
55	0.14	0.14	0.36	0.11	0.75
56	0.20	0.19	0.04	0.29	0.71
57	0.01	0.01	0.02	0.00	0.04
58	0.54	0.46	1.29	0.52	2.80
59	0.24	0.21	1.20	0.31	1.96
5	2.40	1.74	4.75	2.33	11.22
61	0.09	0.02	0.07	0.21	0.39
62	0.10	0.15	0.43	0.16	0.85
63	1.82	0.29	0.35	0.12	2.58
64	0.25	0.41	0.63	0.20	1.50
65	0.99	0.83	1.73	1.16	4.70
66	0.32	0.33	0.64	1.22	2.51
69	0.31	0.42	1.05	0.52	2.30
6	3.88	2.46	4.90	3.59	14.83
71	0.42	0.42	1.54	0.62	2.99
72	1.31	1.09	1.73	1.22	5.35
73	0.15	0.19	0.40	0.30	1.04
74	0.81	1.04	2.76	1.05	5.65
75	0.12	0.48	7.11	1.51	9.23
76	0.26	2.34	6.16	0.90	9.66
77	0.48	6.42	8.73	2.40	18.03
78	0.63	0.74	1.13	1.30	3.81
79	0.39	0.89	2.17	0.13	3.58
7	4.58	13.63	31.72	9.42	59.34
81	0.02	0.02	0.08	0.03	0.15
82	0.12	0.10	0.23	0.20	0.66
83	0.01	0.01	0.15	0.14	0.31
84	0.84	0.82	1.49	1.78	4.93
85	0.16	0.06	0.14	0.36	0.71
87	0.19	0.32	0.93	0.25	1.69
88	0.11	0.32	1.12	0.31	1.85
89	0.28	0.73	2.06	1.26	4.33
8	1.72	2.38	6.20	4.32	14.62
All Manufacturing	12.57	20.20	47.57	19.66	100.00

Manufacturing trade value   13906124

Table A4.2 Continued

SITC 1990	Indonesia	Malaysia	Singapore	Thailand	ASEAN
51	0.59	0.29	1.02	0.55	2.46
52	0.27	0.16	0.19	0.13	0.76
53	0.18	0.10	0.27	0.21	0.76
54	0.09	0.12	0.23	0.13	0.57
55	0.15	0.14	0.31	0.10	0.70
56	0.16	0.15	0.03	0.24	0.60
57	0.01	0.01	0.02	0.00	0.04
58	0.57	0.46	1.10	0.51	2.63
59	0.21	0.20	1.24	0.29	1.94
5	2.24	1.64	4.41	2.17	10.45
61	0.13	0.02	0.07	0.24	0.46
62	0.09	0.16	0.25	0.17	0.66
63	1.73	0.29	0.27	0.10	2.39
64	0.20	0.40	0.58	0.21	1.38
65	1.16	0.75	1.51	1.03	4.45
66	0.26	0.34	0.65	1.42	2.67
69	0.32	0.48	1.02	0.53	2.35
6	3.89	2.43	4.35	3.70	14.37
71	0.42	0.40	1.49	0.88	3.19
72	1.63	1.14	1.66	1.32	5.74
73	0.18	0.25	0.36	0.28	1.08
74	0.88	0.99	2.35	1.15	5.37
75	0.14	0.77	7.64	1.51	10.06
76	0.34	2.51	6.15	1.16	10.15
77	0.52	6.15	7.87	2.41	15.94
78	0.81	0.79	1.16	1.43	4.20
79	0.53	1.19	1.54	0.43	3.69
7	5.45	14.20	30.21	10.56	60.41
81	0.02	0.02	0.08	0.03	0.15
82	0.18	0.12	0.20	0.18	0.69
83	0.01	0.02	0.13	0.14	0.30
84	0.95	0.79	1.42	1.61	4.86
85	0.32	0.07	0.15	0.42	0.95
87	0.18	0.37	0.88	0.23	1.66
88	0.11	0.35	1.18	0.31	1.95
89	0.24	0.88	1.94	1.26	4.32
8	2.01	2.61	5.98	4.17	14.77
All Manufacturing	13.58	20.87	44.95	20.60	100.00

Manufacturing trade value   17743641

Source: Khalifah (1996).

Table A4.3 Profile of ASEAN manufacturing trade, 1991–95 (%)

SITC 1991	Indonesia	Malaysia	Singapore	Thailand	Philippines	ASEAN
51	0.477	0.259	0.961	0.501	0.156	2.354
52	0.199	0.128	0.111	0.098	0.099	0.636
53	0.131	0.086	0.222	0.174	0.039	0.651
54	0.061	0.086	0.195	0.122	0.066	0.529
55	0.155	0.129	0.275	0.071	0.032	0.663
56	0.157	0.088	0.000	0.179	0.124	0.548
57	0.000	0.000	0.000	0.000	0.000	0.000
58	0.444	0.434	0.988	0.431	0.174	2.471
59	0.181	0.162	0.909	0.251	0.082	1.585
5	1.805	1.372	3.661	1.827	0.772	9.437
61	0.121	0.000	0.000	0.212	0.046	0.379
62	0.065	0.162	0.215	0.146	0.027	0.615
63	1.456	0.274	0.240	0.071	0.102	2.143
64	0.220	0.368	0.495	0.191	0.085	1.358
65	1.187	0.719	1.325	0.949	0.516	4.696
66	0.207	0.335	0.614	1.611	0.071	2.837
69	0.332	0.482	0.913	0.401	0.103	2.231
6	3.586	2.339	3.803	3.581	0.949	14.258
71	0.491	0.554	1.400	0.596	0.100	3.141
72	1.622	1.074	1.441	1.217	0.213	5.566
73	0.187	0.273	0.318	0.287	0.026	1.090
74	0.965	1.220	2.223	1.323	0.172	5.904
75	0.108	1.068	6.614	1.443	0.253	9.485
76	0.372	2.863	5.404	1.160	0.352	10.152
77	0.542	5.893	7.411	2.430	1.622	17.898
78	0.606	0.734	0.861	1.023	0.236	3.461
79	0.531	1.265	1.291	0.116	0.109	3.312
7	5.424	14.943	26.965	9.595	3.083	60.009
81	0.000	0.000	0.000	0.000	0.000	0.000
82	0.171	0.119	0.184	0.183	0.079	0.736
83	0.000	0.000	0.081	0.118	0.024	0.224
84	1.022	0.723	1.239	1.635	0.856	5.474
85	0.435	0.047	0.089	0.391	0.060	1.021
87	0.166	0.370	0.812	0.228	0.039	1.615
88	0.101	0.402	0.970	0.350	0.080	1.903
89	0.246	0.858	1.694	1.140	0.294	4.233
8	2.141	2.518	5.069	4.045	1.433	15.205
All manufacturing	12.95	21.173	39.498	19.048	6.237	98.910
Manufacturing trade value			225649140			

Table A4.3 Continued

SITC	Indonesia	Malaysia	Singapore	Thailand	Philippines	ASEAN
1992						
51	0.483	0.285	0.904	0.487	0.144	2.303
52	0.166	0.111	0.106	0.096	0.070	0.550
53	0.131	0.091	0.241	0.197	0.040	0.701
54	0.070	0.101	0.199	0.143	0.068	0.581
55	0.115	0.160	0.310	0.071	0.032	0.688
56	0.125	0.084	0.000	0.190	0.099	0.498
57	0.000	0.000	0.000	0.000	0.000	0.000
58	0.405	0.407	0.780	0.435	0.161	2.188
59	0.170	0.186	0.969	0.265	0.073	1.663
5	1.665	1.425	3.510	1.884	0.688	9.172
61	0.137	0.000	0.000	0.226	0.032	0.394
62	0.080	0.164	0.225	0.163	0.035	0.666
63	1.470	0.350	0.200	0.070	0.059	2.148
64	0.211	0.358	0.425	0.199	0.080	1.273
65	1.527	0.733	1.186	0.960	0.305	4.711
66	0.226	0.373	0.579	0.867	0.089	2.133
69	0.378	0.485	0.815	0.528	0.087	2.293
6	4.028	2.462	3.430	3.012	0.685	13.617
71	0.645	0.577	1.326	0.493	0.153	3.192
72	1.042	0.998	1.251	0.984	0.227	4.501
73	0.193	0.297	0.270	0.218	0.028	1.007
74	0.972	1.229	2.142	1.208	0.173	5.724
75	0.123	1.382	7.133	1.548	0.220	10.406
76	0.566	2.810	4.884	1.242	0.329	9.831
77	0.709	6.059	7.343	2.564	0.803	17.477
78	0.469	0.554	0.930	1.081	0.267	3.302
79	0.317	1.343	1.448	0.484	0.128	3.720
7	5.037	15.249	26.726	9.821	2.327	59.160
81	0.000	0.000	0.000	0.000	0.000	0.000
82	0.188	0.151	0.177	0.187	0.070	0.773
83	0.000	0.000	0.085	0.118	0.020	0.223
84	1.237	0.773	1.154	1.457	0.327	4.948
85	0.500	0.000	0.000	0.367	0.045	0.912
87	0.147	0.372	0.811	0.224	0.037	1.590
88	0.104	0.367	0.937	0.355	0.034	1.798
89	0.311	0.850	1.722	1.233	0.241	4.357
8	2.487	2.514	4.886	3.940	0.774	14.601
All manufacturing	13.217	21.650	38.552	18.657	4.474	96.550
Manufacturing trade value			260279783			

Table A4.3 Continued

SITC 1993	Indonesia	Malaysia	Singapore	Thailand	ASEAN
51	0.277	0.812	0.469	0.127	2.165
52	0.110	0.094	0.090	0.057	0.478
53	0.081	0.257	0.201	0.046	0.716
54	0.077	0.266	0.150	0.068	0.623
55	0.131	0.303	0.071	0.036	0.640
56	0.081	0.000	0.178	0.077	0.420
57	0.000	0.000	0.000	0.000	0.000
58	0.428	0.754	0.415	0.163	2.121
59	0.161	0.902	0.244	0.078	1.557
5	1.347	3.387	1.818	0.652	8.721
61	0.000	0.000	0.209	0.033	0.383
62	0.151	0.216	0.171	0.039	0.641
63	0.508	0.205	0.074	0.041	2.524
64	0.318	0.396	0.198	0.085	1.236
65	0.626	1.056	0.894	0.285	4.112
66	0.360	0.533	0.859	0.069	2.022
69	0.476	0.770	0.545	0.156	2.263
6	2.439	3.177	2.949	0.708	13.181
71	0.552	1.376	0.619	0.270	3.352
72	0.885	1.141	0.915	0.210	4.079
73	0.234	0.245	0.294	0.034	0.929
74	1.240	1.916	1.334	0.205	5.502
75	1.551	7.308	1.512	0.164	10.653
76	3.173	4.730	1.156	0.370	10.077
77	6.708	7.008	2.880	0.882	18.187
78	0.569	0.870	1.360	0.337	3.684
79	0.673	1.249	0.425	0.244	2.900
7	15.586	25.843	10.494	2.717	59.363
81	0.000	0.000	0.000	0.000	0.000
82	0.187	0.155	0.196	0.067	0.829
83	0.000	0.073	0.117	0.018	0.208
84	0.690	0.906	1.393	0.287	4.453
85	0.000	0.000	0.342	0.047	0.927
87	0.340	0.741	0.234	0.052	1.506
88	0.345	0.863	0.299	0.035	1.670
89	0.798	1.521	1.381	0.238	4.302
8	2.361	4.260	3.963	0.744	13.896
All Manufacturing	21.733	36.667	19.225	4.821	82.446

Manufacturing trade value   30251415

Table A4.3 Continued

SITC 1994	Indonesia	Malaysia	Singapore	Thailand	Philippine	ASEAN
51	0.507	0.287	0.757	0.467	0.112	2.130
52	0.117	0.108	0.080	0.075	0.050	0.429
53	0.112	0.081	0.243	0.177	0.039	0.651
54	0.050	0.071	0.266	0.123	0.070	0.579
55	0.097	0.123	0.294	0.066	0.033	0.614
56	0.066	0.070	0.000	0.140	0.079	0.355
57	0.000	0.000	0.000	0.000	0.000	0.000
58	0.331	0.401	0.715	0.436	0.164	2.047
59	0.163	0.198	0.668	0.239	0.071	1.338
5	1.443	1.338	3.022	1.724	0.617	8.145
61	0.122	0.000	0.000	0.195	0.025	0.342
62	0.066	0.135	0.187	0.161	0.034	0.583
63	1.261	0.461	0.149	0.068	0.038	1.977
64	0.221	0.310	0.368	0.192	0.089	1.180
65	0.963	0.590	0.895	0.796	0.261	3.504
66	0.173	0.368	0.521	0.767	0.061	1.890
69	0.259	0.452	0.718	0.564	0.125	2.118
6	3.065	2.316	2.838	2.742	0.633	11.593
71	0.457	0.608	1.186	0.481	0.231	2.962
72	0.795	0.884	1.232	0.857	0.233	4.002
73	0.114	0.249	0.249	0.223	0.024	0.859
74	0.657	1.157	2.143	1.229	0.197	5.383
75	0.124	1.807	8.472	1.702	0.150	12.255
76	0.582	3.449	5.607	1.262	0.411	11.312
77	0.619	7.307	10.508	3.081	0.929	22.444
78	0.691	0.562	0.806	1.279	0.333	3.672
79	0.244	1.377	1.045	0.450	0.212	3.329
7	4.283	17.399	31.249	10.564	2.720	66.217
81	0.000	0.000	0.000	0.000	0.000	0.000
82	0.205	0.201	0.159	0.185	0.063	0.812
83	0.000	0.000	0.074	0.109	0.020	0.203
84	0.854	0.583	0.808	1.185	0.241	3.672
85	0.482	0.000	0.000	0.388	0.046	0.916
87	0.096	0.342	0.885	0.249	0.045	1.617
88	0.103	0.344	0.892	0.282	0.038	1.659
89	0.418	0.743	1.624	1.198	0.221	4.204
8	2.158	2.212	4.442	3.596	0.674	13.081
All manufacturing	10.94	23.265	41.551	18.626	4.644	99.036

Manufacturing trade value   383315101

Table A4.3 Continued

SITC	Indonesia	Malaysia	Singapore	Thailand	Philippine	ASEAN
1995						
51	0.588	0.360	0.832	0.579	0.112	2.472
52	0.109	0.114	0.085	0.075	0.051	0.434
53	0.105	0.074	0.216	0.220	0.037	0.652
54	0.052	0.066	0.264	0.125	0.063	0.571
55	0.090	0.112	0.294	0.064	0.032	0.592
56	0.085	0.071	0.000	0.133	0.073	0.362
57	0.000	0.000	0.000	0.000	0.000	0.000
58	0.354	0.454	0.705	0.466	0.157	2.137
59	0.155	0.241	0.629	0.246	0.062	1.333
5	1.539	1.493	3.025	1.909	0.587	8.553
61	0.092	0.000	0.000	0.166	0.020	0.278
62	0.082	0.122	0.192	0.161	0.034	0.590
63	0.974	0.398	0.100	0.062	0.032	1.566
64	0.263	0.356	0.372	0.232	0.087	1.310
65	0.849	0.567	0.753	0.739	0.241	3.149
66	0.172	0.389	0.542	0.740	0.074	1.918
69	0.216	0.429	0.693	0.598	0.081	2.016
6	2.647	2.260	2.651	2.700	0.570	10.828
71	0.382	0.565	0.982	0.468	0.117	2.515
72	0.846	1.019	1.234	0.916	0.285	4.301
73	0.124	0.353	0.257	0.240	0.044	1.018
74	0.669	1.070	1.881	1.360	0.191	5.171
75	0.155	2.082	8.800	1.822	0.205	13.064
76	0.568	3.374	4.629	1.138	0.444	10.154
77	0.579	7.884	11.694	3.336	0.939	24.433
78	0.701	0.669	0.810	1.254	0.367	3.800
79	0.149	1.080	0.941	0.484	0.130	2.784
7	4.173	18.096	31.229	11.019	2.722	67.239
81	0.000	0.000	0.000	0.000	0.000	0.000
82	0.181	0.191	0.140	0.158	0.058	0.727
83	0.000	0.000	0.065	0.095	0.023	0.183
84	0.721	0.506	0.649	1.058	0.228	3.163
85	0.000	0.000	0.000	0.438	0.032	0.470
87	0.092	0.343	0.868	0.263	0.046	1.612
88	0.097	0.323	0.843	0.272	0.033	1.569
89	0.327	0.693	1.734	1.305	0.212	4.271
8	1.417	2.057	4.299	3.590	0.632	11.995
All manufacturing	9.777	23.906	41.203	19.218	4.511	98.615
Manufacturing trade value			478917451			

Source: Own calculations.

Table A4.4 ASEAN intra-industry trade in manufacturing sector,
     1986-90 (%)

SITC	Indonesia	Malaysia	Singapore	Thailand	Philippin	ASEAN
1986						
51	0.12	0.18	1.41	0.17	0.17	2.05
52	0.18	0.08	0.26	0.05	0.09	0.66
53	0.06	0.03	0.34	0.05	0.00	0.49
54	0.10	0.12	0.78	0.07	0.04	1.10
55	0.18	0.15	0.51	0.08	0.04	0.96
56	0.14	0.14	0.17	0.00	0.57	1.01
57	0.00	0.01	0.02	0.00	0.01	0.04
58	0.01	0.11	1.70	0.28	0.12	2.23
59	0.03	0.43	1.18	0.09	0.09	1.83
5	0.82	1.25	6.36	0.79	1.13	10.35
61	0.02	0.01	0.06	0.10	0.02	0.21
62	0.06	0.19	0.36	0.21	0.02	0.84
63	0.01	0.04	0.54	0.02	0.00	0.61
64	0.20	0.15	0.82	0.19	0.01	1.37
65	0.38	1.10	2.53	1.50	0.19	5.70
66	0.11	0.42	0.49	1.02	0.06	2.10
69	0.01	0.29	1.51	0.29	0.06	2.16
6	0.79	2.20	6.31	3.33	0.35	12.98
71	0.01	0.45	1.75	0.02	0.00	2.23
72	0.02	0.48	2.16	0.21	0.06	2.93
73	0.00	0.03	0.36	0.03	0.00	0.42
74	0.11	0.68	3.77	0.54	0.02	5.13
75	0.00	0.08	5.65	0.37	0.03	6.13
76	0.02	1.52	6.79	0.05	0.02	8.40
77	0.08	12.16	16.62	3.86	1.37	34.08
78	0.00	0.16	0.82	0.11	0.16	1.26
79	0.13	1.03	2.78	0.15	0.01	4.10
7	0.37	16.58	40.70	5.33	1.69	64.67
81	0.01	0.01	0.07	0.02	0.01	0.12
82	0.06	0.07	0.55	0.02	0.01	0.71
83	0.00	0.01	0.12	0.01	0.00	0.14
84	0.02	0.24	1.99	0.04	0.02	2.30
85	0.04	0.05	0.12	0.00	0.00	0.21
87	0.18	0.26	1.27	0.06	0.00	1.76
88	0.05	0.32	1.16	0.23	0.02	1.78
89	0.21	0.74	3.21	0.62	0.20	4.98
8	0.55	1.71	8.48	1.00	0.26	12.00
Manufacturing						
	2.53	21.75	61.86	10.45	3.42	100.00

Table A4.4 Continued

SITC 1987	Indonesia	Malaysia	Singapore	Thailand	ASEAN
51	0.18	0.16	1.38	0.19	1.91
52	0.14	0.05	0.26	0.04	0.49
53	0.02	0.03	0.35	0.07	0.47
54	0.09	0.12	0.67	0.07	0.94
55	0.18	0.16	0.56	0.10	1.01
56	0.23	0.17	0.15	0.00	0.55
57	0.00	0.01	0.02	0.00	0.03
58	0.07	0.14	2.15	0.26	2.62
59	0.06	0.38	1.12	0.10	1.65
5	0.97	1.22	6.65	0.82	9.65
61	0.02	0.02	0.07	0.12	0.21
62	0.05	0.21	0.42	0.20	0.88
63	0.01	0.03	0.69	0.02	0.74
64	0.45	0.19	0.85	0.22	1.70
65	0.75	1.12	2.92	1.96	6.74
66	0.14	0.41	0.58	1.37	2.51
69	0.04	0.33	1.37	0.34	2.09
6	1.46	2.30	6.89	4.22	14.87
71	0.00	0.44	1.87	0.16	2.47
72	0.01	0.44	1.99	0.18	2.62
73	0.00	0.04	0.33	0.01	0.38
74	0.02	0.67	3.77	0.68	5.13
75	0.00	0.14	6.46	0.72	7.32
76	0.04	1.61	8.62	0.11	10.38
77	0.07	11.87	17.16	1.50	30.60
78	0.02	0.18	0.86	0.17	1.23
79	0.11	1.08	2.39	0.01	3.59
7	0.26	16.47	43.45	3.53	63.71
81	0.03	0.03	0.06	0.02	0.13
82	0.03	0.07	0.49	0.02	0.61
83	0.00	0.01	0.15	0.01	0.17
84	0.02	0.20	2.19	0.04	2.45
85	0.01	0.05	0.16	0.00	0.23
87	0.02	0.22	1.46	0.06	1.76
88	0.04	0.31	1.15	0.16	1.67
89	0.21	0.71	3.12	0.73	4.76
8	0.35	1.60	8.79	1.04	11.77
Manufacturing	3.04	21.58	65.78	9.60	100.00

Table A4.4 Continued

SITC	Indonesia	Malaysia	Singapore	Thailand	ASEAN
1988					
51	0.12	0.22	1.49	0.10	0.14
52	0.12	0.05	0.28	0.03	0.08
53	0.03	0.03	0.36	0.06	0.00
54	0.07	0.09	0.53	0.07	0.02
55	0.15	0.14	0.57	0.10	0.04
56	0.25	0.16	0.16	0.00	0.21
57	0.00	0.00	0.03	0.00	0.01
58	0.12	0.14	2.42	0.22	0.10
59	0.04	0.40	0.92	0.12	0.07
5	0.89	1.23	6.76	0.68	0.67
61	0.03	0.02	0.09	0.17	0.01
62	0.03	0.17	0.38	0.19	0.02
63	0.01	0.03	0.60	0.03	0.01
64	0.38	0.28	0.76	0.15	0.02
65	0.68	0.91	2.12	1.49	0.16
66	0.14	0.33	0.53	1.08	0.06
69	0.12	0.31	1.27	0.33	0.05
6	1.39	2.03	5.74	3.43	0.32
71	0.01	37.00	1.73	0.18	0.00
72	0.02	0.42	2.07	0.11	0.04
73	0.00	0.03	0.32	0.05	0.00
74	0.03	0.66	4.09	0.77	0.02
75	0.00	0.21	7.21	1.58	0.06
76	0.06	1.77	8.89	0.33	0.17
77	0.13	9.54	15.59	3.54	1.23
78	0.06	0.10	0.87	0.43	0.05
79	0.07	0.50	2.44	0.02	0.00
7	0.39	13.59	43.21	7.00	1.57
81	0.03	0.03	0.06	0.03	0.01
82	0.03	0.06	0.37	0.03	0.01
83	0.00	0.01	0.16	0.00	1.00
84	0.02	0.15	1.69	0.03	0.02
85	0.01	0.04	0.16	0.00	0.00
87	0.01	0.20	1.36	0.11	0.00
88	0.04	0.28	1.38	0.23	0.02
89	0.21	0.63	2.65	0.83	0.17
8	0.35	1.40	7.82	1.28	0.24
Manufacturing					
	3.01	18.26	63.54	12.39	2.80

Table A4.4 Continued

SITC	Indonesia	Malaysia	Singapore	Thailand	ASEAN
1989					
51	0.21	0.19	1.34	0.09	1.82
52	0.10	0.05	0.23	0.03	0.41
53	0.06	0.05	0.47	0.07	0.65
54	0.04	0.08	0.48	0.05	0.66
55	0.16	0.14	0.47	0.09	0.86
56	0.30	0.18	0.07	0.00	0.55
57	0.00	0.00	0.03	0.00	0.03
58	0.12	0.12	2.10	0.27	2.61
59	0.05	0.25	1.27	0.12	1.68
5	1.04	1.06	6.44	0.72	9.26
61	0.10	0.01	0.08	0.18	0.37
62	0.04	0.17	0.37	0.22	0.79
63	0.02	0.03	0.45	0.03	0.54
64	0.43	0.33	0.71	0.13	1.59
65	0.89	0.84	2.06	1.38	5.17
66	0.21	0.41	0.62	1.91	3.14
69	0.16	0.35	1.35	0.38	2.24
6	1.85	2.14	5.63	4.22	13.84
71	0.02	0.33	1.98	0.22	2.55
72	0.02	0.35	2.17	0.10	2.63
73	0.00	0.03	0.49	0.03	0.55
74	0.04	0.84	4.12	0.71	5.72
75	0.00	0.63	7.52	1.96	10.11
76	0.10	2.38	8.68	1.04	12.19
77	0.19	9.93	13.37	3.09	26.58
78	0.06	0.25	1.06	0.36	1.73
79	0.07	0.88	2.54	0.03	3.51
7	0.49	15.62	41.92	7.53	65.56
81	0.03	0.04	0.07	0.04	0.18
82	0.03	0.07	0.33	0.04	0.47
83	0.00	0.01	0.06	0.02	0.10
84	0.03	0.17	1.59	0.04	1.83
85	0.01	0.04	0.14	0.01	0.20
87	0.01	0.21	1.28	0.09	1.59
88	0.07	0.35	1.47	0.34	2.24
89	0.25	0.72	2.75	1.03	4.74
8	0.42	1.60	7.69	1.62	11.33
Manufacturing	3.80	20.42	61.69	14.09	100.00

Table A4.4 Continued

SITC	Indonesia	Malaysia	Singapore	Thailand	ASEAN
1990					
51	0.18	0.17	1.33	0.12	1.79
52	0.07	0.04	0.23	0.03	0.37
53	0.08	0.06	0.45	0.06	0.65
54	0.04	0.08	0.42	0.06	0.59
55	0.20	0.16	0.40	0.09	0.85
56	0.20	0.12	0.06	0.00	0.39
57	0.00	0.01	0.03	0.00	0.03
58	0.01	0.12	1.87	0.28	2.40
59	0.05	0.15	1.12	0.13	1.44
5	0.95	0.90	5.89	0.78	8.52
61	0.15	0.01	0.08	0.23	0.47
62	0.04	0.17	0.32	0.25	0.77
63	0.03	0.05	0.44	0.05	0.58
64	0.34	0.32	0.66	0.10	1.42
65	0.94	0.80	1.89	1.35	4.97
66	0.16	0.48	0.67	2.07	3.37
69	0.17	0.42	1.36	0.39	2.34
6	1.82	2.26	5.41	4.43	13.92
71	0.03	0.31	1.66	0.23	2.23
72	0.03	0.28	2.04	0.11	2.45
73	0.01	0.04	0.41	0.07	0.53
74	0.04	0.76	3.25	0.87	4.93
75	0.00	1.12	8.37	2.29	1.78
76	0.15	2.61	9.51	1.40	3.67
77	0.21	9.78	12.23	2.99	25.20
78	0.08	0.27	1.04	0.30	1.69
79	0.15	1.23	1.70	0.01	3.09
7	0.70	16.38	40.20	8.27	65.55
81	0.03	0.03	0.07	0.04	0.17
82	0.07	0.09	0.35	0.03	0.54
83	0.00	0.03	0.05	0.01	0.09
84	0.03	0.16	1.76	0.06	2.01
85	0.00	0.04	0.15	0.01	0.21
87	0.02	0.27	1.17	0.13	1.58
88	0.10	0.43	1.52	0.42	2.45
89	0.28	0.88	2.97	1.02	4.96
8	0.52	1.94	7.85	1.71	12.02
Manufacturing					
	3.99	21.47	59.35	15.19	100.00

Source: Khalifah (1996).

*Table A4.5   ASEAN intra-industry trade in manufacturing sector, 1991-
95 (%)*

SITC	Indonesia	Malaysia	Singapore	Thailand	Philippines	ASEAN
1991						
51	0.200	0.253	1.321	0.186	0.079	2.039
52	0.000	0.000	0.000	0.000	0.065	0.065
53	0.000	0.000	0.361	0.082	0.000	0.443
54	0.000	0.000	0.340	0.055	0.000	0.395
55	0.213	0.141	0.357	0.000	0.000	0.711
56	0.089	0.000	0.000	0.000	0.180	0.269
57	0.000	0.000	0.000	0.000	0.000	0.000
58	0.123	0.116	1.713	0.333	0.041	2.327
59	0.000	0.118	0.804	0.278	0.043	1.242
5	0.625	0.628	4.897	0.935	0.407	7.491
61	0.000	0.000	0.000	0.331	0.000	0.000
62	0.106	0.172	0.249	0.204	0.000	0.731
63	0.000	0.000	0.362	0.000	0.000	0.362
64	0.345	0.243	0.539	0.086	0.000	1.214
65	1.376	0.758	1.691	1.552	0.207	5.583
66	0.358	0.500	0.605	1.849	0.122	3.434
69	0.248	0.418	1.155	0.151	0.061	2.033
6	2.433	2.092	4.601	4.172	0.389	13.687
71	0.000	0.422	1.523	0.231	0.000	2.176
72	0.000	0.254	1.764	0.108	0.000	2.126
73	0.000	0.000	0.356	0.000	0.000	0.356
74	0.051	0.950	2.937	0.928	0.000	4.867
75	0.043	1.595	7.302	2.018	0.373	11.331
76	0.319	3.184	8.324	1.652	0.602	14.081
77	0.308	9.399	11.457	3.222	2.577	26.962
78	0.095	0.237	0.913	0.462	0.076	1.782
79	0.182	1.610	1.022	0.107	0.000	2.920
7	0.997	17.650	35.598	8.729	3.627	66.601
81	0.000	0.000	0.000	0.000	0.000	0.000
82	0.171	0.119	0.184	0.183	0.079	0.736
83	0.000	0.000	0.081	0.118	0.024	0.224
84	1.022	0.723	1.239	1.635	0.856	5.474
85	0.435	0.047	0.089	0.391	0.060	1.021
87	0.166	0.370	0.812	0.228	0.039	1.615
88	0.101	0.402	0.970	0.350	0.080	1.903
89	0.246	0.858	1.694	1.140	0.294	4.233
8	2.141	2.518	5.069	4.045	1.433	15.205
Manufacturing						
	4.522	22.551	52.098	15.795	5.034	100.000

Table A4.5 Continued

SITC 1992	Indonesia	Malaysia	Singapore	Thailand	Philippines	ASEAN
51	0.295	0.302	1.239	0.186	0.062	2.085
52	0.000	0.000	0.000	0.000	0.000	0.000
53	0.000	0.000	0.422	0.113	0.000	0.535
54	0.000	0.000	0.336	0.079	0.000	0.415
55	0.187	0.183	0.423	0.000	0.000	0.792
56	0.193	0.000	0.000	0.000	0.120	0.313
57	0.000	0.000	0.000	0.000	0.000	0.000
58	0.107	0.181	1.309	0.293	0.048	1.938
59	0.000	0.143	0.839	0.272	0.042	1.296
5	0.782	0.809	4.568	0.943	0.272	7.374
61	0.000	0.000	0.000	0.387	0.000	0.387
62	0.133	0.182	0.272	0.237	0.000	0.824
63	0.000	0.000	0.300	0.000	0.000	0.300
64	0.284	0.277	0.455	0.099	0.032	1.148
65	1.501	0.810	1.475	1.645	0.169	5.600
66	0.308	0.477	0.559	1.457	0.109	2.911
69	0.301	0.444	0.992	0.556	0.041	2.333
6	2.526	2.191	4.054	4.381	0.351	13.503
71	0.000	0.522	1.521	0.267	0.000	2.310
72	0.071	0.274	1.531	0.142	0.000	2.018
73	0.000	0.000	0.287	0.000	0.000	0.287
74	0.066	1.042	2.877	1.031	0.000	5.016
75	0.190	1.662	7.612	2.203	0.264	11.929
76	0.814	2.651	7.351	1.773	0.555	13.144
77	0.461	9.835	11.419	3.674	1.324	26.714
78	0.247	0.366	1.001	0.452	0.085	2.150
79	0.093	1.684	1.347	0.150	0.000	3.273
7	1.942	18.035	34.945	9.691	2.228	66.841
81	0.000	0.000	0.000	0.000	0.000	0.000
82	0.000	0.000	0.306	0.000	0.000	0.306
83	0.000	0.000	0.000	0.000	0.000	0.000
84	0.000	0.177	1.623	0.000	0.000	1.800
85	0.000	0.000	0.000	0.000	0.000	0.000
87	0.000	0.415	1.199	0.214	0.000	1.829
88	0.144	0.530	1.258	0.626	0.000	2.558
89	0.388	1.139	2.607	1.362	0.293	5.789
8	0.533	2.262	6.993	2.202	0.293	12.282
Manufacturing	5.783	23.296	50.560	17.217	3.144	100.000

Table A4.5 Continued

SITC	Indonesia	Malaysia	Singapore	Thailand	Philippines	ASEAN
1993						
51	0.285	0.324	1.154	0.158	0.048	1.970
52	0.000	0.000	0.000	0.000	0.000	0.000
53	0.000	0.000	0.433	0.183	0.000	0.616
54	0.000	0.000	0.435	0.149	0.000	0.584
55	0.156	0.178	0.431	0.000	0.000	0.765
56	0.117	0.000	0.000	0.000	0.100	0.217
57	0.000	0.000	0.000	0.000	0.000	0.000
58	0.131	0.244	1.273	0.349	0.039	2.035
59	0.000	0.139	0.960	0.219	0.037	1.355
5	0.689	0.886	4.687	1.057	0.224	7.542
61	0.000	0.000	0.000	0.340	0.000	0.340
62	0.106	0.170	0.261	0.252	0.000	0.788
63	0.000	0.000	0.362	0.000	0.000	0.362
64	0.268	0.265	0.446	0.104	0.038	1.121
65	1.323	0.818	1.444	1.531	0.144	5.261
66	0.322	0.476	0.518	1.362	0.102	2.780
69	0.374	0.514	0.903	0.566	0.096	2.452
6	2.392	2.243	3.933	4.155	0.380	13.104
71	0.000	0.547	1.620	0.304	0.000	2.471
72	0.037	0.308	1.550	0.204	0.000	2.099
73	0.000	0.000	0.294	0.000	0.000	0.294
74	0.107	1.117	2.740	1.384	0.000	5.349
75	0.184	1.613	6.561	2.052	0.252	10.662
76	1.129	2.913	6.337	1.768	0.593	12.740
77	0.515	10.866	12.291	4.306	1.464	29.443
78	0.392	0.447	1.109	0.742	0.128	2.818
79	0.180	0.000	1.172	0.284	0.000	1.636
7	2.544	17.812	33.674	11.043	2.437	67.512
81	0.000	0.000	0.000	0.000	0.000	0.000
82	0.000	0.000	0.275	0.000	0.000	0.275
83	0.000	0.000	0.000	0.000	0.000	0.000
84	0.000	0.151	1.399	0.000	0.000	1.549
85	0.000	0.000	0.000	0.000	0.000	0.000
87	0.000	0.368	1.188	0.245	0.000	1.801
88	0.218	0.535	1.287	0.485	0.000	2.525
89	0.357	1.193	2.385	1.440	0.316	5.691
8	0.576	2.247	6.533	2.170	0.316	11.842
Manufacturing						
	6.202	23.188	48.827	18.425	3.357	100.000

Table A4.5 Continued

SITC 1994	Indonesia	Malaysia	Singapore	Thailand	Philippines	ASEAN
51	0.282	0.369	1.000	0.112	0.037	1.799
52	0.000	0.000	0.000	0.000	0.000	0.000
53	0.000	0.000	0.391	0.159	0.000	0.550
54	0.000	0.000	0.416	0.073	0.000	0.489
55	0.128	0.149	0.408	0.000	0.000	0.686
56	0.063	0.000	0.000	0.000	0.085	0.148
57	0.000	0.000	0.000	0.000	0.000	0.000
58	0.103	0.258	1.088	0.352	0.031	1.832
59	0.000	0.260	0.631	0.227	0.030	1.148
5	0.576	1.036	3.934	0.923	0.183	6.653
61	0.000	0.000	0.000	0.276	0.000	0.276
62	0.098	0.144	0.224	0.222	0.000	0.688
63	0.000	0.000	0.240	0.000	0.000	0.240
64	0.214	0.243	0.395	0.141	0.028	1.020
65	0.989	0.731	1.191	1.145	0.150	4.206
66	0.271	0.461	0.428	1.094	0.081	2.335
69	0.278	0.464	0.871	0.532	0.046	2.191
6	1.851	2.043	3.348	3.411	0.304	10.957
71	0.000	0.462	1.357	0.324	0.000	2.144
72	0.028	0.240	1.438	0.134	0.000	1.841
73	0.000	0.000	0.306	0.000	0.000	0.306
74	0.105	1.064	2.781	1.049	0.000	5.000
75	0.149	1.594	8.356	2.012	0.196	12.307
76	0.639	2.672	7.667	1.784	0.573	13.336
77	0.517	10.058	15.039	4.145	1.479	31.237
78	0.264	0.326	0.814	0.723	0.152	2.279
79	0.113	1.551	0.930	0.478	0.000	3.071
7	1.815	17.968	38.688	10.649	2.400	71.520
81	0.000	0.000	0.000	0.000	0.000	0.000
82	0.000	0.000	0.203	0.000	0.000	0.203
83	0.000	0.000	0.000	0.000	0.000	0.000
84	0.000	0.134	1.284	0.000	0.000	1.418
85	0.000	0.000	0.000	0.000	0.000	0.000
87	0.000	0.312	1.123	0.218	0.000	1.653
88	0.145	0.498	1.166	0.451	0.000	2.261
89	0.268	1.066	2.294	1.409	0.299	5.336
8	0.414	2.010	6.070	2.077	0.299	10.870
Manufacturing						
	4.657	23.057	52.040	17.059	3.187	100.000

Table A4.5 Continued

SITC	Indonesia	Malaysia	Singapore	Thailand	Philippines	ASEAN
1995						
51	0.325	0.328	1.102	0.159	0.032	1.947
52	0.000	0.000	0.000	0.000	0.000	0.000
53	0.000	0.000	0.330	0.309	0.000	0.639
54	0.000	0.000	0.400	0.084	0.000	0.484
55	0.125	0.129	0.417	0.000	0.000	0.671
56	0.089	0.000	0.000	0.000	0.080	0.169
57	0.000	0.000	0.000	0.000	0.000	0.000
58	0.203	0.363	1.077	0.474	0.029	2.146
59	0.000	0.366	0.644	0.247	0.025	1.283
5	0.743	1.186	3.970	1.273	0.166	7.338
61	0.000	0.000	0.000	0.215	0.000	0.215
62	0.103	0.122	0.229	0.223	0.000	0.677
63	0.000	0.000	0.148	0.000	0.000	0.148
64	0.217	0.242	0.387	0.229	0.036	1.111
65	0.883	0.782	0.995	1.029	0.142	3.831
66	0.229	0.439	0.461	1.116	0.072	2.317
69	0.281	0.492	0.830	0.499	0.041	2.143
6	1.714	2.077	3.051	3.310	0.291	10.442
71	0.000	0.436	1.143	0.358	0.000	1.936
72	0.107	0.280	1.403	0.109	0.000	1.899
73	0.000	0.000	0.314	0.000	0.000	0.314
74	0.096	1.097	2.397	1.144	0.000	4.734
75	0.160	1.857	8.770	1.999	0.295	13.081
76	0.723	2.566	6.124	1.608	0.536	11.557
77	0.538	10.837	16.975	4.255	1.453	34.058
78	0.248	0.310	0.794	0.483	0.159	1.993
79	0.072	1.082	0.689	0.423	0.000	2.266
7	1.944	18.466	38.608	10.379	2.442	71.839
81	0.000	0.000	0.000	0.000	0.000	0.000
82	0.000	0.000	0.147	0.000	0.000	0.147
83	0.000	0.000	0.000	0.000	0.000	0.000
84	0.000	0.103	0.975	0.000	0.000	1.078
85	0.000	0.000	0.000	0.000	0.000	0.000
87	0.000	0.284	1.097	0.207	0.000	1.588
88	0.133	0.482	1.177	0.411	0.000	2.202
89	0.281	0.941	2.378	1.446	0.319	5.365
8	0.414	1.810	5.774	2.064	0.319	10.381
Manufacturing						
	4.814	23.539	51.403	17.027	3.217	100.000

Source: Own calculations.

Table A4.6 Grubel-Lloyd indices for ASEAN manufacturing trade,
1986-90

SITC	Indonesia	Malaysia	Singapore	Thailand	Philippines	ASEAN
1986						
51	7.33	25.67	66.38	13.77	22.15	31.70
52	16.70	19.50	61.53	16.89	25.06	25.80
53	15.02	20.14	68.27	14.06	1.30	30.71
54	29.90	30.33	98.38	17.73	15.05	51.59
55	51.62	42.19	65.50	36.98	34.55	52.76
56	30.81	35.92	93.80	23.00	91.35	46.42
57	0.00	26.20	45.63	0.00	70.98	28.63
58	0.73	15.29	79.21	29.81	23.23	37.86
59	5.61	70.93	90.15	15.36	36.22	54.60
5	12.89	33.06	76.78	17.21	37.20	38.71
61	30.38	54.89	60.71	37.58	36.49	42.09
62	20.28	69.60	67.28	73.47	21.70	57.13
63	0.29	6.63	61.26	5.73	1.20	11.05
64	41.34	17.43	60.92	40.99	4.48	40.31
65	25.87	65.85	58.61	60.94	24.15	53.27
66	17.30	71.07	33.73	59.56	46.08	46.39
69	1.21	37.70	65.35	41.63	26.56	44.32
6	10.92	45.79	57.65	54.10	18.89	41.92
71	0.77	55.26	64.92	3.49	1.15	37.25
72	0.75	28.90	75.91	17.04	14.01	33.68
73	0.21	16.30	67.19	14.74	3.58	33.99
74	5.76	37.89	79.72	38.75	6.16	50.03
75	0.86	16.92	64.00	38.16	27.75	57.26
76	2.99	53.96	74.79	5.41	15.23	62.08
77	5.33	85.71	85.46	85.60	69.00	81.94
78	0.13	15.32	61.08	9.94	61.31	22.00
79	7.53	56.01	61.34	55.97	14.42	48.91
7	2.99	66.87	75.32	48.10	44.79	60.95
81	22.74	22.90	38.48	74.10	82.35	39.78
82	96.05	80.60	87.90	10.40	2.66	55.87
83	45.00	43.83	43.54	5.95	11.74	33.30
84	1.00	18.10	64.92	1.48	1.84	24.78
85	87.11	57.78	36.14	1.28	1.22	23.69
87	33.13	42.93	69.09	14.47	1.52	51.05
88	16.61	54.69	63.20	49.88	17.51	54.39
89	32.19	60.57	79.65	41.50	32.36	62.11
8	17.41	42.69	69.74	18.22	12.42	44.59
Manufacturing						
	8.68	58.15	72.40	38.22	31.89	52.62

Table A4.6 Continued

SITC 1987	Indonesia	Malaysia	Singapore	Thailand	ASEAN
51	13.48	24.40	64.25	13.25	34.29
52	13.13	13.79	62.75	13.22	22.83
53	5.38	18.47	73.10	16.40	32.39
54	32.22	34.83	98.54	19.35	57.60
55	63.28	48.58	70.83	40.94	60.51
56	72.65	45.75	89.81	26.00	43.37
57	0.42	27.77	55.44	1.69	30.78
58	4.88	16.70	79.99	25.56	43.55
59	7.34	66.61	93.24	15.56	52.55
5	16.30	33.07	77.40	17.19	42.05
61	12.45	59.98	55.78	31.93	33.86
62	24.83	64.30	72.24	72.94	63.93
63	0.24	3.55	69.18	4.51	11.27
64	80.06	23.16	60.77	39.87	51.46
65	47.72	66.19	63.23	74.20	64.14
66	29.67	74.05	40.50	66.71	55.33
69	5.67	41.72	63.98	42.92	46.33
6	17.95	46.15	61.08	60.14	47.33
71	0.26	42.18	63.39	20.33	38.25
72	0.46	31.99	70.86	12.30	31.88
73	0.22	16.84	47.75	5.33	24.20
74	0.95	40.43	79.37	39.61	51.87
75	0.71	32.59	57.54	54.42	55.45
76	5.31	51.37	78.62	12.64	66.44
77	4.96	85.39	85.57	31.67	76.32
78	0.91	22.15	51.98	10.97	21.65
79	13.22	84.27	61.69	6.11	58.55
7	2.34	69.00	73.68	27.61	59.63
81	47.26	57.93	44.97	61.02	49.57
82	38.26	60.61	91.67	7.25	58.35
83	70.12	63.51	45.19	2.94	34.43
84	1.55	13.28	63.17	1.04	24.93
85	15.50	50.34	53.72	8.00	23.52
87	2.25	37.86	75.97	15.14	49.31
88	21.64	55.29	62.39	36.95	54.82
89	61.31	56.97	74.51	38.24	62.11
8	12.72	38.33	69.04	14.29	43.74
Manufacturing					
	10.84	58.81	71.83	30.19	53.16

Table A4.6 Continued

SITC	Indonesia	Malaysia	Singapore	Thailand	Philippines	ASEA
1988						
51	10.25	32.38	73.68	7.95	26.13	36.87
52	17.04	16.09	66.41	10.42	35.28	29.08
53	10.86	21.59	77.77	15.13	4.31	35.56
54	37.01	32.77	97.49	25.57	7.92	52.85
55	74.30	52.53	77.07	47.61	37.14	65.92
56	75.70	40.51	99.59	0.02	70.45	47.36
57	0.26	14.37	49.62	0.72	91.44	37.88
58	10.72	16.02	82.40	23.28	22.73	47.59
59	7.60	78.66	87.76	21.08	31.63	55.10
5	20.02	35.60	80.53	15.89	31.41	45.05
61	23.18	67.98	66.98	48.97	26.95	47.09
62	20.14	60.94	72.58	74.16	24.15	60.54
63	21.00	5.17	68.75	12.60	3.14	12.33
64	84.96	38.13	61.09	39.32	8.33	52.61
65	45.01	66.26	63.93	70.91	25.46	60.03
66	30.15	64.38	43.56	65.84	41.53	53.68
69	26.17	45.83	65.54	39.44	28.94	51.09
6	20.76	49.29	62.18	59.31	20.95	47.18
71	82.00	50.14	62.84	20.18	1.22	41.16
72	1.02	25.86	68.97	6.11	6.91	29.62
73	0.16	14.99	47.19	11.21	3.04	23.03
74	1.76	41.22	83.46	40.55	4.75	54.78
75	1.85	46.55	60.45	70.90	44.13	60.58
76	12.75	56.63	78.82	34.65	60.44	69.68
77	16.63	84.45	83.43	75.75	75.69	81.01
78	5.26	10.28	48.93	20.29	12.73	23.45
79	15.72	75.40	77.34	20.40	0.63	54.38
7	4.83	65.91	74.29	43.57	42.33	61.70
81	87.74	73.75	50.30	67.48	63.22	63.00
82	21.60	46.20	83.18	8.2	2.50	36.18
83	38.17	53.30	47.74	3.23	16.51	29.92
84	1.62	11.33	59.89	1.07	3.21	21.12
85	6.95	44.58	55.90	0.95	3.85	19.01
87	1.84	39.37	76.90	25.14	1.84	53.63
88	24.56	54.20	67.40	52.16	22.39	59.92
89	48.78	58.62	71.23	45.63	33.22	59.37
8	14.01	37.59	67.86	18.54	13.28	42.01

Manufacturing

| | 13.93 | 57.18 | 72.76 | 37.51 | 30.58 | 54.63 |

Table A4.6 Continued

SITC	Indonesia	Malaysia	Singapore	Thailand	ASEAN
1989					
51	17.86	33.26	69.14	7.98	38.28
52	16.15	14.74	59.63	10.54	25.49
53	18.62	26.18	93.15	17.49	46.23
54	26.48	33.56	96.80	20.56	56.43
55	61.95	57.81	72.52	47.64	64.27
56	83.26	53.82	93.64	0.04	42.90
57	2.72	24.69	68.70	4.80	42.70
58	12.39	14.94	90.76	28.90	51.83
59	11.00	63.96	58.86	22.29	47.84
5	24.11	34.06	75.43	17.16	45.96
61	57.78	42.60	63.94	47.88	52.97
62	20.54	60.40	47.50	75.58	52.02
63	0.66	5.26	71.35	15.75	11.53
64	94.43	44.92	62.37	35.01	59.25
65	50.39	56.22	66.49	66.07	61.20
66	37.10	68.78	53.33	86.71	69.58
69	29.47	45.45	71.62	41.15	54.27
6	26.58	48.29	63.97	65.45	51.96
71	2.00	43.57	71.83	19.91	47.39
72	0.65	18.01	69.76	4.50	27.39
73	0.40	8.18	68.14	5.37	29.28
74	2.76	45.12	83.25	38.06	56.34
75	0.29	72.19	58.90	72.04	60.97
76	21.68	56.60	78.44	64.03	70.26
77	21.53	86.03	85.25	71.61	82.02
78	5.66	19.05	52.01	15.16	25.31
79	9.25	54.82	65.01	13.43	54.54
7	5.95	63.80	73.57	44.49	61.49
81	86.49	83.49	54.36	71.13	66.52
82	13.30	38.15	79.72	9.91	39.68
83	25.43	64.94	21.24	9.56	17.62
84	1.91	11.37	59.19	1.36	20.62
85	2.34	38.09	55.54	1.17	15.28
87	1.85	35.80	76.69	21.28	52.47
88	38.80	62.15	73.01	61.90	67.36
89	48.83	54.36	73.34	45.62	60.96
8	13.71	37.41	69.08	20.81	43.14
Manufacturing					
	16.84	56.25	72.18	39.87	55.65

Table A4.6 Continued

SITC 1990	Indonesia	Malaysia	Singapore	Thailand	ASEAN
51	15.92	30.81	70.16	11.59	39.20
52	13.38	14.31	62.70	13.76	26.18
53	22.44	31.18	90.66	16.62	46.17
54	23.72	36.42	97.64	22.80	56.12
55	73.42	60.37	69.52	47.64	65.30
56	66.68	41.78	97.13	0.70	34.89
57	0.77	47.16	71.20	19.68	51.21
58	13.06	14.16	91.54	29.73	49.17
59	12.22	38.97	48.60	23.62	39.86
5	22.87	29.59	71.95	19.22	43.86
61	63.51	38.62	57.86	51.22	55.02
62	25.91	58.00	68.77	79.52	63.30
63	0.96	9.79	87.58	27.22	12.95
64	88.89	43.81	61.57	26.49	55.28
65	43.73	57.20	67.37	70.24	60.18
66	32.59	76.76	55.24	78.36	68.08
69	28.08	47.64	71.60	39.34	53.50
6	25.23	50.04	66.96	64.50	52.18
71	3.32	40.80	59.93	14.27	37.55
72	1.05	13.11	66.15	4.34	22.98
73	1.63	8.60	60.56	13.90	26.27
74	2.70	41.31	74.52	40.78	49.39
75	0.62	78.58	58.97	81.61	63.06
76	23.58	55.92	83.34	65.17	72.51
77	21.53	85.60	83.75	66.75	65.09
78	5.37	18.03	48.14	11.39	21.64
79	15.14	55.46	59.66	1.80	45.17
7	6.86	62.13	71.67	42.18	58.43
81	74.44	73.30	48.57	60.72	58.31
82	20.74	40.60	92.91	9.37	40.40
83	11.92	92.24	21.77	4.56	16.60
84	1.91	11.01	66.80	2.02	22.75
85	0.68	35.01	54.63	1.66	11.79
87	4.48	40.01	71.41	30.00	51.43
88	47.05	65.40	69.05	72.57	67.72
89	62.52	53.96	77.34	43.55	61.91
8	14.04	39.90	70.69	22.08	43.81
Manufacturing	15.82	55.39	71.11	39.7	53.85

Source: Khalifah (1996).

Table A4.7 Grubel-Lloyd indices for ASEAN manufacturing trade,
           1991-95

SITC	Indonesi	Malaysia	Singapore	Thailand	Philippines	ASEAN
1991						
51	23.954	55.748	78.542	21.234	28.712	49.481
52	0.000	0.000	0.000	0.000	37.469	5.847
53	0.000	0.000	93.198	26.985	0.000	38.926
54	0.000	0.000	99.666	26.036	0.000	42.680
55	78.394	62.247	74.112	0.000	0.000	61.261
56	32.420	0.000	0.000	0.000	83.091	28.030
57	0.000	0.000	0.000	0.000	0.000	0.000
58	15.770	15.275	99.128	44.177	13.594	53.799
59	0.000	41.679	50.544	63.115	29.588	44.788
5	35.268	26.132	87.739	29.228	30.146	52.704
61	0.000	0.000	0.000	89.203	0.000	49.919
62	93.839	60.781	66.137	79.673	0.000	67.901
63	0.000	0.000	86.064	0.000	0.000	9.644
64	89.931	37.802	62.241	25.830	0.000	51.100
65	66.213	60.275	72.889	93.437	22.899	67.931
66	98.989	85.435	56.342	65.572	98.525	69.168
69	42.644	49.619	72.294	21.495	33.854	52.081
6	56.459	79.993	70.898	76.955	45.170	68.566
71	0.000	43.490	62.150	22.180	0.000	39.580
72	0.000	13.536	69.915	5.066	0.000	21.823
73	0.000	0.000	64.083	0.000	0.000	18.681
74	3.036	44.489	75.494	40.081	0.000	47.107
75	22.601	85.370	63.091	79.936	84.163	68.264
76	48.965	63.543	88.018	81.347	97.778	79.259
77	32.431	91.144	88.334	75.772	90.807	86.086
78	8.949	18.448	60.551	25.811	18.258	29.428
79	19.531	72.725	45.234	52.635	0.000	50.382
7	10.503	83.558	98.348	62.530	69.842	79.535
81	0.000	0.000	0.000	0.000	0.000	0.000
82	0.000	0.000	97.956	0.000	0.000	24.492
83	0.000	0.000	0.000	0.000	0.000	0.000
84	0.000	11.912	75.456	0.000	5.441	19.503
85	0.000	0.000	0.000	0.000	0.000	0.000
87	0.000	55.275	84.742	45.097	0.000	61.621
88	61.991	78.689	76.649	92.372	93.050	79.890
89	83.176	74.522	85.871	60.836	77.186	76.067
8	31.598	69.408	91.085	35.202	30.585	58.555

Table A4.7 Continued

SITC	Indonesia	Malays	Singapore	Thailand	Philippines	ASEAN
1992						
51	23.954	55.748	78.542	21.234	28.712	49.481
52	0.000	0.000	0.000	0.000	37.469	5.847
53	0.000	0.000	93.198	26.985	0.000	38.926
54	0.000	0.000	99.666	26.036	0.000	42.680
55	78.394	62.247	74.112	0.000	0.000	61.261
56	32.420	0.000	0.000	0.000	83.091	28.030
57	0.000	0.000	0.000	0.000	0.000	0.000
58	15.770	15.275	99.128	44.177	13.594	53.799
59	0.000	41.679	50.544	63.115	29.588	44.788
5	35.268	26.132	87.739	29.228	30.146	52.704
61	0.000	0.000	0.000	89.203	0.000	49.919
62	93.839	60.781	66.137	79.673	0.000	67.901
63	0.000	0.000	86.064	0.000	0.000	9.644
64	89.931	37.802	62.241	25.830	0.000	51.100
65	66.213	60.275	72.889	93.437	22.899	67.931
66	98.989	85.435	56.342	65.572	98.525	69.168
69	42.644	49.619	72.294	21.495	33.854	52.081
6	56.459	79.993	70.898	76.955	45.170	68.566
71	0.000	43.490	62.150	22.180	0.000	39.580
72	0.000	13.536	69.915	5.066	0.000	21.823
73	0.000	0.000	64.083	0.000	0.000	18.681
74	3.036	44.489	75.494	40.081	0.000	47.107
75	22.601	85.370	63.091	79.936	84.163	68.264
76	48.965	63.543	88.018	81.347	97.778	79.259
77	32.431	91.144	88.334	75.772	90.807	86.086
78	8.949	18.448	60.551	25.811	18.258	29.428
79	19.531	72.725	45.234	52.635	0.000	50.382
7	10.503	83.558	98.348	62.530	69.842	79.535
81	0.000	0.000	0.000	0.000	0.000	0.000
82	0.000	0.000	97.956	0.000	0.000	24.492
83	0.000	0.000	0.000	0.000	0.000	0.000
84	0.000	11.912	75.456	0.000	5.441	19.503
85	0.000	0.000	0.000	0.000	0.000	0.000
87	0.000	55.275	84.742	45.097	0.000	61.621
88	61.991	78.689	76.649	92.372	93.050	79.890
89	83.176	74.522	85.871	60.836	77.186	76.067
8	31.598	69.408	91.085	35.202	30.585	58.555

The Macroeconomics of East Asian Growth

Table A4.7 Continued

SITC	Indonesia	Malaysia	Singapore	Thailand	Philippines	ASEAN
1993						
51	33.572	65.859	80.129	19.019	21.490	51.309
52	0.000	0.000	0.000	0.000	0.000	0.000
53	0.000	0.000	95.240	51.307	0.000	48.566
54	0.000	0.000	92.129	55.914	0.000	52.813
55	88.701	76.589	80.250	0.000	0.000	67.377
56	79.388	0.000	0.000	0.000	73.378	29.184
57	0.000	0.000	0.000	0.000	0.000	0.000
58	20.460	32.157	95.254	47.384	13.414	54.132
59	0.000	48.721	60.083	50.526	26.615	49.075
5	27.890	37.082	87.565	32.789	19.382	52.873
61	0.000	0.000	0.000	91.966	0.000	50.133
62	91.816	63.475	68.179	83.209	0.000	69.356
63	0.000	0.000	99.649	0.000	0.000	8.086
64	63.212	46.946	63.501	29.633	25.501	51.154
65	59.657	73.784	77.090	96.635	28.526	72.159
66	90.343	74.605	54.818	89.450	83.253	77.552
69	66.798	60.886	66.091	58.522	34.800	61.119
6	47.116	98.060	69.884	95.726	42.053	72.634
71	0.000	55.849	66.406	27.717	0.000	41.593
72	2.257	19.597	76.630	12.551	0.000	29.017
73	0.000	0.000	67.573	0.000	0.000	17.839
74	7.510	50.831	80.663	58.510	0.000	54.834
75	87.668	58.663	50.639	76.552	86.764	56.450
76	98.191	51.788	75.569	86.273	90.429	71.311
77	40.918	91.373	98.927	84.352	93.635	91.311
78	40.303	44.318	71.956	30.762	21.382	43.142
79	32.947	0.000	52.914	37.736	0.000	31.827
7	30.388	92.317	89.642	69.133	50.603	80.218
81	0.000	0.000	0.000	0.000	0.000	0.000
82	0.000	0.000	99.849	0.000	0.000	18.674
83	0.000	0.000	0.000	0.000	0.000	0.000
84	0.000	12.304	87.040	0.000	0.000	19.626
85	0.000	0.000	0.000	0.000	0.000	0.000
87	0.000	61.041	90.423	59.096	0.000	67.453
88	96.540	87.504	84.092	91.311	0.000	85.279
89	55.471	84.294	88.467	58.811	74.650	74.618
8	23.460	68.575	92.023	37.021	47.299	57.287

Table A4.7 Continued

SITC 1994	Indonesia	Malaysia	Singapore	Thailand	Philippines	ASEA
51	34.418	79.803	81.873	14.845	20.277	52.356
52	0.000	0.000	0.000	0.000	0.000	0.000
53	0.000	0.000	99.816	55.790	0.000	52.361
54	0.000	0.000	97.091	36.957	0.000	52.358
55	81.656	74.928	85.901	0.000	0.000	69.150
56	59.283	0.000	0.000	0.000	67.273	25.887
57	0.000	0.000	0.000	0.000	0.000	0.000
58	19.320	39.870	94.280	49.978	11.829	55.469
59	0.000	81.627	58.587	58.805	26.263	53.182
5	28.487	47.995	89.788	33.179	18.409	54.670
61	0.000	0.000	0.000	88.065	0.000	50.169
62	92.875	66.041	74.228	85.353	0.000	73.164
63	0.000	0.000	99.423	0.000	0.000	7.515
64	59.793	48.533	66.474	45.718	19.563	53.606
65	63.680	76.824	82.492	89.140	35.551	74.385
66	97.248	77.592	50.927	88.411	81.817	76.574
69	66.602	63.611	75.180	58.490	22.841	64.133
6	51.365	98.419	73.121	98.249	41.866	76.660
71	0.000	47.151	70.946	41.777	0.000	44.849
72	2.220	16.836	72.333	9.688	0.000	28.513
73	0.000	0.000	76.019	0.000	0.000	22.063
74	9.936	57.000	80.455	52.903	0.000	57.574
75	74.092	54.683	61.128	73.301	81.040	62.243
76	68.054	48.014	84.757	87.616	86.418	73.073
77	51.745	85.323	88.703	83.371	98.708	86.265
78	23.716	35.959	62.542	35.042	28.216	38.469
79	28.647	69.795	55.152	65.710	0.000	57.182
7	36.456	94.028	96.716	74.037	54.684	86.767
81	0.000	0.000	0.000	0.000	0.000	0.000
82	0.000	0.000	78.808	0.000	0.000	15.475
83	0.000	0.000	0.000	0.000	0.000	0.000
84	0.000	14.234	98.442	0.000	0.000	23.933
85	0.000	0.000	0.000	0.000	0.000	0.000
87	0.000	56.666	78.696	54.129	0.000	63.373
88	87.516	89.778	81.057	99.050	0.000	84.473
89	39.794	88.933	87.540	72.890	83.874	78.674
8	22.011	72.890	84.698	42.154	52.149	58.989

Table A4.7 Continued

SITC 1995	Indonesia	Malaysia	Singapore	Thailand	Philippines	ASEA
51	34.713	57.252	83.050	17.225	18.133	49.427
52	0.000	0.000	0.000	0.000	0.000	0.000
53	0.000	0.000	96.021	88.006	0.000	61.488
54	0.000	0.000	95.202	42.134	0.000	53.210
55	87.258	71.805	89.135	0.000	0.000	71.098
56	65.328	0.000	0.000	0.000	68.958	29.236
57	0.000	0.000	0.000	0.000	0.000	0.000
58	36.049	50.165	95.813	63.851	11.515	63.027
59	0.000	95.448	64.263	62.934	25.570	60.406
5	34.142	51.339	92.268	41.839	17.759	58.294
61	0.000	0.000	0.000	80.923	0.000	48.363
62	79.560	62.852	75.084	86.635	0.000	71.960
63	0.000	0.000	93.206	0.000	0.000	5.948
64	51.796	42.648	65.306	61.863	26.173	53.215
65	65.292	86.566	82.995	87.374	36.836	76.354
66	83.603	70.850	53.332	94.657	60.757	75.838
69	81.760	71.965	75.235	52.331	31.810	66.706
6	52.717	96.839	72.233	95.363	43.342	76.845
71	0.000	48.377	72.985	47.975	0.000	48.318
72	7.937	17.247	71.357	7.487	0.000	27.721
73	0.000	0.000	76.596	0.000	0.000	19.325
74	9.021	64.356	79.969	52.786	0.000	57.458
75	64.942	55.971	62.551	68.875	89.955	62.844
76	79.851	47.743	83.027	88.631	75.738	71.435
77	58.288	86.267	91.102	80.058	97.110	87.487
78	22.180	29.123	61.507	24.159	27.161	32.918
79	30.226	62.913	45.945	54.856	0.000	51.088
7	37.321	93.662	96.272	71.757	58.287	86.355
81	0.000	0.000	0.000	0.000	0.000	0.000
82	0.000	0.000	66.289	0.000	0.000	12.722
83	0.000	0.000	0.000	0.000	0.000	0.000
84	0.000	12.794	94.202	0.000	0.000	21.391
85	0.000	0.000	0.000	0.000	0.000	0.000
87	0.000	51.906	79.306	49.451	0.000	61.813
88	86.282	93.487	87.562	94.711	0.000	88.101
89	53.996	85.227	86.084	69.531	94.237	78.837
8	33.224	73.304	84.288	43.496	56.609	62.705

Source: Own calculations.

NOTES

1. A complete list of all the 149 manufacturing industries at the three-digit level is provided in the appendix to this chapter.
2. According to Chalmers (1991, p.195), the activities of the electronics industry can be categorised into three groups: "production of 'consumer electronics', consisting of mostly video and audio products (TVs and radios); production of 'electronic components' such as semiconductors (i.e diodes, transistors & integrated circuits); and production of 'industrial electronics' including computers and telecommunications equipment." Khalifah (1996) hence indicates that production in Division 75 refers to 'industrial electronics', while Division 76 refers to 'consumer electronics' and Division 77 refers to 'electronic components'.
3. Data for any commodity in the *International Trade Statistics Yearbook*, vol I (United Nations, various years) are given only if the value in any year is greater than or equal to 0.3 percent of the total trade value for that year.
4. Table A4.6 was extracted from Khalifah (1996) in her study of AFTA and Intra–Industry Trade, while Table A4.7 was own calculations using trade data from the *International Trade Statistics Yearbook*, vol 1 (United Nations, various years).
5. The inclusion of non-manufacturing data for the analysis of IIT is computed due to the ambiguity of certain commodity products. In Thailand, exports of processed food are classified as a primary commodity according to the SITC, but would be classified differently as a manufactured good by industry data. This problem has been stressed by Hirata (1988). Similarly, Indonesia's IIT in petroleum and related materials is not considered to be a manufactured product according to the SITC.
6. As previously explained, at the 2-digit level, this is likely to contain a large element of spurious intra-industry trade, and hence contain a higher risk of exaggerating intra-industry trade.

5. The Role of Productivity Growth

Why have East Asian economies achieved unprecedented high rates of growth? This question has attracted lively debate among economists and social commentators. The fact underlining this debate is that the 'Asian Tigers' (Hong Kong, Singapore, Korea and Taiwan) have achieved per capita growth rates of GDP around 6 per cent for the past four decades. The performance of other economies from East Asia (for example, Malaysia, Indonesia, Thailand and China) has also been impressive. Explanation of these growth 'miracles' is important as it could provide an 'East Asian model' for development. Also, inability to explain East Asia's success would represent a major defeat for economists (Sarel 1995).

Despite a large volume of literature, there has been no consensus on the sources of growth in East Asia. The emerging view is that either factor accumulation or technological progress is the source of growth. The former has been supported by growth accounting studies from Young (1992, 1994) and Kim and Lau (1994) who found relatively low rates of total factor productivity (TFP) growth in the East Asian economies. These results were popularised by Krugman's (1994) controversial article comparing the growth of East Asia to that of the Soviet Union and its demise in the 1990s. The conclusion drawn by Krugman is that diminishing returns to capital will eventually result in a slowdown of growth. The East Asian model can therefore be replicated through increasing capital stocks but it should not be practised or preached.

Advocates of the new growth theories have a less pessimistic view of East Asia. They look at the role of technology in economic growth and the factors that could drive technological progress. A short list of possible factors includes trade, government intervention, human capital and foreign investment. Sustained growth can be made possible by influencing private and public involvement with these factors.

To resolve this debate, growth accounting is often employed to decompose growth into factor-input growth and TFP growth. However, because of the large disparities between the results, the numerous growth accounting studies have yet to provide a consensus on the sources of growth in East Asia. In order to shed some light on this debate, a re-examination of some of the important issues will be undertaken. Section 5.1 compares the theories associated with explaining growth in East Asia. These conflicting theories and views are sometimes referred to as the 'growth debate'. Section 5.2 examines growth and the estimates of TFP. It will illustrate the sensitivity of TFP results obtained from different methodologies. The rest of the chapter is devoted to a case study of Taiwan. Section 5.3 offers an alternative approach to estimating TFP and examines structural change and its effect on technological growth. An empirical study of the possible determinants of TFP in Taiwan is conducted in section 5.4. Finally, summary remarks are presented in the conclusion.

5.1   THE GROWTH DEBATE

The phenomenal growth of the Asian Tigers has led to many debates on the source and sustainability of growth. The growth debates can be divided into two camps, the traditional neoclassical and the 'new growth theories'. The neoclassical view is that the growth experience of the Asian Tigers can be explained by factor accumulation. The high levels of investment maintained by the Asian Tigers supports this view. The key assumption in Solow's (1956) neoclassical model is that diminishing returns to factors make sustained growth impossible if growth is based solely on factor accumulation. Other assumptions include constant returns to scale and exogenous technological progress.

The speed at which the four Tigers were able to grow can be explained by the 'catch-up hypothesis', that is, followers tend to catch up faster if they are initially more backward (Abramovitz 1986, p.387). Imports of inputs from industrialised countries and increasing foreign direct investment resulted in imports of superior technology. The introduction of new techniques into production led to rapid growth as the economy was able to bypass the slow process of technological innovation. Under this hypothesis, it is predicted that developing countries will eventually catch up with industrialised countries and all countries will converge to a steady-state growth rate.

However, in light of the East Asian growth experience, much literature has been devoted to the new growth theories. These new theories have come about because of the empirical shortcomings and theoretical limitations of the neoclassical model. [1] First, the neoclassical model failed to explain technological progress. This was treated as an exogenous component in the Solow model. Solow (1957) himself recognised that factor accumulation could not explain all growth. Solow found that 80 per cent of per capita income growth in the United States during 1909–49 was due to technological progress. But the essential difference between Solow's case and that of the Asian Tigers is that annual growth of GNP per capita was only 1.8 per cent for the United States, whereas the Asian Tigers have grown at well over 6 per cent on average for 30 years.

The convergence issue is also an ongoing debate and has not yet reached a final conclusion. In support of the Solow model, Mankiw, Romer and Weil (1992) correctly pointed out that different steady-state income levels can occur among countries because of variations in savings and population growth rates. However, their augmented Solow model can be criticised for its strict assumptions of perfect competition and smooth exogenous technological change across all countries. The role of perfect competition ensures that economic actors can make the correct economic decisions through price signals. But price distortions in the East Asian region have been well documented. For example, the governments of Korea and Taiwan limited entry into exporting industries by offering tariff exemptions and lifting quantitative restrictions on inputs into some exporting industries (Hughes 1995). The industries that received these protection offsets were hand picked by the governments as they were perceived as 'winners' or having future potential. Barriers to entry ensured profits and economies of scale. These examples highlight the inappropriate assumption of perfect competition in the neoclassical models. The perfect competition assumption can, however, be applied to Hong Kong and Singapore as they are generally regarded as free trading states.

Perfect competition also implies that information is treated as a pure public good and can be freely obtained across countries. This assumption ensures that developing countries can catch up with industrialised countries if income differences are due to differences in technology. However, this assumption ignores the existence of patents and copyrights which protect new discoveries and information flow from rival bodies. If information flows can be protected, firms can charge for access to information and earn profits (imperfect markets) since the opportunity cost of information is zero (Romer 1994).

Another criticism of the neoclassical approach is the assumption that technological progress grows at a constant rate. Consider the Cobb–Douglas production function:

$$Y_t = A_t K_t^{\alpha} L_t^{1-\alpha} \qquad (5.1)$$

In the neoclassical model, A_t (the multiplicative factor of aggregate production) represents the state of technology and is assumed to be exogenous (Mankiw, Romer and Weil 1992). This assumption is debatable. Is the process of gaining new technology predictable or is it random? Is it entirely exogenous or can it be determined by other variables? Romer (1994) argued that technological progress is actually endogenous in the production equation. He believes that if more emphasis is placed on discovery and research the aggregate rate of discovery will certainly rise.

Some new growth models assume that technology is related to the level of investment. However, not all types of investment will lead to higher levels of technology (for example, the purchase of an additional tractor). But at the aggregate level many firms (especially in imperfect markets) do set aside some proportion of profits for investment in research and development. If the level of investment increases with profits, this should also drive research and hence improve technology.

The simplest version of a new growth model is the spillover production function with constant returns to capital.[2] It takes the form:

$$Y_t = AK_t^{\theta}K_t^{\alpha}L_t^{1-\alpha} \tag{5.2}$$

where $\theta > 0$.

In equation (5.2), the output of the aggregate economy is determined by capital and labour inputs plus spillovers from capital. Equation (5.2) attempts to model imperfect competition by allowing for increasing returns to scale in the aggregate economy. Investment in capital will also increase output due to some positive externalities θ. Despite individual firms having diminishing returns to capital, constant returns to capital for the aggregate economy will exist because of the externalities.

Solow (1994) argues that constant returns to capital is a fragile assumption. He notes that any hint of diminishing returns will lead us back to the neoclassical model, but more importantly, increasing returns to capital will lead to very explosive results. When using a model with a small degree of increasing returns, Solow predicts that a country such as France or Germany will have infinite levels of output in 200 years. Constant returns to capital is therefore an inadequate approach to explain growth because of the volatile 'knife edge' characteristic.

Although the spillover model is inadequate, it provides a valuable insight into the possibility of sustained growth. More elaborate models such as Romer (1986) have since been developed. In his model, technological progress is an endogenous function of expenditure on research and development. Solow notes that once we assume diminishing returns to capital, the standard neoclassical results of steady-state growth are still possible, even when we take account of imperfect markets (increasing returns to scale). He also argues that technological progress is difficult to model because of the exogenous components.

Growth Accounting and Growth Theories

The purpose of growth accounting is to relate the theoretical debate in the previous section to the empirics. First, can growth be totally explained by factor accumulation? Second, is there evidence of technological change? These two questions are very important. If growth can be totally explained by factor accumulation, then growth follows the neoclassical model. If much of the growth is the result of technological change, further questions can be raised about how this is achieved.

From equation (5.1), a Cobb-Douglas production function can be converted into its dynamic form as follows:

$$\frac{\Delta Y}{Y} = \frac{\Delta A}{A} + \alpha \frac{\Delta K}{K} + (1 - \alpha) \frac{\Delta L}{L} \qquad (5.3)$$

The interpretation of (5.3) is that the percentage change in output should be equivalent to the product of the capital share (α) and the percentage change in capital plus the product of the labour share ($1-\alpha$) and the percentage change in labour force plus $\Delta A/A$ which is the growth of TFP. In equilibrium, the values of α and ($1-\alpha$) can be regarded as elasticities of inputs into production when there are constant returns to scale.

The purpose of deriving equation (5.3) is to decompose output growth into factor growth (capital and labour) and growth in TFP. Therefore, TFP growth is the residual that measures the 'unexplained' difference between output and input growths within the neoclassical framework. TFP growth can also be regarded as a measure of improved efficiency, quality and technology. As noted before, new growth theories have implied that TFP growth can be influenced within the model through increasing research, reducing market distortions and producing positive externalities. Therefore, many have argued that significant TFP growth represents the inability of the neoclassical model to explain growth.

There are some problems associated with using the neoclassical model for growth accounting. First, this method ignores quality changes in capital and labour. The Asian Tigers have experienced significant change in the level of education of the workforce, which represents the quality of workforce. Measuring increases in the quality of capital is also problematic. TFP may be mismeasured because inputs between two periods are assumed to be identical. Many such as Toh and Low (1996) have tried to account for labour–augmenting technological progress by considering increasing average labour productivity over time, that is, $L = L_t e^{\lambda t}$. In this formula, λ measures the rate of labour-augmenting technological progress. However the choice of λ is ambiguous. Alternatively, by not taking account of quality changes, TFP can be a measure of the quality changes that have come about due to technological changes.

Second, a neoclassical model will result in biased TFP estimates if the assumption of constant returns to scale is wrong. We have already discussed the existence of imperfect markets in South Korea and Taiwan. If increasing returns to scale exist, TFP estimates will be biased upwards under the assumption of constant returns to scale. Third, many have argued that the growth accounting framework will mismeasure TFP because it measures TFP as a residual and thus includes shocks and cyclical factors. However, as long as there is a large sample period, these cyclical factors should not matter in the long run.

Although growth accounting provides a useful analysis of the composition of growth in terms of inputs and technology, the results from the exercise are meaningless unless they can be explained. Barro and Sala-i-Martin (1995, p. 352) acknowledge that since growth accounting does not provide an explanation for the changes in inputs and technology, it cannot be regarded as a theory. Large TFP residuals will simply show a failure of the assumptions of the model and will be suggestive of an alternative (Ito 1995, p. 291). Hence, growth accounting is designed to stimulate and develop ideas about economic growth.

5.2   THE COMPLEXITY OF ESTIMATING TFP

Estimating the rate of TFP growth would provide useful insights into the growth debate. However, the correct procedure for estimating TFP is debatable. Differences in the choice of data and methodology have led to conflicting results. This section aims to compare and contrast the various methodologies developed for growth accounting.

Empirical Evidence

Table 5.1 presents a survey of various TFP estimates of the Asian Tigers. The literature surveyed in this table is Young (1995), World Bank (1993) and Chen (1979). These three studies used different sample periods and hence a suitable comparison cannot be drawn. However, this table still provides a good illustration of the contrasting results. According to this table, the consensus is that the Asian Tigers achieved high rates of output growth (over 7 per cent for each country). The great difference is between Young's (10.3 per cent) and the World Bank's (7.9 per cent) estimates for South Korea. The results should be quite similar once we take account of the differences in the sample period and data sets.

Although the estimates of output growth are quite similar across the countries, the estimated rates of TFP growth are very different. Singapore consistently has the lowest rates of TFP growth ranging from 0.2 per cent (Young) to 3.6 per cent (Chen). The World Bank estimates of the TFP growth rate are also substantially higher than those by Young but are lower than those by Chen. These varying TFP estimates will give conflicting conclusions about the source of growth for the economy in question. Consider the case of Singapore. Young's results indicate that only 2 per cent of total growth is due to TFP growth, while the rest of growth is attributable to factor accumulation.

On the contrary, the World Bank results indicate that 17 per cent of growth is attributable to TFP. These inconsistent findings may be due to data inaccuracy and methodological variation.

Table 5.1   Previous estimates of TFP growth (%) for the Asian Tigers

Source	Country	Period	GDP growth(%)	TFP growth (%)
Young	Hong Kong	1966–91	7.3	2.3
(1995)	Singapore	1966–90	8.7	0.2
	South Korea	1966–90	10.3	1.7
	Taiwan	1966–90	9.4	2.6
World	Hong Kong	1960–89	7.1	3.6
Bank	Singapore	1960–89	7.0	1.2
(1993)	South Korea	1960–89	7.9	3.1
	Taiwan	1960–89	7.3	3.7
Chen	Hong Kong	1955–70	9.3	4.3
(1979)	Singapore	1957–70	6.6	3.6
	South Korea	1955–70	8.8	5.0
	Taiwan	1955–70	8.0	4.3

Sources: Young (1995), World Bank (1993) and Chen (1979).

Data Inaccuracy

The two inputs in standard TFP analysis are labour and capital. Other inputs considered by various studies include land and human capital. Many studies have measured labour by the number of people employed in the economy. This is calculated using the participation and unemployment data from the national accounts. However, a more appropriate measure of labour is annual person–hours.[3] This takes account of falling working hours associated with income growth.

Capital is usually measured by the perpetual inventory method. There are two complications associated with this method. First, the original capital stock must be estimated at the beginning of the period. With a large sample, any reasonable initial rate of capital stock should be acceptable because of a positive depreciation rate. The second complication concerns choice of the depreciation rate. Young (1992, 1995) used a series of different depreciation rates for residential, non-residential, transport, machinery and inventory capital. Others such as van Elkan (1995) used a single approximated rate.

The different methodologies used to estimate capital stock will influence the estimated rate of TFP growth, since capital can be a major contributor to growth. Toh and Low (1996) demonstrated that TFP estimates for Singapore were sensitive to the calculation of capital stock using various depreciation rates from 4 to 6 per cent.

Van Elkan (1995) used land as an input by measuring increases in the area used for agricultural and built-up classifications in Singapore. On average, land remained unchanged for Singapore between 1961 and 1991. Since land is a very slow growing input, many have opted to omit this factor. However, land inputs may play a role in growth for countries such as Korea and Taiwan where land usage was increased. Young (1995) addressed this problem by limiting his analysis to the non-agricultural economy where land input was minimal for Korea and Taiwan.

Many arguments have been put forward to stress the importance of human capital on the growth of developing countries. The measurement and treatment of human capital is difficult and debatable and is often omitted. Proxies used to measure human capital have included the population in secondary school (Mankiw, Romer and Weil 1992) and educational attainment (Barro and Lee 1993). Sarel (1996) argues that TFP will be underestimated by including education as a pure investment good. This occurs because it exaggerates the causality between investment in education and economic growth.

Technological Variation

Following the conventional definition, TFP represents the ratio of output over a combined input. The combined input depends on the value of factor shares. Thus, the procedure that is used to estimate factor shares is crucial for growth accounting. Table 5.2 illustrates the sensitivity of TFP estimates to different values of capital shares. The average capital shares estimated for Singapore range from 38.2 per cent (van Elkan 1995) to 53.3 per cent (Young 1992). The TFP estimates are 1.8 per cent and –0.8 per cent respectively. The trend in this table shows that the contribution of TFP to growth in Singapore falls as the capital share rises.

This outcome is attributable to the high rates of capital growth in Singapore and hence are likely occur in other East Asian economies. Higher capital shares imply that more weight should be placed on capital growth as a source of output growth. For example, Young's (1992) results of negative TFP growth for Singapore during 1970–90 were based on a relatively high capital share. Sarel (1996) has discussed the sensitivity of TFP estimates to different values of capital shares. In his sensitivity analysis of six countries, Sarel demonstrated that Singapore's TFP growth can be higher than that of the United States (and vice versa), depending upon the chosen value of capital share (α).

There are generally two methods commonly used to measure factor shares: regression and national accounts. The former derives factor shares by estimating production functions. This approach was used by Chen (1979) to estimate the capital shares for Japan, Korea and Taiwan. From his regression results, Chen concluded that the capital shares could be assumed to be 40 per cent for Korea and Taiwan and 30 per cent for Japan.[4] Because of the lack of data, Chen also assumed that the capital shares for Hong Kong and Singapore should be the same as those in Taiwan and Korea. This assumption is open to criticism. A close examination of the industrial and trade policies in Singapore, Taiwan, Korea and Hong Kong will indicate that these economies are different. The industrial structure of Hong Kong and Singapore is also very different from that of Korea and Taiwan. The most notable difference is the size of the agricultural sector.

Table 5.2   Selected TFP estimates and capital shares for Singapore

Source	Period	Average capital share (percent)	TFP as a % of output growth
Chen	1957–70	40.0	55.2
Young	1970–90	53.3	– 8.0
Young	1966–90	49.1	2.2
van Elkan	1961–91	38.2	22.5

Sources: Chen (1979), Young (1992, 1995) and van Elkan (1995).

Statistical problems will also arise from the regression procedure. These problems can occur because of low degrees of freedom arising from the lack of observations. Chen used the regression approach for the period 1955–70 for Japan and Taiwan and the period 1960–70 for Korea. Six of the 14 estimates presented by Chen (1979, p.63) were insignificant at the 5 per cent level. By using small samples, efficiency problems and low confidence will always exist in the regression estimates. Another criticism of the regression approach is the assumption that output growth is endogenous, while growth of factors is assumed to be exogenous. Sarel (1996) argues that the regression approach will overestimate the capital shares because of this assumption. Rather, capital growth should be treated as an endogenous variable to output.

Cross-country regressions have also been used to estimate factor shares. The advantage of this approach is that it allows for cross-country comparisons and the use of more observations. However the problem with using cross-country regressions is that the economies in the sample are assumed to have similar production functions and factor shares. The World Bank (1993) used a sample of 87 economies and derived a capital share estimate of 17.8 per cent.[5] This low estimate was influenced by the inclusion of the developing countries in the sample and is therefore inappropriate. The World Bank re-estimated the same regression using a sample of high-income economies and derived a capital share of 39.9 per cent. Not surprisingly, the estimates of TFP growth were lower for the Asian Tigers using the high income sample (see Table 5.3).

Table 5.3   World Bank estimates of TFP

Economy	TFP growth (%) (full sample)	TFP growth (%) (high income sample)
Hong Kong	3.64	2.41
Korea	3.10	0.23
Singapore	1.19	−3.01
Taiwan	3.76	1.29

Source: World Bank (1993, p64).

The study showed that the results could be sensitive to the chosen sample. The estimates of TFP using the full sample are unreliable, being biased upwards due to the use of low capital shares. The use of the high-income sample is therefore more appropriate and gives more reliable TFP estimates. However, the East Asian economies might not be similar to the OECD countries in the high-income sample. If not, these results can be misleading. A better method is to classify countries into various groups (for example, high performing countries).[6] This is an attractive proposal, but lack of observations will reduce the efficiency of the estimates.

Cross–country research also requires comparable cross-country data. Data from national accounts for each country must be deflated and converted into a common monetary unit. Some of the common data sets include the Penn World Tables (PWT), developed and described in detail by Summers and Heston (1991), and the International Comparison Project (ICP) of the United Nations. These data sets provide a wide range of samples useful for research in growth and are internationally comparable. However their quality is questionable, especially for the developing countries. First, one must take account of the differences in the quality of national accounts data from different countries. Disparities can arise from the different ways in which countries measure output, labour and capital formation. Second, the data from the PWT will be of low quality if the estimates are based on extrapolations. For example, Summers and Heston's quality rating ranged from a grade of 'C' to 'D' for the African nations. The data quality problems encountered with cross-country research will therefore give flimsy results.

The national accounts method measures factor shares by measuring the share of income distributed to the factors. It has been used by van Elkan (1995) and Young (1992, 1995). Under the assumption of perfect competition, income shares of the factors should reflect output elasticities. This approach also assumes that the additional income to factors should be equivalent to the marginal product of the input.

Because incomes to capital are hard to measure and may not reflect the marginal product of capital, most researchers tend to directly estimate the labour share. To derive labour share, Young (1992) multiplied the data for compensation to paid employees (as a percentage of GDP) by the ratio of the total working population to paid employees to take account of unpaid, self-employed, or implicit income. Assuming constant returns to scale, the capital share is derived by simply subtracting the labour share from one.

This approach has several disadvantages. First, market imperfections such as labour unions and monopolist firms may affect the level of wages by increasing the prices of products. Hence wage rates will not reflect the marginal product of labour and income shares will not reflect factor shares. Second, the classification and measurement of income to workers who are not paid employees, will certainly vary from country to country and may not be readily available. To derive the amount of income earned by unpaid workers, self employed workers, and employers, Young (1995) estimated their implicit wages by setting their wages proportionate to paid employees with similar sex, age, educational and industrial characteristics. Sarel (1996) argues that this type of classification is problematic since the data are based on labour surveys (conducted once every ten years) and questionable interpolations. Sarel also argued that employees and employers should not have the same wage structure determined by sex, age, educational and industrial characteristics.

To overcome the problems associated with the conventional approaches, Sarel (1996) proposed an alternative method. In the following section, this method is applied to estimate TFP growth for the Taiwanese economy.

5.3   TFP GROWTH IN TAIWAN

Economic Background

The traditional Taiwanese economy was based heavily on agriculture aided by Taiwan's semi-tropical climate, which provides suitable conditions for rice and sugar production. The development of the agricultural sector was also strengthened by investment in infrastructure during the occupation by Japan starting in 1895. During 1920–29, total exports consisted mainly of primary goods, namely rice (19 per cent) and sugar (50.6 per cent). Manufacturing exports played only a small role during this period, making up 7.4 per cent of total exports (Ho 1978, p.30). Taiwan's main trading partner was Japan and trade consisted of agricultural exports and machinery imports. This partnership produced a substantial trade surplus for Taiwan and enabled the development of a small but sophisticated non-agricultural sector by the 1930s.

By the end of World War II and the subsequent end of Japanese rule, political and economic instability resulted in high inflation and population pressures (due to refugees from mainland China). These events marked the beginning of structural change towards manufacturing, as political and national security interests led to the desire for rapid industrialisation. This desire resulted in the development of protectionist policies directed towards import substitution. Despite directing resources towards import substitution, success was limited in the period 1949–54.

Table 5.4   Economic indicators of Taiwan, 1952–94

Indicator	1952	1965	1980	1994
GDP per capita (NT $000 at 1991 prices)	21	40	118	280
GDP per capita real annual growth (%)	8.3	7.9	5.1	5.1
Population annual growth rate (%)	3.3	3.1	1.9	0.8
Agriculture/GDP (%)	32.2	23.6	7.7	3.6
Manufacturing/GDP (%)	12.9	22.3	36.0	29.0
Gross domestic saving/GDP(%)	11.9	17.5	31.4	21.4
Gross domestic investment/GDP (%)	15.3	22.6	33.7	23.7
Exports/GDP (%)	5.8	11.5	36.1	46.1
Imports/GDP (%)	12.5	14.2	33.1	44.0
Literacy (%)	57.9	76.9	89.7	94.2
Labour participation (%)	66.5	58.2	58.3	59.0

Source: Council for Economic Planning and Development (1996).

By the late 1950s, the Taiwanese economy became sluggish and the trade balance was unacceptably high.[7] 'The domestic market reached its saturation point during the mid-1950s and enterprises had to compete fiercely for the limited domestic market.' (Chou 1995, p.108).

Faced with economic difficulties, the government began the task of implementing gradual reforms to shift trade policy from import substitution to export promotion. The 19-point economic reform program in 1960 included: the gradual devaluation of the $NT (Taiwan's dollar), the removal of trade controls from importables (although tariffs were still high), the expansion of export promotion schemes, and the provision of tax incentives for imports-into-export production.

These policies marked the beginning of export-led growth for Taiwan. They also led to a structural transformation in manufacturing as exports moved away from consumer goods towards technologically advanced items. The velocity of trade growth was remarkable. Taiwan's growth in exports increased from 5.8 to 36.1 per cent between 1952 and 1980 (see Table 5.4).

The current account deficit was eliminated by the mid-1960s and Taiwan has since maintained a trade surplus.

The development of education, health and other public infrastructure during the growth phase also aided the development of human capital. In recent years, an increasing demand for higher living standards has seen a rise in the expenditure on social security. The expansion of public investment projects and the promotion of industrialisation increased the investment ratio to 33.1 per cent by 1980 but this declined to 23.7 per cent by 1994 due to a fall in public investment. Investments were financed through increases in the savings ratio, but this ratio has also declined in recent years.

TFP Growth: An Alternative Approach

If Taiwan's economic growth was the result of export and capital growth, can growth be sustained? The historical evidence has demonstrated that the initial conditions in the 1950s were below optimum. By the 1990s, investment ratios had fallen and education and literacy levels are now comparable to those of high-income economies. Has Taiwan reached the point of diminishing returns? The continued growth of output, despite a slowdown in capital input has implied that other factors (eg. technology, spillovers) may have contributed to Taiwan's success. To determine the extent of TFP growth in Taiwan during 1966–95, a new approach developed by Sarel (1996) is employed in this study.

Sarel's approach aims to explain the reasons why factor shares should differ across countries. There are two main reasons for such differences. First, there are differences in the structure of production in each country. For example (assuming two sectors), if country A has a relatively higher agricultural intensity than country B, and agriculture has a higher labour share, we will expect country A to have a relatively higher aggregate labour share. Second, the differences in development across countries will affect the technology and production techniques in each sector. Countries at a higher development level are expected to have better techniques and different factor shares (for example, the agricultural sectors of USA and Zambia). To estimate factor shares, the following assumptions are made:

- Each economic sector/industry follows Cobb-Douglas production technology and exhibits constant returns to scale.
- Factor shares are constant for each activity but may vary across different activities.
- Technologies are not drastically different over time and across countries.
- Differences between technological factor shares and income shares are not systematic.

Given the aforementioned assumptions, the aggregate capital share can be calculated as $\alpha_t = \Sigma w_{it} \varphi_I$, where α_t is the aggregate capital share for the economy at time t, w_{it} the relative intensity of sector i at time t and φ_{it} the capital share of sector i.

TFP growth at time t can be estimated as:

$$TFP_t = \ln\left(\frac{Q_t}{Q_{t-1}}\right) - \alpha_t \ln\left(\frac{K_t}{K_{t-1}}\right) + (1 - \alpha_t)\ln\left(\frac{L_t}{L_{t-1}}\right) \qquad (5.4)$$

This approach has several attractions. First, it captures the effect of structural change on factor shares. The Taiwanese economy experienced a transition away from agriculture to manufacturing after World War II. Agriculture declined significantly while sectors such as manufacturing and tertiary sectors began to increase. The economy's aggregate factor share should vary during this transitional phase because different production technologies are assumed for the sectors. Hence, this approach argues against using constant aggregate factor shares over time (at least for the growth phase) in contrast to the regression approach. Second, the use of sectoral factor shares improves the national accounts approach as it removes the need for using questionable labour compensation data.

Estimating factor shares
The first step in the estimation procedure is to estimate the individual factor shares (φ_i) of each sector. This is the most difficult task of the estimation procedure. Fortunately, estimates of eight major economic sectors are available from Sarel's 1995 paper. The estimates in Table 5.5 were derived using panel data of various countries and sectors. Sarel's results show that capital shares were indeed different across sectors and the level of development did not have a significant effect on capital shares. The eight economic sectors listed in Table 5.5 accounted for over 90 per cent of Taiwan's GDP. The sectors not included in Table 5.5 will be classified as 'unaccountable' and will be removed from total output and our estimation procedure.

To calculate the aggregate capital share, we simply sum the products of each sector's capital share by its relative intensity. The relative intensity of each sector is simply the share of GDP (adjusted for indirect taxes and unaccountable) of each sector. Under constant returns to scale, the labour share is derived by subtracting the capital share from one.

Measuring output and inputs
The main source of data is the Council for Economic Planning and Development, *Taiwan Statistical Yearbook 1996*. Other data calculations and

estimates are detailed in the appendix to this chapter. Output and capital are deflated and expressed in 1991 prices. They are all measured in new Taiwan dollars. Output is measured as real GDP adjusted for indirect taxes. Unaccountable sectors are also removed from the calculation of output.

Table 5.5   Taiwan: capital shares for individual sectors

Activity (i)	Capital share (φ_i)
Agriculture	0.27
Manufacturing	0.31
Utilities	0.54
Construction	0.19
Commerce	0.23
Transport and communications	0.32
Financial and business services	0.60
Government and other services	0.08

Source: Sarel (1996).

Labour inputs are calculated by multiplying the employed workforce by the average monthly working hours. For a more accurate measurement, the workforce was disaggregated by its sector and labour was calculated by summing the average monthly working hours of each sector multiplied by the number of employees of each sector. Working hours declined significantly in utilities, and transport and communications, while only small reductions were seen in the construction sector. Unavailable working hours for 1965–76 were estimated using ordinary least squares for those industries that exhibited declines in working hours.

With capital inputs, data for real capital accumulation are available for the period 1952–95.[8] The capital accumulation series was forecasted backwards for the period 1900–52 using a logarithmic extrapolation and an initial capital stock of zero. To estimate capital stock, the perpetual inventory method was used with a depreciation rate of 5 per cent.

The results of output, inputs and TFP growth for 1966–95 are presented in Table 5.6. The estimated average capital shares are also included. According to these results, the estimated capital shares have averaged around 31.2 per cent. But importantly the capital share increased gradually from 29.1 per cent to 33.6 per cent during this period. The increased capital share may reflect an increase in the marginal productivity of capital during the period and hence higher rates of capital accumulation.

Although capital grew by 10 per cent per annum and was a large contributor to growth, it was not the largest contributor. The results show that capital and labour growth contributed to 39.4 per cent and 9.4 per cent of total growth respectively while TFP contributed to more than half of total growth during the period considered.

Table 5.6   Taiwan: contributions to growth, 1966–95

	Growth (%)			Capital share	Contribution (as a % of growth)		
	Output	Capital	Labour		Capital	Labour	TFP
1966	8.0	11.5	0.8	29.1	41.9	7.5	50.5
1967	8.6	10.8	2.9	29.1	36.5	24.2	39.3
1968	8.8	12.8	3.0	29.3	42.6	23.8	33.6
1969	6.4	13.9	4.4	29.5	63.9	48.0	−0.1
1970	12.2	12.9	1.8	29.5	31.3	10.1	58.6
1971	13.6	13.8	1.6	29.5	30.0	8.4	61.5
1972	12.0	14.4	1.0	29.8	35.7	6.0	58.3
1973	12.0	14.0	2.1	30.1	35.3	12.2	52.5
1974	1.4	14.6	4.9	30.2	316.3	246.8	−463.1
1975	4.0	16.7	1.2	30.1	126.6	20.2	−46.8
1976	13.0	12.0	−0.9	30.3	28.0	− 4.9	76.9
1977	9.9	12.3	1.0	30.3	37.6	7.1	55.3
1978	12.3	11.2	3.5	30.5	27.8	20.0	52.2
1979	7.3	11.5	2.1	30.8	49.0	20.0	31.0
1980	8.1	12.6	1.4	31.0	47.9	11.8	40.3
1981	7.8	11.9	−1.8	31.5	48.2	−16.0	67.8
1982	5.0	10.3	0.9	31.4	64.3	11.8	23.8
1983	7.6	7.9	0.6	31.5	32.6	5.1	62.3
1984	11.0	7.3	3.3	31.7	20.9	20.4	58.7
1985	6.0	7.1	0.8	31.9	37.8	9.0	53.2
1986	12.4	5.5	0.2	31.8	14.1	1.3	84.6
1987	11.4	5.5	2.7	32.1	15.6	15.8	68.7
1988	7.8	7.8	1.7	32.3	32.5	15.1	52.4
1989	7.7	9.3	−1.1	33.0	39.9	−9.8	69.9
1990	5.4	9.1	−0.1	32.8	55.4	−1.7	46.3
1991	7.6	8.5	−0.6	32.6	36.3	−5.2	68.9
1992	6.1	8.7	0.6	32.8	47.0	6.6	46.3
1993	5.8	9.6	1.5	33.0	54.6	17.3	28.1
1994	6.3	9.3	0.0	33.5	49.4	0.4	50.2
1995	6.1	8.6	0.0	33.6	47.0	−0.3	53.3
Mean	8.8	10.4	1.2	31.2	39.4	9.4	51.2

To correct for cyclical and irregular components, the TFP series is
smoothed using a five-year moving average and displayed in Figure 5.1. TFP
growth seems to vary substantially, with high rates during the early 1970s and
1985–89 and low rates during 1973–76. The results also indicate that TFP
growth has declined in recent years. Despite this variability, TFP growth has
remained significantly high on average and has played a major role in output
growth.

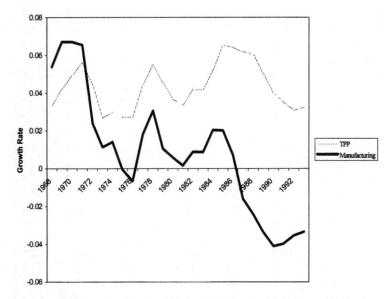

Notes: Growth rates are in natural logarithms. 1974–75 was omitted from the calculations of
averages.

*Figure 5.1   Taiwan: total factor productivity and manufacturing growth as
% of GDP (five year moving average) 1966–95*

Figure 5.1 illustrates the relationship between TFP growth and the growth
of manufacturing intensity. The manufacturing sector experienced growth (in
output shares as a percentage of GDP) from 1965 to 1971 but then stagnated
and eventually declined after 1986. As for TFP, it grew substantially from
1968 to 1971 and experienced a decline thereafter with a sharp drop after
1985. Kuznets (1974) observed this relationship between productivity growth
and changes in sector proportions. Kuznets recognised that one characteristic
of economic growth is the transition from agriculture to industrial sectors, and
then at a later stage, a transition from industry to service sectors.

Kuznets (1989) argued that some sectors in the economy are naturally more productive than others and that these productivity differences will affect the aggregate growth and productivity in the economy. For example, if the industrial sector has a higher rate of productivity relative to the agricultural sector, income and productivity will naturally grow as the industrial sector dominates the shrinking agricultural sector. Kuznets assumed that industrial sectors (manufacturing, utilities, transport and communications) are more productive because these sectors place more emphasis on technology relative to the agricultural sector.

For Taiwan, the manufacturing sector is one of the important industrial sectors. As discussed earlier, Figure 4 revealed the relationship between TFP growth and the growth of the manufacturing sector. This relationship suggests that manufacturing is a major contributor to TFP and output growth. However, if the manufacturing sector continues to decline (TFP growth has declined 3.3 percentage points from 1986 to 1993 as the manufacturing sector declined from 39 to 30 per cent of GDP), can Taiwan achieve sustained growth? The decline of the manufacturing sector is considered to be a natural growth process and the service sector is assumed to continue to rise and eventually become the largest contributor to total output. It has also been suggested that the manufacturing sector contributes less to TFP growth as the economy becomes more developed (Syrquin 1988).

The present analysis points to a bleak outcome for sustained growth in Taiwan. However, this analysis assumes that the manufacturing sector is the only productive sector and all other sectors are inferior. Historically, productivity tends to be more evenly diffused across sectors as the economy develops. Therefore, to increase TFP, the economy must place more emphasis on improving the capabilities of the emerging sectors (eg. the service sector) rather than increasing the emphasis on manufacturing. Other factors that could drive TFP growth cannot be ignored. These include research, education, trade and market reform. They could have contributed to the increasing rates of TFP growth during 1981–86, as these rates cannot be totally explained by the changes in manufacturing intensity.

Sensitivity Analysis

One of the controversial aspects of Sarel's methodology is the assumption that factor shares are constant over time for the individual sectors. This is a rather stringent assumption since structural changes could bring about new technologies to the individual sectors in Taiwan. Technological change can affect production in two ways. It could be either factor neutral or factor biased. In the first case, the production isoquant has shifted outwards as a result of technological change. More importantly, the production technology does not change (as indicated by the identical marginal rates of technological substitution for each capital to labour ratio on the new isoquant) and therefore the factor shares should remain the same. This example of factor-neutral growth is implied in Sarel's approach.

Alternatively, in the case of factor biased growth, technological change has resulted in higher output and changes in production process. At each level of capital and labour, the new marginal rate of substitution is higher than that of the previous isoquant. The variability of factor shares caused by this type of growth effect will therefore contradict the assumption from the previous section. The purpose of this section is to relax this assumption for industries exhibiting factor-biased growth and assess its effect on TFP growth.

One of the first tasks of this section is to identify the industries affected by biased technological growth. Jorgenson and Fraumeni (1981) conducted such an analysis using a sectoral production model for 36 sectors in the United States economy and modelled technological biases by looking at the relationship between factor shares, factor prices and technological change. Productivity is considered to be factor using (saving) if increase in the factor price diminishes (increases) the rate of productivity growth. Their results supported the view that technological change will lead to biases towards production technology, as productivity growth was found to be related to factor prices.

The sensitivity analysis performed in this section will be based on the conclusions and findings drawn from Jorgenson and Fraumeni's study. It is important to emphasise that their results may not have direct relevance to our study since their findings were based on United States data and derived using four factors (capital, labour, energy and materials). However, the purpose of this sensitivity exercise is to examine the fragility of TFP results by relaxing some of the assumptions. The study by Jorgenson and Fraumeni (1981, p.44) will be used as a guide to determine those industries affected by factor biases and the direction of those biases:

- Capital using and labour using: agriculture; mining (metal and non metallic); manufacturing (textiles, apparel, furniture, printing, leather, gas, metals, electrical, motor vehicles and instruments); financial and business (finance, insurance and real estate); commerce (services); government enterprises; transport and communications.
- Capital using and labour saving: construction and manufacturing (petroleum refining).
- Capital saving and labour using: utilities (gas) and manufacturing (primary metals, paper, chemicals, rubber, stone, clay and glass, non-electrical machinery and transportation equipment).

According to the above classification, some sectors are classified as both capital and labour using. Under constant returns to scale, total biases must sum to zero and therefore simultaneous increases to both factor shares are not possible (that is, labour and capital using). This result was possible for Jorgenson and Fraumeni's model, as there were additional factors (material and energy). Material and energy shares were able to fall to allow for the simultaneous increase in capital and labour shares. For simplicity, capital and labour using industries will be assumed to be factor neutral (factor shares don't change).

The construction and utilities industries have had apparent biases. For the sensitivity analysis, the capital shares for these affected industries will be arbitrarily varied for each 10-year interval. Construction will have an increasing capital share as it is capital using while utilities will have a decreasing capital share as they are capital saving. The manufacturing sector it can be treated as capital using, saving or neutral. In the analysis, we will consider these three possible scenarios since manufacturing played an important role in TFP growth.

The results of the sensitivity analysis are presented in Table 5.7. The sectoral capital shares are arbitrarily varied according to the type of bias. The affected capital shares were increased (decreased) by 10 percentage points at every 10-year interval with the exception of the capital saving manufacturing sector in scenario IV (these were decreased by 5 percentage points). Surprisingly, these variations to sectoral capital shares had only minor effects on TFP for the entire period. In the four scenarios, TFP growth varied between the narrow range of 3.9 and 4.3 per cent. Hence, although factor neutral growth is a rather weak assumption in Sarel's analysis, the effect of biased technological growth on TFP growth is only minor.

5.4   THE DETERMINANTS OF TFP GROWTH

As discussed earlier, much of the focus of the new growth theory has centred around endogenous technological change. The purpose of this section is to contribute to this debate by examining the factors (if any) that could have driven TFP growth during our sample period. The studies on how economies acquire technology are vast and sometimes inconclusive. Factors frequently surveyed in the growth literature include: (1) equipment investment; (2) human capital; (3) government intervention; (4) trade; and (5) foreign direct investment. In the following analysis, a review of these factors will be conducted in the context of Taiwan.

Equipment Expenditure

Many new growth models place much emphasis on capital investment as a source of technological progress. However, not all types of investment will contribute to technological improvements. Investment that could lead to technological improvements includes research, development, and equipment.[9] Equipment is believed to promote technology through absorption of foreign technology and development of new skills through learning by doing. In Taiwan, most equipment expenditure is on manufacturing. The relationship between manufacturing and TFP has already been discussed in Section 5.3. The high level of equipment expenditure, due to the growth of the manufacturing sector, can therefore be a determinant of TFP growth.

Table 5.7   Sensitivity analysis using different sectoral capital shares

	Capital share (%)			TFP growth
	1966–75	1976–85	1986–95	
Scenario I				4.2
All sectors (factor neutral)				
Scenario II				4.2
Construction (capital using)	18.9	28.9	38.9	
Utilities (capital saving)	53.8	43.8	33.3	
Other sectors (factor neutral)				
Scenario III				3.9
Construction (capital using)	18.9	28.9	38.9	
Utilities (capital saving)	53.8	43.8	33.3	
Manufacturing (capital using)	30.8	40.8	50.8	
Other sectors (factor neutral)				
Scenario IV				4.3
Construction (capital using)	18.9	28.9	38.9	
Utilities (capital saving)	53.8	43.8	33.3	
Manufacturing (capital saving)	30.8	25.8	20.8	
Other sectors (factor neutral)				

It has also been apparent that the state promoted the transfer of foreign technology from imports. Technology embodied in machinery imports into Taiwan was somewhat aided by relatively low tariff protection. The relationship between equipment investment and growth has been discussed by De Long and Summers (1991). Using cross-country analysis, they demonstrated a relatively large, positive relationship between growth and equipment investment. On causality, De Long and Summers argued that if growth caused equipment expenditure, the higher rentals of economic structures should result in a decline in equipment expenditure. However, high equipment expenditure occurred during times of high growth. Hence, De Long and Summers argued that equipment expenditure caused growth.

Human Capital

Many studies have shown that returns to schooling are significantly greater than the opportunity cost of capital. [10] Macroeconomic studies such as Mankiw et al. (1992) have also pointed out that human capital can be treated as a neoclassical factor in the Solow model. In this analysis, the emphasis on human capital will be on the externalities that drive TFP growth.

On acquiring technology, Nelson (1990) argued that most technology is acquired through education in science and engineering. Although science and engineering play a role in technological improvements, other forms of education can also play roles for improving labour quality and efficiency. For example, labour training and vocational education at any level of the production process will enable growth of technology by removing bottlenecks and increasing the quality of production. Sanjaya (1996) pointed out that technological capabilities of an industry depend upon how well the industry can function as an organisation. Through better management and organisation skills, flows of information and interactions among the members of the organisation will be greater than the sum of individual skills and knowledge. When new technology is acquired (for example, foreign equipment), investment in management and vocational education will be required to maintain and improve this organisational synergy.

Government Intervention

The role of government intervention in economic growth is very controversial. The views on public policy can range from a *laissez faire* (neoclassical) approach to a revisionist (interventionist) approach. An examination of the public policies in Taiwan will indicate that the state has played an important role in guiding the economy through its growth process. Government intervention in Taiwan has included trade protection (subsidies and tariffs), foreign exchange controls, biased industry promotion (subsidised credit, monopoly rights and tax holidays) and price controls. However, critics have argued that growth was inhibited by these policies.

Nevertheless, the emphasis on research and development through state-sponsored programs cannot be ignored. Simon (1992) outlined the five main technological contributions of the state: (1) financial and tax policies to encourage firms to undertake innovation; (2) development of programs and institutions to facilitate the diffusion of existing technologies; (3) policies aimed at improving the utilisation of foreign technology; (4) investments in education and training; and (5) providing the means to collect and disseminate economic and technological information so that firms can be aware of market changes. However, the role of state-owned enterprises (usually monopolies) should be mentioned in this context. Public corporations in Taiwan accounted for 56.7 per cent of total manufacturing output in 1966 but by the early 1980s this figure had declined to less than 20 per cent (Amsden 1985, p.91). This fall in public ownership may have been attributable to the inefficiencies of state intervention.[11]

Trade

The implementation of favourable trade policies is considered to be one of the central themes of economic development. As mentioned before, the story of Taiwan's growth was one based on trade and export expansion. However, it must be emphasised that trade expansion in Taiwan did not result from free trade. On the contrary, tariffs in Taiwan remained significantly high despite reforms to promote export expansion. Traditional trade models of comparative advantage and efficient resource allocation (through market allocation) will be inappropriate for Taiwan. More emphasis should therefore be placed on the role of trade in promoting externalities and technology.

The basic assertion of the benefit of trade is that it could provide new production technologies by absorbing foreign technology and improving production. These new technologies result from improving production by adapting to technologically-embodied foreign inputs. The process of absorbing foreign technology can also lead to further externalities by instigating and developing human capital. Smith and Jordan (1990) recognised that the skill base of the labour force will be enhanced by adapting to new technology from trade.

Trade can also help acquire new technology for globally competitive firms. Instead of producing commodities for the domestic market only (as in import-substitution industries), the export-competing industries in Taiwan must cater for the tastes of the world market. Exporting firms will therefore undergo the process of investing in research and development and developing more advanced production lines in order to increase their global market shares.

Foreign Direct Investment (FDI)

In traditional growth models, the role of FDI is to boost the level of aggregate funds required for investment. However, the new line of thinking suggests that FDI can play a role in promoting technology. FDI is usually associated with long-term investment in an economy. As foreign investors become stakeholders in the economy, their investments are usually coupled with the transfer of foreign technology. The recent emergence of multinational corporations (MNCs) has led to an increasing amount of foreign technology transfer. MNCs played an important role in investment in Taiwan in the

1960s and 1970s, as they brought new forms of technology and human capital from their home countries.

Critics of MNCs argue that the diffusion of technology from these corporations will be slower, thus not benefiting domestic producers. For example, MNCs may restrict the diffusion of technology to ensure that their technology is monopolised in the domestic market. However, these criticisms are not evident in Taiwan. Industries in Taiwan have flourished with the inclusion of MNCs (Myers 1984).[12] With the television industry of the 1970s, the transfer of technology was attributable to the departure of foreign managers and workers from MNCs to native firms. This transfer of human capital from European colour television companies resulted in the development of a higher proportion of native television producers. The Singer Sewing Company also transferred technology by providing training seminars and using mostly domestic parts in production. This technology soon filtered through to other Taiwanese firms.

Empirical Analysis

To shed some light on the factors that drive TFP growth, some simple econometric models are estimated using variables discussed in the preceding sections. Consider the production function:

$$Y = AK^{\alpha}L^{1-\alpha} \qquad (5.5)$$

In its dynamic form:

$$\frac{\Delta Y}{Y} = TFPG + \alpha \frac{\Delta K}{K} + (1-\alpha)\frac{\Delta L}{L} \qquad (5.6)$$

where $\qquad TFPG = f(.....).$ $\qquad (5.7)$

From the above equation, TFP growth is treated as an endogenous component to output. By estimating a model for TFP growth equation (5.4), this model can be substituted into equation (5.3) to explain growth in terms of physical input growth and technological input growth. The technological inputs that are believed to affect TFP growth are *EQUIP* (equipment investment), *EDU* (vocational education), *GOV* (level of government expenditure), *TRADE* (level of trade), and *FDI* (foreign direct investment). The descriptions of these variables are detailed in the appendix to this chapter. The estimation results of five model specifications are presented in Table 5.8. First-order lags have been included to take account of the delayed effects and possible serial correlation. From these five regressions, trade and government expenditure consistently have significant positive effects on TFP growth. Foreign direct investment also has significant positive effects on TFP for two of the models.

Table 5.8   Estimates of five TFP models

Regressor	(1)	(2)	(3)	(4)	(5)
Intercept	−0.010	0.039**	−0.010	0.006	−0.006
EQUIP	−0.050	0.027		−0.133**	0.125**
EQUIP(−1)	−0.013	−0.111		0.073	−0.137**
DEDU	−0.066	0.050		0.211	−0.415*
DEDU(−1)	0.026	0.317		0.084	0.0471
GOV	0.152**		0.152**		0.297**
GOV(−1)	0.048		0.054**		0.067
TRADE	0.306**		0.283**	0.438**	
TRADE(−1)	0.141		−0.173**	−0.286**	
FDI	0.017	0.046*	0.013	0.036**	
FDI(−1)	0.004	−0.017	−0.010	−0.012	
TFP(−1)	0.445**	0.213	0.491**	0.554**	0.384*
Serial correlation	0.010	0.059	0.636	2.644	1.244
Functional form	0.199	0.391	0.519	0.843	0.000
Normality	0.122	0.260	0.853	0.133	1.296
Hetero–scedasticity	0.159	2.655	1.190	2.022	0.079
Adjusted R^2	0.820	0.288	0.830	0.766	0.680
SEE	0.015	0.030	0.015	0.017	0.020

Notes: The diagnostic tests are the LM test for serial correlation; Ramsey's RESET test for functional form; asymptotic chi-squared test for normality; and asymptotic chi-squared test for heteroscedasticity.
   **denotes significance at 1%.
   *denotes significance at 5%.
   (−1) denotes lagged variable.

As for education, the results are ambiguous. Education has different signs in the five models and is negative and significant in model (5). Although insignificant, the lagged education variables are positive for the five cases. The effect of equipment investment is also inconclusive from the five models. The coefficient for this variable is positive and significant for model (5) but negative and significant for model (4).

Nested tests are conducted to examine the suitability of the specifications outlined in Table 5.8. Tests of models (2) to (5) against the general model (1) are shown in Table 5.9. From these tests, the results show that model (1) is rejected in one test. More importantly, these tests have showed that education and equipment expenditures are insignificant in explaining TFP growth and hence can be ignored.

Table 5.9 Nested tests of models against the general specification.

Model	Variables excluded	F–statistics	Decisions
2	Trade and government	$F(4,16) = 15.8107$	Reject
3	Education and equipment	$F(4,16) = 0.7160$	Do not reject at 10%
4	Government	$F(2,16) = 3.7326$	Reject
5	Trade and FDI	$F(4,16) = 4.888$	Reject

Finally, a predictive failure test was conducted to examine the forecasting ability and the overall robustness of model (3). The model was re-estimated over the sample period 1967–85 and the observations for 1986–95 were used for forecasting. Figure 5.2 illustrates the predictive power of model (3). From this figure, we can see that the forecasts match the actual trends closely. The good forecasts given by this model indicate its robustness and insensitivity to small changes in the sample size.

5.5 CONCLUSIONS

In this study the sensitivity of TFP estimates with respect to the choice of methodology and the estimated factor shares is discussed and investigated empirically. An alternative approach developed by Sarel (1996) was used for the Taiwanese case and revealed significant levels of TFP growth during 1966–95. However, it must be emphasised that this alternative approach (and any other) is subject to criticism. In this study, estimated sectoral factor shares from Sarel's paper are applied to the case of Taiwan.

The results from the application of this methodology show a relationship between TFP growth and structural change in Taiwan. In particular, TFP growth in Taiwan appears to be strongly correlated with the growth of manufacturing. The empirical results found that the growth of government expenditure and trade had significant positive effects on TFP. Other factors such as education (vocational), foreign investment and equipment expenditure were found to have played a less significant role. However these factors should not be ignored in the development of technology. The proxies used for education, foreign investment and equipment expenditure may not give a true representation of their effects on technology. More importantly, the role of education may have had partial effects on technology by enabling a higher rate of technology diffusion from trade and government expenditure. Further and more elaborate analysis in this area is still required.

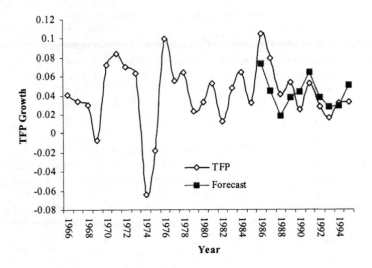

Figure 5.2　Actual TFP and forecasted values

The results from this study point to a positive role for government intervention in sustainable economic growth. Rather than just playing a passive role (that is, maintaining good fundamentals), the government should directly promote technology through facilitating research and development, subsidising education and providing incentives for the private sector to undertake research. Government intervention should focus on promoting the capabilities of the emerging sectors (for example, service sector, finance). The role of manufacturing in Taiwan has now reached a point of diminishing returns in terms of technology, as observed from the declining trends in manufacturing as a percentage of GDP. The stage of development in Taiwan is well past the transitional phase. To achieve sustained growth, the promotion of hi-tech industries and the utilisation of human capital resources is necessary.

As for trade, the 1997 Asian economic crisis and global instability certainly affected the level of trade and TFP growth in Taiwan. The positive role of trade in promoting technology transfers is noted in this study. However, trade with foreign countries, especially with those in the East Asian region, will depend largely on the health of the global economy rather than domestic policies. External arrangements with multilateral organisations (such as APEC) should be encouraged to promote regional trade growth.

In conclusion, Paul Krugman's (1995) 'sausage maker' analogy of East Asian economies is questionable. Impressive TFP growth for Taiwan over the period 1966–95 confirms that sustainable growth can exist but it will depend on the strength of TFP-inducing factors. Finally, it must be emphasised that the conclusions derived in this study should be used with caution. Strong differences between East Asian economies do exist in terms of their economic structure and their development policies. Further investigation into this region is still worthwhile.

APPENDIX TO CHAPTER 5

Data for activity shares and monthly working hours (1974–95) are from the Council for Economic Planning and Development (1996), *Taiwan Statistical Data Book 1996*. Some manipulations of this data are detailed as follows:

- Calculation of unaccountable sectors as a share of GDP:

  GDP shares/intensities for the eight sectors are available for Taiwan. The unaccountable sector's share is simply the sum of the eight sector's shares less one.

- Estimation of average working hours 1966–75:

  Agriculture: Data are not available for 1966–1995. Average monthly hours are approximated by taking the average of the seven sectors. Tertiary includes government, financial and business services.

The data for the technological inputs are from the Council for Economic Planning and Development (1996), *Taiwan Statistical Data Book 1996*. The data used for total factor productivity growth is the series derived in Section 5.3.

EQUIP is measured as the growth of equipment expenditure. The data used here is the growth rate of capital formation in machinery and other equipment (adjusted for 1991 prices). The proxy used for human capital (*EDU*) is the growth of the percentage of the population receiving vocational education. Vocational education includes agricultural, industrial, commercial, marine products, nursing and mid wifery, home economics and other studies.

GOV (Government intervention) is approximated by the growth of current government expenditure (in 1991 prices). Current government expenditure may be a good proxy for the expenditure in R&D and technology institutions, however it must be emphasised that the other types of intervention (eg. tariffs, foreign exchange controls) are ignored by this variable. Trade growth

(*TRADE*) is measured as the growth of total trade (exports plus imports) in 1991 NT dollars, and foreign direct investment (*FDI*) is measured as the growth of approved private foreign and overseas Chinese investment (in 1991 $US) in Taiwan.

Table A5.1   OLS forecasts for working hours (1966–75)

Sector	Intercept	Year	Adjusted R^2
Log (manufacturing)	16.7738*	−0.00576*	0.861
Transp/communication	2695.7857*	−1.25414*	0.978
Commerce	3830.6857*	−1.82782*	0.915
Construction	1707.1286*	−0.76015*	0.748
Utility	5322.8000*	−2.57895*	0.851
Tertiary	1999.8000*	−0.91053*	0.893

Note: *denotes significance at 1%.

Table A5.2   Tests for unit roots

Variable	Trend	Test	Test stat	Critical value
TFP	No	DF	−4.106	−3.029
EQUIP	No	DF	−3.280	−3.029
TRADE	No	DF	−4.989	−3.029
GOV	No	ADF(10)	−3.339	−3.029
FDI	No	DF	−3.884	−3.029
EDU	No	ADF(3)	−1.510*	−3.029
DEDU	No	ADF(2)	−5.678	−3.040

Note: Critical values at 95% significance.

Tests for unit roots were conducted on each of these variables using the Dickey-Fuller and Augmented Dickey-Fuller tests (see Table A5.2). With the exception of *EDU*, the tests concluded that the variables were stationary. Ordinary least squares regression can therefore be conducted on these stationary variables. As for *EDU*, the variable was found to be stationary when it was first differenced (*DEDU*).

NOTES

1. See Lucas (1988) and Romer (1986).
2. Also referred to as the *AK* model.
3. For example, see Chen (1979) and van Elkan (1995).

4. Chen's (1979, p.63) actual estimates of α are: Korea 38.9 per cent; Taiwan 37.1 per cent and Japan 30.6 per cent.

5. The World Bank (1993) included human capital as an additional factor using Barro and Lee's (1993) measure of educational attainment.

6. The high performing economies are Hong Kong, Indonesia, Korea, Malaysia, Singapore, Taiwan and Thailand.

7. This was aided by increased importation of intermediate goods for production and the deliberate overvaluation of the $NT which hindered the export competing sector.

8. Interpolations were conducted for missing years between 1952–55, 1955–60 and 1960–65.

9. Although Romer (1986) considers R&D to be a vital factor in technological progress, data for R&D in Taiwan for the period 1966–95 is non-existent. This factor is therefore unfortunately omitted from our empirical analysis.

10. For example, see Psacharopoulos (1973).

11. Amsden (1985) noted that 14 of 15 state enterprises were 'in the red' by 1981.

12. Government regulation of MNC activity also existed. Policies were implemented to ensure MNCs' activities were consistent with the technological priorities of Taiwan (Simon 1992).

6. Mechanics of Growth:
   The Singaporean Experience

Between 1965 and 1990, the economies of Hong Kong, South Korea, Singapore, Taiwan, Japan, Indonesia, Malaysia and Thailand grew twice as fast as the rest of East Asia, three times faster than Latin America and South Asia, and 25 times faster than Sub-Saharan Africa (World Bank 1993). The four Tigers and Japan are considered to be the first wave of 'miracle' economies. China, Indonesia, Malaysia, Thailand and Vietnam form the second wave. Each economy grew at its own pace depending on initial conditions and the type of public policy pursued. Endogenous and human-capital-augmented neoclassical growth models have been put forward to explain the growth phenomenon. This study will consider the macroeconomic determinants of growth for a particular country over time. Three alternative engines of growth are hypothesised: trade, public policy, and investment. The trade engine is based on studies finding general empirical support for export-led growth (Balassa 1978, Henriques and Sadorsky 1996). The second engine models the role of government in providing a stable macroeconomic framework and improving basic infrastructure to continually attract foreign investment. Finally, investment as an engine of growth encompasses investments in human and physical capital as both are common features of the East Asian 'miracle'.

   The aim of this study is to determine which engine has propelled the Singaporean economy in recent years. The following sections examine the relative importance of each engine of growth and attempt to explain Singapore's sustained growth over the last decade. Section 6.1 presents a review of the literature on rival trade policies, multinational corporations, and their impact on economic growth. Implications from the McCombie-Thirlwall (1994) model are briefly examined. The role of public policy is viewed in the light of productive government expenditure and macroeconomic stability. The importance of investment in physical and human capital is also examined. Section 6.2 relates the theoretical issues to Singapore's experience. A note on the TFP debate is included. Competing engines of growth are specified in Section 6.3 and issues in econometric modelling are considered. In Section 6.4 error correction models are derived for each engine and non-nested tests are employed to compare the three models. Recent evidence is compared with the results. Section 6.5

summarises the chapter and presents conclusions for Singapore's future growth prospects.

6.1 THEORETICAL FOUNDATIONS AND DEBATES

This section reviews the literature on the key macroeconomic variables that define the three possible engines of growth: trade, public policy and investment. While neoclassical and endogenous growth models are theoretically useful, they suffer from several drawbacks in practice. Besides the unsatisfactory treatment of technical progress and omission of human capital, the standard neoclassical model does not appear to fit the facts (Mankiw 1995). Todaro (1994) highlighted the inability of endogenous growth models to consider the inefficiencies of inadequate infrastructures and institutions common in developing countries; the effects of short- and medium-term growth are also omitted. It may be more meaningful to study the interrelations between economic agents within a macroeconomic framework. Pack (1994, p.66) argued that in practice it would seem 'necessary to examine one country at a time, insofar as there is no identical international production function along which changes in capital exert their effect'.

Trade

It has been suggested that an adverse balance of payments constrains growth to the extent that countries with current account deficits tend to invest less, leading to slower growth, *ceteris paribus*. McCombie and Thirlwall (1994) derive a demand-side model from the balance-of-payments identity and use the elasticity approach to estimate the balance of payments-constrained growth rate.

Fischer (1993) found that adverse changes in the terms of trade reduce growth mainly through their effect on productivity growth; small open economies are especially vulnerable. One has to be cautious when interpreting the terms of trade trends as different measures of the terms of trade yield different results. Changes in transportation costs as well as the quality and composition of manufactured exports must also be considered. Balassa (1989) argues that the terms of trade based on unit values ignores decreases in transport costs and is generally biased upwards for manufactured products since quality improvements are more readily captured than in the case of primary commodities. He further argues that using price indices would thus show a deterioration rather than an improvement in the terms of trade. In other words, changes in terms of trade based on price indices may be inversely related to income levels.

The model does not consider the response of domestic savings and investment to the aggregate wealth implications of rising external liabilities, and hence the current account deficit may not be corrected. This shortcoming highlights the important role of savings in mitigating such potential problems resulting from the long run impact of receiving foreign aid or when multinational corporations (MNCs) repatriate more funds than they invest through foreign direct investment (FDI). High and rising net external liabilities create uncertainty as to how the government may correct the adverse balance of payments and this may reduce investment and hence growth. For a developing country relying largely on FDI, further problems are envisaged when MNCs withdraw their operations in response to a poor economic outlook, for which they may be responsible. Furthermore, correcting the current account deficit through currency devaluation will generate inflationary pressures, *ceteris paribus*. These implications stress the need to control the free mobility of capital flows by making clear the conditions of MNC operations through legislation, for instance by providing incentives for MNCs to re-invest part of their intended profit repatriation in local projects.

Public Policy

The role of the state in public policy has been downplayed in models of growth and development. Attempts have been made to model the contributions of government expenditure to growth. The role of the state as an engine of growth is based on the argument that the government has to provide basic infrastructure and macroeconomic stability before trade policies can be pursued. This leads to the question of the extent of state intervention required for economic success.

Barro (1990) incorporated government consumption into an endogenous growth model and found a negative correlation with growth.[1] This may be due to government consumption crowding out private-sector investment. However, government spending in the form of public investment may stimulate private investment. Such productive government expenditures include those on education, health and on improving infrastructure. Foreign and local investors are attracted by a large pool of skilled labour and continuous improvement in infrastructure. In this study, government activity is assumed to be a productive input into private sector production and this includes expenditures on national security, economic services and education.

Barro's model assumes that expenditures require financing through distortionary taxation which in turn reduces growth. Further work undertaken by Dowrick (1995) found support for Barro's model when government consumption (not considered to be directly productive) was used. He also found that productive government spending does stimulate growth.

Investment

The transition from labour- to capital-intensive industries cannot be made without sufficient investment in human and physical capital. Saving behaviour is motivated for reasons such as borrowing constraints, bequests, uncertainties and taking advantage of investment opportunities including education. The level and growth of saving depend on life expectancy and demography. Gersovitz (1988) suggested two ways the government can affect the level of national savings. First, it can select the level of government saving by deciding on how much revenue to raise via taxation and how much to spend. Second, the government can indirectly affect foreign and private savings (comprising corporate and personal savings) through its influence on the incentives to save faced by households and corporations. The assumption of close substitutability between private and government consumption may explain why some countries provide retirement pensions through pay-as-you-go schemes. By reducing uncertainty through the provision of insurance programs, governments may encourage greater private investment. However, Andersen and Gruen (1995) showed that maintaining a high national savings rate is not sufficient for generating or maintaining high economic growth rates.

It is now widely accepted that accumulation of human capital plays an important role in sustaining or raising growth rates. Levine and Renelt (1992) acknowledged that investment in physical capital, and either the level or the rate of change of human capital, increase the rate of growth. Human capital can be accumulated through better health and nutrition, education, on-the-job training and skills upgrading, which in turn raise labour productivity and hence output. Birdsall et al. (1995) argued that over some range, spillover benefits raise productivity, that is when one more-educated worker (manager) motivates the entire group of workers (on the production line) to become more productive. However, the World Bank (1995) found that the relationship between investment in human capital and productivity growth is weaker than that between investment in physical capital and productivity growth, but argued that investment rates and initial endowments of education are robust predictors of subsequent growth.

This section has briefly reviewed the literature on most of the key macroeconomic variables on which the three engines of growth are based. These models will be specified and tested to determine which engine best explains the data. The following section highlights some features of the Singaporean economy in relation to the theoretical treatment of the macroeconomic variables outlined above.

6.2   ECONOMIC GROWTH IN SINGAPORE

In the space of three decades, Singapore has become the envy of many developing countries still struggling to break out of the poverty trap. Krugman (1994) believes that the East Asian success is not sustainable and that the recent slowdown is due to structural factors such as total factor productivity (TFP). This section seeks to relate Singapore's experience to the theories considered previously and to set the stage for empirical work to be undertaken in the next section. The TFP controversy will be brought up later in this section.

Export-Oriented Industrialisation

Among the Tiger economies Singapore has the smallest domestic market and almost no natural resources. The decision to adopt the import-substitution industrialisation (ISI) strategy for survival was reinforced when South Korea and Taiwan appeared to enjoy initial success. It was not until they ran into serious economic problems during the 1960s that Singapore retreated from ISI and adopted the export-oriented industrialisation (EOI) stance. During the same period, manufacturers in industrialised countries reached the stage of the product cycle where they focused on product innovation and capital-intensive production techniques. With an abundance of labour in Asia, the costs of outsourcing relatively less efficient labour intensive activities were low. From Singapore's perspective, there appeared to be a comparative advantage in exporting intermediate products. Singapore was also blessed with its location at the gateway between East and West. Sachs (1997a) proposed that physical geography mattered in that landlocked countries grew slower than coastal ones by about 0.7 percent per annum.

In order to overcome the problems of technological disadvantage and lack of entrepreneurial experience, the government drew up a list of tax incentives to encourage foreign enterprises to set up branches in Singapore.[2] However, poorly designed tax holidays can deter investment. The World Bank (1993) cited the example of South Korea where constant changes to the tax regime resulted in manufactured export growth of 3 percent during the period 1962–1982.

MNCs are vital to Singapore's success in that they link Singapore directly to their respective domestic markets. This linkage becomes especially important when their home governments impose trade restrictions to protect their domestic markets from relatively cheaper exports from developing countries. While recognising the importance of FDI in expanding the manufacturing sector, Singapore has also identified the need to study the technology and superior managerial/marketing skills of MNCs, as it has yet to join the ranks of developed countries.[3] Any form of FDI is closely monitored by government agencies to ensure that exploitation opportunities do not arise. Joint training centres have been encouraged for local firms to learn from joint research projects and for MNCs to develop the skills required to cater to world markets. Lifting foreign exchange controls on the repatriation of profits and tax incentives have effectively deterred the practice of transfer pricing. Thailand and Indonesia have been less successful in this area.

Although current account deficits were persistent until 1985, they were not as substantial as those of other developing countries. FDI increased substantially over the years and appeared to generate more spillover benefits to the economy than necessary to offset the capital outflow.

By the mid-1980s, MNCs accounted for 70 percent of gross output in the manufacturing sector, 53 percent of employment and 82 percent of direct exports (Bello and Rosenfeld 1990). Total exports grew to 191 percent of GDP at the end of 1987. In the 1980s, the EOI strategy was extended to more capital- and skill-intensive as well as higher-productivity type activities. This led to the government picking 'winners' in the manufacturing sector, namely chemicals and more importantly electronics. Table 6.1 shows that the value-added share of gross output for electronics fell over the years from 1978 to 1992 despite an overall increase for all the industries in the same period. This reflects the Korean experience with its selected 'winner'– heavy and chemical industries – and reinforces the conclusion that promoting specific industries does not work. Despite this decline, electronics still accounted for 38.5 percent of total manufacturing value-added (MVA) in 1992 and half of total manufacturing output, which in turn contributes more than 25 percent of national output today.

Table 6.1   Singapore's manufacturing value-added (MVA) as a percentage of output[a] (1973–1992)

	1973	1978	1984	1992	% of total MVA, 1992
All industries	32.0	26.3	27.0	34.6	100.0
Electronic products & components	n.a.	32.2	29.9	27.9	38.5
Electrical machinery & apparatus	39.0[b]	33.7	37.6	38.7	4.4
Transport equipment	46.8	47.4	51.7	45.2	8.6
Machinery except electrical/electronic	39.9	49.1	45.7	38.5	6.4
Fabricated metal products	36.8	34.5	38.7	37.8	7.1

Notes: [a] Figures include petroleum refineries and products.
          [b] Includes electronic products.

Source: Huff (1995, p.743).

Manufactured exports affect the economy through various channels. In addition to generating saving, investment and jobs, productivity also improves. This view is also shared by the World Bank (1993, p.317) which argues that the 'relationship between exports and productivity growth may arise from exports' role in helping economies adopt and master international best-practice technologies'. Singapore's experience provides supporting evidence of this conclusion. A cycle is complete when higher total factor productivity (TFP) growth feeds back into higher export growth. However, the role of TFP is controversial and will be discussed later.

Role of Government

There is an increasingly popular view that the role of public policy in resource allocation and infrastructural development is more important than trade as an engine of growth. Contrary to Barro's (1990) model, the case for Singapore is not clear since it has a small government which is also alleged to be highly interventionist (Bello and Rosenfeld 1990; Huff 1995). It may be argued that a positive correlation between government expenditure and economic growth should apply to Singapore since the tax rates are comparatively lower than those in the West. Barro's assumption of a distortionary tax effect may not be relevant to Singapore. A study by Kormendi and Meguire (1985) found that growth in the ratio of government consumption to output does not adversely affect economic growth. Figures 6.1 and 6.2 using Singapore data appear to support their findings. Government consumption seems to be positively correlated with real GDP.

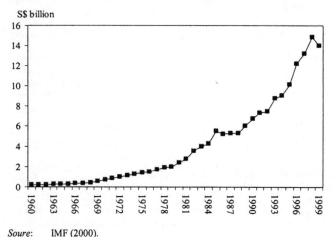

S$ billion

Soure: IMF (2000).

Figure 6.1   Government consumption in Singapore, 1960–1999

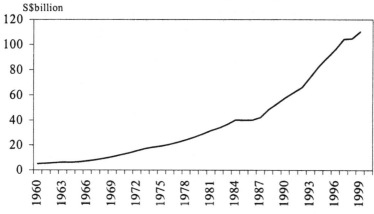

S$billion

Source: IMF (2000).

Figure 6.2 Singapore's real GDP, 1960–1999

The Structure of Savings

Saving and investment are the two major pillars in Keynesian macroeconomics. The virtues of saving have been propagated from the individual to national level. Upgrading of infrastructure and other development programs require financing. The government chose to raise funds by creating voluntary and compulsory savings schemes. These schemes are preferable to printing money (strong inflationary tendencies) and foreign loans (external liabilities can adversely affect the balance of payments). Both serve to slow down the painful recovery process should the economy experience adverse external shocks.

Postal saving has been a popular way of establishing a voluntary saving scheme. Governments in Japan, Malaysia, Singapore, South Korea and Taiwan have run these institutions at relatively low administrative costs, tapping a non-traditional source of financial savings provided by small savers desiring greater security and accessibility than that provided by the private sector (World Bank 1993). Tax exemptions are granted on interest-bearing deposit accounts to attract depositors. In Singapore, the habit of saving was inculcated in primary schools during the 1970s, when the government took over management of the postal institutions, which did not actively promote saving.

Compulsory saving schemes should complement voluntary savings to raise the overall savings rate but studies have yielded inconclusive results. Only Japan, Malaysia and Singapore have developed such schemes. The impact of forced savings on aggregate savings depends on the extent of substitution for voluntary savings (World Bank 1993). Such schemes appear to work for

Singapore's Central Provident Fund (CPF), set up to provide funds for old-age financial security. All employees and their respective employers are required by law to contribute to the personalised accounts of employees. Each member has three accounts. The Ordinary Account may be used for housing, insurance, approved investments and education purposes; the Medisave Account is used for medical insurance and hospitalisation expenses; and the Special Account is for old age and contingency purposes. CPF deposits are interest bearing and the full amount may only be withdrawn after retirement. The Monetary Authority of Singapore estimated the CPF scheme raised the overall saving rate by 3.8 percent between 1967 and 1989. Such a social security scheme avoids most of the problems evident in the West and reduces the need to save more in lieu of uncertainties so that these intended funds may be invested elsewhere. Goh (1977) added that it also reduces the upward pressure on prices as the economy grows and provides the government with a non-inflationary source of funds for development programs.

Macroeconomic Management

Contrary to views about the negative correlation between inflation and economic growth, the World Bank (1993) argued that this relationship is not robust to small changes in that below-average inflation rates for a long period of time do not always imply a high growth rate. Low inflation is necessary but not sufficient for growth; India experienced low inflation rates and low growth. It is clear that uncertainty about future inflation effectively reduces investment. Even if it is known that it will be equally high in subsequent periods, the measures taken to reduce it will often discourage investment and hence growth.

Singapore, despite its openness to trade, keeps the inflation rate low by allowing the exchange rate to appreciate in line with foreign inflation but not without taking steps to prevent 'internalisation' of the local currency (Huff 1995).[4] A stable local currency has the added advantage of stimulating export growth. Singapore's consistently low inflation rates have minimised relative price distortions and lead to more efficient allocation of resources. Part of this consistency is due to the government's quick response to external shocks and to aggressive export-promotion strategies. A set of strong and credible measures is in place to mitigate any potential economic damage inflicted. Singapore relied mainly on manufactured exports and was a major re-exporter of refined petroleum products at the time of the oil price shocks. This made the economy less susceptible to inflationary pressures as compared to oil-importing South Korea and Taiwan. Even the ensuing global recession elicited a quick response to stabilise the economy. Slower responses and/or policy mismanagement makes the recovery process a slow and painful one. Mexico's two "lost years" of adjustment translated into a "lost decade" of growth (World Bank 1993).

The Contribution of Education

The high-performing East Asian economies not only invest substantially in education, they also strive to continually improve the quality of education. The rapid attainment of universal primary education has generated an excess demand for secondary and tertiary education. It should be noted that education and training contribute to rapid and sustained growth but do not by themselves make growth possible (World Bank 1993). The measure of improvements in human capital varies according to assumptions and techniques, therefore different conclusions have been drawn. The World Bank (1993) supports universal primary education across most East Asian economies as being vital to success but this is not necessarily correct.

Table 6.2   Social rate of return/private rate of return ratio (%)

Country	Primary	Secondary	Tertiary
Hong Kong	n.a.	81	49
Singapore	n.a.	88	60
South Korea	n.a.	87	83
Taiwan	54	97	112
Philippines	73	85	91
Thailand	54	90	79
India	88	69	82

Notes: Years studied are 1976 (Hong Kong), 1966 (Singapore), 1986 (South Korea), 1972 (Taiwan), 1988 (Philippines), 1970 (Thailand) and 1978 (India).

Source: Lim (1996, p.172).

Table 6.2 shows that despite the private rate of return exceeding the social rate of return (except for tertiary education in Taiwan), secondary education yielded a relatively higher rate of return to society compared to tertiary education in Hong Kong, Singapore, South Korea and Thailand. In contrast, primary education in India should be emphasised. Secondary education appears to be justified for Singapore since its export base is becoming more diversified (in the manufacturing and service sectors). Higher wage premiums are paid to workers in these expanding sectors and scarce jobs are allocated on the basis of higher educational qualifications (Todaro 1994). One important implication of education from a national development point of view is summarised by Hughes (1995, p.98). Hughes argued that access to quality tertiary graduate and post-graduate degrees in industrial countries had played a very important role in the transfer of 'hand' production technologies as well as 'soft' skills such as business and economic management. She observed that the East Asian countries innovated to increase productivity in education, and that schools were used for two shifts during the day and for continuing education at night.

The latter is popular in Singapore and Taiwan as fees for night courses are usually subsidised. With such opportunities, many women are putting off marriage in favour of career advancement. In Singapore, fertility rates (measured per 1000 females) fell from 5813 in 1960 to 1707 in 1995. Birdsall et al. (1995) and the World Bank (1995) argued that when fertility rates decline, families invest more in each child who then benefits from the higher quality of education provided. This is evident in South Korea and Singapore. More married women in Singapore have entered the workforce since 'guest workers' such as housemaids are increasingly being employed to perform household chores and mind children. Family units are getting smaller with each succeeding generation, and the government is attempting to avert the ageing-population problem by offering attractive tax relief for families with three or more children and raising the retirement age.

The Total Factor Productivity Controversy

While increases in labour productivity through education and training are desirable, an ideal measure would be TFP. Krugman (1994, p.67) argued that 'mere increases in inputs, without an increase in the efficiency with which those inputs are used, must run into diminishing returns'. By efficiency he means TFP which is the difference between growth of output and growth of all factor inputs, better known as the Solow residual in a neoclassical context. The problem is that this residual is subject to measurement problems which may explain why other studies have found higher estimates of productivity growth (*Economist* 1997).

Work by Tsao (1985) among others concluded that TFP growth in Singapore was close to zero over different periods of time. However, other studies have shown different results. Goh and Low (1996) recognised that productivity gains from skills training and (information) technology are difficult to measure, as are productivity and service quality. It is therefore not supring that different TFP estimates have been derived. Much depends on the specification of the production function representing the economy. It has also been argued that Krugman failed to recognise that part of technological progress embodied in capital equipment exported from industrialised economies may be productivity growth of another form (*Economist* 1997).

In summary, it is clear that TFP estimates are fragile due to factors such as the sample period for estimation, measurement errors, difficulty in distinguishing between TFP growth and capital investment as well as in measuring intangibles such as service quality and their improvement, and specification of the appropriate production function and its functional form. With a better understanding of the Singaporean economy, it is now appropriate to consider which engine of growth accounts for Singaporean success in recent years.

6.3 DATA AND MODELLING ISSUES

Many studies on economic growth apply regression techniques using cross-sectional or panel data to study convergence or policy effectiveness across countries. However, Quah (1996) argues that such applications capture 'representative economy dynamics' rather than those of the entire distribution. He maintains that panel data techniques are only used for a restricted class of economic problems. Some authors argue that using these techniques implicitly imposes a naive assumption about some common economic structure, such as identical production technologies, being adopted by countries at various stages of their development. Although cross-country regressions are useful in summarising correlations in the data, they do not explain how countries with good macroeconomic management policies manage to grow relatively faster (Fischer 1991). These arguments justify the use of time-series regressions on one country at a time.

In this study, models of growth engines are kept simple by considering only the most relevant variables. For expositional convenience, these hypothetical models are referred to as the trade, state, and investment models. A log-linear functional form is chosen as it may be more meaningful to model the responsiveness of real GDP to each percentage point change in the explanatory variable of interest. The first differences of such transformed variables may be interpreted as the rate of growth. The study utilises seasonally unadjusted quarterly data compiled from various issues of the *Monthly Digest of Statistics (Singapore)*, the *Economic Survey of Singapore* and the *Monthly Bulletin of Statistics* (United Nations).[5] Monthly data are converted to quarterly data by taking the average of three months except in cases where data are measured at the end of the period as is the case with CPF balances. All variables are measured in aggregate. Monetary units are measured in millions of Singapore dollars (S$) and are adjusted to 1990 prices using the consumer price index. Presentation of data changes over time as old statistics are either discontinued or replaced by an improved classification. This restricts the sample periods of the trade model (1979(1) to 1995(4)) and the state and investment models (1985(1) to 1995(4)).

Trade Model

The trade model is based on the export-led growth hypothesis. The proposed model is similar to the one specified by Henriques and Sadorsky (1996). It is expressed as

$$logY_t = \alpha_0 + \alpha_1 logTOT_t + \alpha_2 logMFDX_t + \alpha_3 logTOUR_t + \epsilon_t \qquad (6.1)$$

where Y_t represents the real gross domestic product (GDP) of Singapore, TOT_t the term of trade, $MFDX_t$ the real value of manufactured exports, and $TOUR_t$ the number of visitors to Singapore.[6]

State Model

Government policies are instrumental in the East Asian success stories. A hypothetical model may be specified as

$$logY_t = \beta_0 + \beta_1 logGS_t + \beta_2 logGEC_t + \beta_3 logCPF_t + \beta_4 logCPI_t + \epsilon_t \qquad (6.2)$$

where GS_t represents real government recurrent expenditure on the administration of national defence, the judicial system and the police force; GEC_t real government recurrent expenditure on economic services encompassing national development programs and improvements in transport and communications; CPF_t compulsory savings, and CPI_t the general price level.

Investment Model

Singapore is claimed to be an investment-driven economy so the final model may be expressed as

$$logY_t = \gamma_0 + \gamma_1 logGED_t + \gamma_2 logGEC_t + \gamma_3 logINV_t + \epsilon_{tt} \qquad (6.3)$$

where GED_t is real government recurrent expenditure on education at all levels and INV_t real private-sector investment in physical capital.[7]

Seasonality

As seasonally unadjusted quarterly data are used, seasonality is expected to be present in most of the series. Leong (1997) reviewed one method of testing for seasonality by running an auxiliary regression

$$\Delta Y_t = \alpha + \delta_1 S_{1t} + \delta_2 S_{2t} + \delta_3 S_{3t} + \varepsilon_t \qquad (6.4)$$

where $\Delta Y_t = Y_t - Y_{t-1}$; α is a constant term and S_{it} is a seasonal dummy variable (taking a value of 1 in quarter i, where i =1,2,3 and 0 elsewhere). The regression is run for full and split samples. Considering split samples allows one to check whether seasonal fluctuations have changed over time. Regression results (not presented here) suggest that the series logY, logTOUR, logGS and logGEC exhibit seasonal fluctuations. The estimated coefficients of the seasonal dummy variables are found to be similar, implying that the pattern of seasonality has remained relatively constant over the sample period. An exception is the logGED series of which the results tentatively suggest that seasonal unit roots may be present.

Seasonality can be either deterministic or stochastic. Conventional augmented Dickey-Fuller (ADF) tests cannot detect seasonal unit roots. Hylleberg, Engle, Granger and Yoo (1990; henceforth HEGY) developed a test for unit roots at zero, semi-annual and annual frequencies for seasonally unadjusted data. [8] The HEGY regression of the following form is run[9]:

$$a_t = \alpha + \delta t + \gamma_1 S_{1t} + \gamma_2 S_{2t} + \gamma_3 S_{3t} + \pi_1 b_t + \pi_2 c_t + \pi_3 d_t + \pi_4 e_t + \varepsilon_t \quad (6.5)$$

where

$a_t = (1 - L^4)\, y_t;$
$b_t = (1 + L + L^2 + L^3) y_{t-1};$
$c_t = -(1 - L + L^2 - L^3) y_{t-1};$
$d_t = -(1 - L^2) y_{t-2};$
$e_t = -(1 - L^2) y_{t-1};$

L is the lag operator and ε_t are independently and identically distributed error terms.

Using the critical values tabulated by HEGY (1990), the hypotheses to be tested are:

   (i) H_0: $\pi_1 = 0$ (zero frequency unit root) against H_A : $\pi_1 < 0$;
   (ii) II_0: $\pi_2 = 0$ (semi-annual unit root) against H_A : $\pi_2 < 0$; and
   (iii) H_0: $\pi_3 = \pi_4 = 0$ (annual unit root) against H_A : $\pi_3 \neq 0$ or $\pi_4 \neq 0$

The last column of Table 6.3 suggests the appropriate differencing filter to apply in order to obtain stationarity. For those series with the suggested filter (1–L), conventional ADF tests may be used. In addition, the series that exhibit deterministic seasonality (Y, TOT, MFDX) require the inclusion of seasonal dummy variables in the error correction model to capture the pattern of seasonality. Series exhibiting stochastic seasonality (TOUR, GS, GED, GEC) require the appropriate differencing filter and seasonal dummy variables to induce stationarity and account for the seasonal pattern.

Nonstationarity and Unit Root Tests

Regressing nonstationary series will almost always lead to biased estimates and hence wrong inferences will be drawn since the conventional t- and F-tests are designed based on the assumptions of the classical linear regression model. Engle and Granger (1987) found that among the seven test statistics they considered, the ADF test was most favoured. This test will be used here. The ADF regression to be run is

$$\Delta Y_t = \alpha + \beta Y_{t-1} + t_i + \sum_{j=1}^{J} \delta_j \Delta Y_t \, _j + \varepsilon_t \qquad (6.6)$$

where ΔY_t, α and ε_t are defined in (6.4); and t is a deterministic time trend.[10] Using critical values from the Dickey-Fuller distribution, the hypothesis to be tested is H_0: $\beta = 0$ (presence of a unit root) against H_A: $\beta < 0$.

Table 6.3 HEGY test for seasonal integration

Variable[a]	H_0:π_1=0	H_0:π_2=0	H_0:π_3=0	H_0:π_4=0	H_0:π_3=π_4	Differencing filter
Y	−1.65	−4.899*	−4.993*	−4.299*	34.646*	$(1-L)$
TOT	−3.327	−3.324*	−3.980*	−4.403*	25.517*	$(1-L)$
MFDX	−2.208	−3.487*	−4.864*	−5.232*	49.923*	$(1-L)$
TOUR	−2.295	−2.117	−5.886*	−4.361*	48.962*	$(1-L^2)$
GS	−2.937	−2.612	−4.448*	0.753	10.635*	$(1-L^2)$
GEC	−1.931	−2.059	−2.519	−1.087	4.239	$(1-L^4)$
GED	−3.102	−2.368	−3.827	0.136	7.355*	$(1-L^2)$
CPF[b]	−2.083	−4.571*	−3.997	−5.716*	39.281*	$(1-L)$
CPI[b]	−2.564	−4.437*	2.779*	−7.537*	44.080*	$(1-L)$
INV[b]	−3.004	−3.906*	−6.334*	−4.367*	55.738*	$(1-L)$

Notes: [a] All variables are in logarithms.

[b] HEGY regressions do not include seasonal dummy variables.

* denotes significance at 5% level.

The results in Table 6.4 suggest that CPI is stationary while the other series require first differences to induce stationarity in the data. The four series exhibiting seasonal unit roots are not included since the differencing filter used in the ADF test is inappropriate. Determining the appropriate differencing filter is important otherwise OLS estimates of each correction model may be biased.

Structural Breaks

It has been shown that structural changes in the series tend to bias the conventional tests for a unit root toward non-rejection. Perron's (1989) test procedure suffers from the drawback that there is a single change in the structure occuring at a known time. If such an event cannot be accounted for by experience, the test becomes a meaningless exercise. The hypotheses are specified as follows:

A.   One-time jump in the level of the series:

H_0: $Y_t = \alpha + \phi Y_{t-1} + \mu_1 D_p + \varepsilon_t$ against H_A : $Y_t = \alpha + r_t + \mu_2 D_L + \varepsilon_t$

Table 6.4   ADF test results for levels, first differences and diagnostic test statistics

Variable[1]	ADF Statistic[2]	95% critical value	Suggested I(d)	H_0: no serial correlation	H_0: homo–scedasticity
Y	ADF(7) = –0.362	–3.485	1	F(4,46)=1.581	F(1,58)=1.796
ΔY	ADF(6) = –3.793	–2.910	0	F(4,48)=1.854	F(1,58)=0.224
TOT	ADF(3) = –3.280	–3.480	1	F(4,54)=1.749	F(1,62)=0.022
ΔTOT	ADF(2) = –7.695	–2.907	0	F(4,56)=2.505	F(1,62)=0.621
MFDX	ADF(4) = –2.878	–3.481	1	F(4,52)=0.695	F(1,61)=1.189
ΔMFDX	ADF(2) = –4.728	–2.907	0	F(4,56)=2.110	F(1,62)=0.325
CPI	ADF(1) = –4.101	–3.478	0	F(4,58)=1.528	F(1,64)=1.200
CPF	ADF(1) = –1.498	–3.478	1	F(4,58)=2.232	F(1,64)=0.098
ΔCPF	DF = –4.478	–2.906	0	F(4,60)=1.991	F(1,64)=1.769
INV	DF = –2.894	–3.477	1	F(4,60)=1.463	F(1,65)=0.023
ΔINV	DF = –7.966	–2.906	0	F(4,60)=1.83	F(1,64)=1.955

Notes: [1] All variables are in log-form.
   [2] Lag lengths are given in parentheses. ADF regressions include a constant term and a time trend is included for variables in levels. None of the computed diagnostic test statistics are statistically significant.

B.   Permanent change in magnitude of the drift term:
$H_0: Y_t = \alpha + \phi Y_{t-1} + \mu_2 D_L + \varepsilon_t$ against $H_A : Y_t = \alpha + r_t + \mu_2 D_L + \mu_3 D_T + \varepsilon_t$

C.   Change in both level and drift term of the series:
$H_0: Y_t = \alpha + \phi Y_{t-1} + \mu_1 D_p + \mu_2 D_L + \varepsilon_t$ against
$H_A : Y_t = \alpha + r_t + \mu_2 D_L + \mu_3 D_T + \varepsilon_t$

where D_p is a pulse dummy variable, $D_p = 1$ if $t = \tau + 1$ and zero otherwise; D_L is a level dummy variable, $D_L = 1$ if $t > \tau$ and zero otherwise; $D_T = t - \tau$ if $t > \tau$ and zero otherwise; and τ is the time of break. Perron's test is an extension of the unit root test in which appropriate dummy variables are now included in the DF regression.[11] For example, the regression in case A is

$$\Delta Y_t = \alpha + \beta Y_{t-1} + r_t + \mu_2 D_L + \varepsilon_t \tag{6.7}$$

The t-ratio for the null of a unit root is compared to the appropriate critical value (Table 6.5).[12]

Table 6.5   Perron's test for unit roots with a structural change

Variable	Model	Lag length	Test statistic	95% critical value
Y	A	4	−5.5414	−3.72
MFDX	A	4	−4.5833	−3.76
GEC	A	3	−1.9793	−3.76
INV	C	0	−3.1966	−4.22

Notes: The model classification follows Perron (1989, p.1364). Critical values are taken from Tables IVB and VIB in Perron (1989, pp.137–77). All variables are in log-form.

Both Y and INV have a break in the series at 1984(4) preceding the year-long recession in 1985. The economy recovered with substantial foreign investment in the manufacturing sector particularly in the electronics industry where exports were boosted (hence the break at 1987(1) for MFDX) to meet global demand for semiconductors and other peripherals. Government expenditure on infrastructural development (GEC) increased in 1990(2) to develop the tertiary sector. Transport (including construction of the Mass Rapid Transit system and highways) and communications were improved to encourage MNCs to expand their operations. The above results suggest that for Y and MFDX, including a level dummy variable in the ECM is warranted: ignoring it implies a nonstationary outcome. For GEC, a non-rejection of the null may suggest a pulse effect but note that the small sample size could have caused this result. For INV, including dummy variables did not result in a stationary process.

The purpose of this section is to specify the three alternative engines of growth, examine issues in econometric modelling and provide a description of the data used. However, the presence of seasonality and structural breaks in some series may not have yielded reliable test results as these features were treated separately.

6.4   EMPIRICAL RESULTS

Error Correction Models

Each growth engine is tested for cointegration in the hope deriving a suitable long run equilibrium relationship for inclusion in the respective ECM (see Table 6.6). However, it was found earlier that four series exhibited stochastic seasonality, implying the possible existence of seasonal cointegration. At most two seasonal unit roots are present in each model but seasonal cointegration may not be found in such relations (Kunst 1993). A simplifying assumption is that these series are treated as I (1) in order to proceed.

Table 6.6   Cointegration tests

	Y	TOT	MFDX	TOUR	T
Normalised estimates of cointegrating vectors for trade model					
Vector 1	−1.000	−0.8864	0.1023	−1.0570	0.0311
Vector 2	−1.000	−5.8192	−1.1540	2.0953	−0.0115
	Y	GS	GEC	CPF	T
Normalised estimates of cointegrating vectors for state model					
Vector 1	−1.000	0.0533	0.2294	−2.0817	0.0502
Vector 2	−1.000	0.6197	0.3201	−1.7929	0.0307
	Y	GEC	GED	INV	T
Normalised estimates of cointegrating vector for investment model					
Vector 1	−1.000	−0.1722	−1.0169	0.1940	0.0387

Notes: Estimates for trade and state are based on VAR (6) with maximal eigenvalue and trace test at 95% critical value. Estimates for investment are based on VAR(4) with trace test at 95% critical value. All variables but T are in log-form.

Some authors (Henriques and Sadorsky 1996) use information criteria to determine the order of the vector autoregression (VAR). The approach taken here is to specify various lags (n) of the VAR (subsequently denoted by VAR(n)) and apply cointegration likelihood ratio tests based on the maximal eigenvalue and trace test statistics. [13] The tests suggest the number of cointegrating vectors and their coefficients are estimated using Johansen's (1988) maximum likelihood estimation procedure. None of the estimated cointegrating vectors is perfectly consistent with theory and only the vectors deemed more reasonable are presented.

The signs for TOUR in Vector 1 and MFDX in Vector 2 are wrong while the magnitudes for TOT and TOUR in Vector 2 are too large. According to Table 6.6, the declining terms of trade for Singapore appears to be consistent with its high-value imports of capital-intensive foreign technology relative to export value of assembled components and other goods and services. Manufactured exports and to a lesser extent, tourism are responsible for generating the revenues needed to develop the economy, hence they should be positively correlated with Y.

The signs in both vectors are consistent with theory but the estimated coefficients for CPF appears to be too large. Government expenditure on security and economic services is instrumental to Singapore's success. Forced savings represent a leakage in the economy. Unless they are used entirely for productive purposes (public investment), they will only dampen growth.

The magnitudes of the estimates are reasonable but the signs on GEC and GED are wrong. It has been well established that private-sector investment has played a critical role in the East Asian 'miracle', especially in the investment-driven economies of Singapore and Hong Kong. Thus the positive correlation between Y and INV is justified.

Variables in Table 6.6 are lagged one quarter since most of them do not affect GDP within the quarter. Foreign payments for manufactured exports and returns to investment may take months before affecting GDP. For notational convenience, the cointegrating vectors are equivalently expressed as the negative of their cointegrating residuals. The error correction model for each hypothetical engine combines its respective (long run) cointegrating residuals and corresponding (short run) differenced variables. As these are stationary, OLS may be used to estimate the ECMS.

Since macroeconomic determinants of growth are considered, the variables of interest (except CPI) are expected to be positively correlated with growth. The results in Table 6.7 show that for the general model, growth in manufactured exports, government expenditure on economic services and education, and compulsory savings influence GDP growth negatively. What is of interest is the other models. For the state and investment models, Δ_4LGEC and ΔLCPF appear to have the wrong signs. One plausible explanation is that Singapore's infrastructure was already well developed and additional expenditures on upgrading over the last decade might have been counter-productive. Contrary to previous studies, growth in compulsory savings does not appear to be a significant contributor to economic growth. This result may suggest that current regulations on the withdrawal of funds are too restrictive although it does not mean that compulsory savings are not necessary for growth. For the state model, growth in government expenditure on maintaining national security contributes to economic growth by maintaining a stable and safe climate for the enterprises. This perception is bolstered by the result that stable prices appear to contribute to growth as

Table 6.7   OLS estimates of the ECMs

Regressors	General 1985(1)–1995(4)	Trade 1979(1)–1995(4)	State 1985(1)–1995(4)	Investment 1985(1)–1995(4)
Intercept	6.3460* (2.1262)	0.13056 (0.36006)	0.74174 (0.35463)	0.11568 (1.43480)
ΔLTOT	–0.20999 (1.3767)	–0.07635 (0.83729)		
ΔLMFDX	–0.00311 (0.05885)	0.03355 (0.79692)		
Δ_2TOUR	0.07545 (0.94910)	0.02644 (0.70551)		
Δ_2LGS	0.01163 (0.41173)		0.01685 (0.61901)	
Δ_4LGEC	–0.03704 1.3781)		–0.01396 (0.61447)	–0.00925 (0.5216)

ΔLCPF	-0.19444		-0.30969	
	(0.9316)		(1.3120)	
LCPI	0.21547		0.04025	
	(1.6127)		(0.70525)	
Δ_2LGED	-0.00461			0.00159
	(0.25937)			(0.1007)
ΔINV	0.07169			0.02854
	(0.47039)			(0.19303)
$\hat{R}D_1$	-0.00727	-0.00916	-0.02934	-0.01419
	(0.43902)	(0.38960)	(0.30453)	(1.1946)
$\hat{R}D_2$	-0.21633*	0.00345	-0.00417	
	(2.3784)	(0.28887)	(0.06773)	
$\hat{R}D_3$	-0.16535			
	(1.5846)			
S_1	-0.02499	-0.03569**	-0.03626**	-0.04434**
	(1.4073)	(2.2299)	(3.7040)	(3.9290)
S_2	0.00716	0.02321*	0.04113	0.02662*
	(0.14952)	(2.1831)	(1.1364)	(2.1995)
S_3	0.2077	0.01346	0.04285	0.01910
	(0.41608)	(1.5662)	(1.2074)	(1.9902)
DSLMFDX	(0.01385)	0.00848		
	(1.1914)	(1.7789)		
DPLGEC	0.01237		-0.00778	-0.00856
	(0.39683)		(0.31939)	(0.43225)

Descriptive statistics				
Adjusted R^2	0.65131	0.68347	0.64030	0.65621
S.E. of regression	0.01855	0.01727	0.01885	0.01842
F-statistic	5.2851**	16.5945**	7.9425**	10.3052**
Diagnostic test				
Serial correlation	$F(4,18)=0.4437$	$F(4,52)=1.0148$	$F(4,25)=0.4782$	$F(4,27)=0.3338$
Functional form	$F(1,21)=4.6673*$	$F(1,55)=0.0744$	$F(1,28)=3.5641$	$F(1,30)=3.4311$
Hetero-scedasticity	$F(1,38)=0.7002$	$F(1,64)=1.6035$	$F(1,38)=0.7530$	$F(1,38)=0.7048$

Notes: Dependent variable is ΔLY. The absolute values of t-ratios are given in parentheses. 'General' specification is based on VAR (1) with the maximal eigenvalue test at 95% critical value. $\hat{R}D_j$ represents the cointegrating residual where i is the number of residuals (j = 1, 2 and 3). S1, S2, S3 represent seasonal dummy variables for the first, second and third quarter respectively. The operator Δ is defined as $\Delta_k X_t = X_t - X_{t-k}$.
$\Delta = \Delta_1$
* denotes significance at 5% level.
** denotes significance at 1% level.

well. For the investment model, investment in human capital does not seem to have growth-enhancing effects although it is positively correlated with GDP growth. Private-sector investment seems also to contribute to economic growth positively but not significantly.

The adjusted R-square and F-statistics for the regressions indicate that they are useful.[14] The trade, state and investment models are also statistically adequate as the computed diagnostic test statistics reveal an absence of serial correlation, functional form misspecification and heteroscedasticity. Non-nested testing procedures are used to determine which modelled engine contributes most to sustaining growth.

Tests of Non-nested Hypotheses

Two competing models are described as non-nested when the variables in one model cannot be expressed as a linear combination of the variables in the other model.[15] The three error correction models will be tested on the basis of bi-directional paired tests where the null and alternative hypotheses are reversed for each test. McAleer (1995) argued that the Davidson-McKinnon J-test was the most popular while the Wald-type (W) and adjusted Cox (NT) tests were less frequently used despite their vintage. As each test has its strengths and weaknesses, additional tests including the Cox (N), Fischer-McAleer (JA) and F tests are employed to reduce the possibility of biased inferences.

Discussion of Results

Results in Table 6.8 are also supported by the Akaike and Schwartz-Bayesian information criteria. The trade model is favoured over the state and investment models while the investment model explains the data better than the state model. This suggests that Singapore is still highly dependent on world trade and manufactured exports to sustain its high growth rate. However, none of the variables have any significant effect on real GDP growth. This may be due to an inadequate sample size. The terms-of-trade changes are negatively correlated with GDP growth and this result appears to support Balassa's (1988) hypothesis. Singapore may be considered to be on a par with developed countries. The deterioration in terms-of-trade may be the result of maintaining price competitiveness in exports and increasing productivity that lowers the price of exports relative to imports of intermediate and capital-intensive goods which tend to have a higher price. When the number of visitors grows by one percentage point over a six-month period, real GDP grows by 0.026 of a percentage point in one quarter. Although Singapore serves as a major tourist destination, it does not appear to contribute to GDP as much as manufactured exports. For a percentage point growth in the real value of manufactures exported, real GDP grows by 0.034 of a percentage point per quarter. Manufacturing accounts for over 25 per cent of Singapore's national output with electronics making up half of total manufacturing output. Recently published statistics appear to support the empirical evidence that trade is the most important engine of growth.

Table 6.8   Tests of non-nested specifications

Test statistic	Trade v state	State v trade
N	−1.8523	−4.4882
NT	0.7015	−0.1948
W	0.7319	−0.1925
J	2.4497*	2.9552**
JA	−1.3572	−1.4284
F	0.9319	1.5717
(Decision)	(Do not reject null)	(Reject null)

Test statistic	Trade v investment	Investment v trade
N	−4.2237	−5.8834
NT	0.5249	−0.0924
W	0.5377	−0.0919
J	2.0675*	2.7981**
JA	−1.2040	−1.2213
F	0.7818	1.2407
(Decision)	(Do not reject null)	(Reject null)

Test statistic	State v investment	Investment v state
N	−2.6647**	−1.4402
NT	0.2785	0.8157
W	0.2817	0.8546
J	1.4104	1.3476
JA	0.8344	−0.6472
F	0.6767	0.5276
(Decision)	(Reject null)	(Do not reject null)

Notes: * denotes significance at 5% level.
          ** denotes significance at 1% level.

Table 6.9 shows that the manufacturing sector contracted 6.7 percent in 1997(1) due mainly to a downturn in the global electronics market. Related industries such as precision engineering and plastics were adversely affected and overall exports shrank by 2.7 percent. Quarterly GDP growth subsequently slowed to 3.8 percent. This appears to support the notion that developed countries play the role of the engine and developing countries are pulled along behind (Riedel 1984). While Lewis (1980) prescribed trade among developing countries as an alternative source of fuel, Riedel (1984) suggested that developing countries should exploit the opportunities they have in the market of developed countries. Havrylyshyn and Civan (1985) showed that intra-industry trade among NICs is generally lower than between NICs and the rest of the world. This is particularly true for Singapore and hence Riedel's view appears to be more readily acceptable. However, Lewis' (1980) view is not entirely misplaced as Singapore's success depends on the prosperity of the West.

Table 6.9   Growth rates of Singapore's main sectors (%)

| | 1996 | | 1997 |
	First quarter	Annual	First quarter
Overall growth	11.5	7.0	3.8
Manufacturing	13.6	3.4	−6.7
Construction	26.9	18.4	10.7
Commerce	10.4	6.0	3.0
Transport and communications	10.7	8.1	7.6
Financial and business services	9.1	8.2	10.5

Source: Economic Survey of Singapore, various issues.

The alternative models are rejected for several reasons. The role of the government in the state model is to create a conducive environment in order to encourage local and foreign investment. However, this role has diminished in recent years although it may not be the case at the start of economic take-off. Government expenditure on economic services and the compulsory saving scheme were found to retard growth. Investment is an important ingredient in Singapore's long-term success. However the investment model is not entirely satisfactory as investment is proxied by loans and advances and hence measurement errors are introduced.

6.5   CONCLUSIONS

This chapter has looked into the theory and evidence surrounding the debates between proponents of different engines of growth, each purporting to explain the East Asian 'miracle'. Three competing engines of growth were investigated for Singapore: trade, the role of public policy and investment. A review of the literature on the macroeconomic determinants of growth and certain issues in economic development was provided before the competing models were specified.

The role of manufactured exports has been crucial to Singapore's survival in the past and accounts for its success today. MNCs have contributed to Singapore's growth in the areas of providing capital, linking Singapore to their home markets and engaging in joint ventures with institutions in both public and private sectors. Yet others have argued that the state has implemented the appropriate policies to create conditions favourable to growth. Good macroeconomic management boosts consumer and investor confidence. Singapore has been described to be investment rather than productivity driven. Investments in physical and human capital complement each other. A decline in fertility rates permitted an improvement in the quality of education per child at school for a given level of government expenditure. TFP has been shown to be less useful in explaining economic growth given that estimates are sensitive to several factors including sample period and accuracy of data. In Singapore, the growth of output in the manufacturing sector over the 1970s was associated with zero TFP growth.

The empirical evidence suggests that trade is the driver of the Singapore economy over the 1980s and 1990s. This may not be surprising given Singapore's unique geographical advantage and established tradition as a major trading centre. However, the results should only be taken as tentative since some empirical issues are not satisfactorily accommodated. First, the sample size is small and may have contributed to insignificant estimates. Another issue concerns the inappropriate treatment of seasonal unit roots in cointegration. Many studies have investigated the direction of causality between each macroeconomic variable and real GDP growth. This may not yield any useful inferences as some variables may be closely linked and so must be considered jointly in order to explain growth satisfactorily.

A number of implications and lessons can be drawn from this study. Replicating the East Asian success may not be possible as each country is unique in terms of physical geography, initial conditions and the type of economic policies pursued. This applies to both achieving and sustaining high growth rates. The latter may be harder to target as it requires a continual global search for niche markets where scale economies may be realised so that new products can be sold at competitive prices and the cycle continued. In other words, new comparative advantages must be created over time. Lafay (1992) suggested that conservation of previously established advantages usually leads to an erosion of these advantages and probably explains why today's industrialised countries were unable to sustain their 'miracle' growth beyond the immediate post-war period. In this respect, Singapore is aiming to become a global service centre providing a plethora of financial, commercial, construction and consulting services so that it can rely less on manufactured exports characterised by high demand elasticities and extended (forward and backward) linkages to other industries. However, the valuation of services is difficult and unless further research is undertaken to effectively capture the contribution of services to economic growth, the renewal of comparative advantages in services could easily be mistaken for an economic slowdown. Further research may also be directed at the role that economic integration might play in growth. For instance, Singapore is an active foreign investor in China's special economic zones and in Vietnam. Such an arrangement is mutually beneficial as the host country can gain in much the same way as Singapore did from MNCs. while Singapore can benefit from trade with the host country and avoid problems related to land scarcity by setting up industrial parks there. Nevertheless, the Asian success depends very much on the prosperity of the West, and the link between them is trade.

NOTES

1. Dowrick (1995) noted an inconsistency with Barro's theoretical and empirical modelling.
2. See Bello and Rosenfeld (1990, p.292) for a comprehensive list of such incentives.
3. Although Singapore's per capita GDP ranks higher than that of some industrialised countries, it has yet to earn the developed country status as much of its income is still dependent on foreign technology.
4. This is achieved by levying a withholding tax on the returns of assets held by non–residents within Singapore and restricting loans in local currency to non-residents or residents for use outside Singapore.
5. Seasonally adjusted data would have simplified the analysis but are not available. Attempts to seasonally adjust the data using a technique suggested by Pindyck and Rubinfeld (1991) have not been successful.
6. This is an important variable as it contributes nearly 6 percent to GDP. Hazari and Sgro (1995) argued that the tourist moves to consume non-traded goods and services in the host country rather than the goods and services the moving to foreign countries for consumption. These goods and services and may thus be treated as exportable items but traded at the local price.
7. This differs from military expenditure alone which has been found to be negatively correlated with growth. See Choi and Beladi (1996) and Todaro (1994). Its first difference implies a measure of inflation and is used as an indicator of macroeconomic stability. This includes primary, secondary, vocational training, tertiary and others (curriculum development and related institutions). The variable is used to proxy investment in human capital.
8. See Leong (1997) for a useful discussion on the seasonality issue.
9. In the presence of serial correlation, the regression may be augmented by lagged dependent variables to remove it.
10. Equation (6.6) is a reparameterised (and augmented) version of the DF regression $Y_t = \alpha + \beta^* Y_{t-1} + \gamma_t + \mu_t$, so that the t-ratios may be computed. Note that $\beta = \beta^* - 1$.
11. The regression may be augmented by lagged first differenced dependent variables to remove any serial correlation.
12. For some series exhibiting seasonality and structural breaks, it may be more appropriate to consider unit root tests incorporating both simultaneously. This is briefly discussed in Franses (1996, pp. 323–4). Research into this area is still continuing.
13. Cheung and Lai (1993) found that the trace test is more robust to both skewness and excess kurtosis than the maximal eigenvalue test. The test results are also not presented here as the procedures are purely statistical.
14. It should be noted that the structural break dummy variables for logY and logINV are not used as including the former does not enable the application of non-nested tests while estimation of the investment model is not possible if the latter is included.
15. McAleer and Pesaran (1986) provide a comprehensive survey of the literature on nested and non-nested econometric models.

7. Asian Financial Crisis and Recovery

The 1997 Asian financial crisis caught the world by surprise. The Asian crisis differed from other currency crises in a number of fundamental respects. The key features in this regard are that the crisis was a private sector rather than a public sector problem and that there was no significant public deficit or debt build-up in the affected countries. Furthermore, the key private sector variable was investment growth, not consumption growth, so that the widening current account surpluses were not seen as being problematic (Ostry 1997).

Why the crisis became such a rout is a complex question and can probably be explained in conjunction with a number of necessary conditions for a currency crisis. These, combined with domestic financial fragility and with an element of 'herding' behavior in foreign capital and currency markets, create extreme devaluation of currencies and stock markets. It is postulated that in the presence of large foreign-exchange-denominated debt, a greater devaluation is required so that export gains will be large enough to offset debt-burden losses.

However, the Asian countries did not benefit from their increased competitiveness after the large exchange-rate depreciation following the 1997 crisis. In fact, export volumes from the crisis-affected economies responded with a notable lag. One reason for the failure to benefit from devaluation is the degree of intra-regional trade on which they depend and the fact that falling incomes in the region (and Japan) constrain their growth.

The literature on the Asian financial crisis is expanding rapidly. [1] In particular, with detailed information available over time, more rigorous studies will appear. The objective of this chapter is to present a brief review of some of the emerging issues and thus contribute to an understanding of the causes underlying the upheaval that gripped the Asian economies in late 1997. Section 7.1 looks at the background of the Asian countries before the crisis evolved. Section 7.2 discusses the various explanations advanced so far for the causes of the crisis. Section 7.3 provides further evidence on various countries in order to understand the process during which Asia collapsed into crisis. Section 7.4 analyses the consequences of the crisis. Section 7.5 sheds some light on the recovery and outlook for growth in Asia.

7.1   THE ASIAN FINANCIAL CRISIS

The Economic Background

The crisis came as such a surprise partly due to the region's long track record of economic success. In Malaysia, Indonesia and Thailand, average income more than quadrupled between 1965 and 1995, and in Korea, income rose seven fold. Average incomes in these economies climbed from 10 per cent of the US average in 1965 to around 27 per cent in 1995. Table 7.1 shows that the average life expectancy at birth rose from 57 years in 1970 to 68 years in 1995, and that the average adult literacy rate jumped from 73 to 91 per cent. Notably, the benefits of economic growth were widely shared throughout the population. Incomes of the poorest quintile of the population grew just as fast as average incomes and poverty rates fell substantially in each country.

Table 7.1   Development indicators in selected Asian countries

	Indonesia	Korea	Malaysia	Philippines	Thailand	Mean
Life expectancy at birth (years)						
1970	48	60	62	57	58	57
1995	64	72	72	66	69	69
Adult literacy rate (%)						
1970	54	88	60	83	79	73
1995	84	98	85	95	94	91
Average income of the poorest 20%						
1970	392	303	431	218	361	341
1990	908	2071	1070	435	726	1042

Source: World Bank (1997b).

The economic transformation experienced in East Asia from the 1950s to the 1990s is without precedent. East Asia has been the most rapidly growing region in the world: it has had two decades of double-digit economic growth rates. The share of measured global production accounted for by the economies of East Asia (defined here as Japan, Korea, China, Taiwan, Hong Kong, and the Association of South East Asian Nations (ASEAN) economies) has more than doubled, to reach 21 per cent, while their share of merchandise trade has risen to a similar 22 per cent (World Bank 1997b).

As shown in Table 7.2, East Asia's share of the external trade of the current 15 European Union (EU) economies rose from 6 to 21 per cent between 1965 and 1995. East Asia's share of the external trade of the North

American Free Trade Area (NAFTA) economies rose from 15 to 42 per cent during the same period. Both NAFTA and the EU now trade more with East Asia than with each other. Meanwhile, the Asian economies' internal trade has also grown just as rapidly as their external trade. Table 7.3 clearly illustrates that the share of their intra-regional trade in their total trade increased from 37 per cent in 1968 to 51 per cent in 1995, compared with North America's intra-regional trade of 36 per cent and Western Europe's 69 per cent in 1995. The Asian region's dependence on intra-regional trade is approaching that of Europe.

Table 7.2   Inter-regional trade: volume and percentage share

	East Asia	NAFTA	EU	ROW	External trade
1965					
East Asia		3.8 (39.6)	2.1(21.3)	3.8 (39.1)	9.7(100)
NAFTA	3.8 (15.1)		10.3(41.2)	10.9 (43.7)	24.9(100)
EU	1.8 (5.9)	7.2 (23.7)		21.4 (70.5)	30.4(100)
ROW	3.9 (11.9)	7 (21.2)	22.2(67)		33.1(100)
1995					
East Asia		318.1(46.2)	190.2(27.6)	180.5 (26.2)	688.8 (100)
NAFTA	196.0 (42.4)		138.3(29.9)	127.8 (27.7)	462.1 (100)
EU	161.4 (21.3)	154.5(20.4)		441.0 (58.3)	756.9 (100)
ROW	172.9 (28.9)	113.6(19)	312.5(52.2)		598.9 (100)

Notes: The volume of trade is in billions of US dollars. The numbers in parentheses are percentage shares.

Source: World Bank (1997b).

Table 7.3   Intra-regional trade: percentage share

	1968	1979	1990	1995
Western Europe	63	66	72	69
Eastern Europe	64	54	36	19
North America	37	30	32	36
Asia	37	41	45	51
World	47	46	52	52

Source: IIF (1998).

Onset of the Crisis

No one central element in the causation of the East Asian currency crisis can be found in the dynamics of international investment flows. The role of international lenders and investors in the onset of the crisis is unclear. Wolf (1998) argued that foreign lenders, i.e. commercial banks, were the main agents in producing the rapid capital outflows and the pronounced overreaction to the underlying fundamental weaknesses. Sachs (1997b) even compared the crisis to the bank runs in Europe and the US during the 1930s.

Worries about the financial and macroeconomic environment began to affect the perceptions of investors in Thailand and Korea from early 1996. Through 1996, Thai economic commentary was focused on a slowdown in export growth and the effects of over-borrowing by a number of Thai financial firms (Warr 1997). As prominent indicators, it is useful to look at exchange rates and stock market indices.

Table 7.4   Exchange rates and stock market indices

	Indonesia	Malaysia	Philippines	Korea	Thailand
Exchange rate					
25 Jun. 1996	2432	2.52	26.4	888	25.3
3 Dec. 1997	5570	3.89	40.5	1635	47.0
24 Jun. 1998	14750	3.95	41.5	1381	41.1
Stock market index					
3 Dec. 1996	637	1238	3171	651	832
3 Dec. 1997	401	589	1869	376	366
24 Jun. 1998	431	455	1713	302	268

Note: The exchange rates are in units of domestic currency per US dollar.

Source: *Economist*, various issues.

Table 7.4 shows the changes in exchange rates and stock indices in East Asia between June 1997 and June 1998. The Thai index had been moving downwards since 1997, and there are hardly any signs of immediate recovery in 1998. The Korean index remained extremely weak. The stock market index continued to rise in Malaysia until mid-1997. By then, investment behavior was being influenced by speculative capital outflow in Thailand. The Indonesian index also continued to rise for a long time, until the devaluation and collapse of the Thai baht in July 1997.

As shown in Table 7.4, the three worst affected countries (Korea, Thailand, and Indonesia) also experienced the biggest falls in exchange rates. Malaysia and the Philippines, generally regarded as having escaped lightly, had exchange rate declines of not much less than Thailand and Korea.

7.2 UNDERSTANDING THE CRISIS

There are broadly three types of explanation, though Radelet and Sachs (1998) divide them into five groups, which have been advanced so far for the causes of the crisis. Each of these incorporates some explanation of the boom which preceded the crisis and then the factors that contributed to the bust. The first is a supply-side explanation which concentrates on aspects of investment behavior in these economies. The second explanation involves financial-structure stories, which put most of the blame on asset price booms combined with financial mismanagement followed by a bank-run type phenomenon. The third explanation involves macro-mismanagement and currency models that focus on the problem of inappropriate exchange-rate policies and open capital markets.

Supply-Side Effects

Diminishing returns to investment Before the crisis, there was debate about productivity growth and whether there had been 'too much investment' in the Asian economies. Krugman (1994), famously quoting the work of Young (1992) and Kim and Lau (1994), likened capital-intensive growth in Asian economies to that of the Soviet Union. He pointed out that 'if growth in East Asia has been primarily investment driven', then it was likely that 'capital piling up is beginning to yield diminishing returns'. That interpretation has been challenged by Radelet and Sachs (1997).

Sachs (1997b) argued that good economic policies and a favorable economic structure helped raise the returns to capital and thereby stimulate rapid investment in capital. Without those economic fundamentals, the returns to capital would be much less, and, as a result, capital accumulation would be much lower and overall growth would be much slower. However, Sachs agrees that growth is the result of capital accumulation and that it will slow down as capital deepening takes place. In East Asia, rates of return on capital have declined as capital accumulation has progressed, suggesting that both capital accumulation and growth will taper off in the future. However, this decline in profit rates is mitigated by two factors: improvement in TFP (which thereby raises the marginal productivity of capital), and high substitutability of capital for labor in the basic production function.

It is still an empirical question whether productivity growth and returns to capital have been low for some time, or high but falling. Krugman (1998a) cited capital outflow from the region as evidence that returns have been low (and he would presumably claim capital inflow since the mid-1990s as evidence of a bubble). Radelet, Sachs and Lee (1997) provided further evidence that the rate of return on capital in Korea declined gradually from around 22 per cent in the mid-1980s to about 14 per cent in 1994 and that similar declines occurred in Singapore, Hong Kong and Taiwan. While these declines do confirm the neoclassical prediction of declining returns to investment, rates of return on capital were still well above the worldwide average returns of 11 per cent on US foreign direct investment (Radelet, Sachs and Lee 1997).

In the context of the present crisis, Krugman (1998b) describes the problem as one of short-term boom 'papering over the cracks' of fundamental problems in Asia. One must assume this means that despite low and falling rates of return to investment, capital flowed into the region and domestic investment continued at high rates of growth like a bubble. When the bubble subsequently burst, the fundamental fissures opened up. However, Radelet and Sachs (1998) argued that it would be misleading to attribute the entire massive contraction to the inevitable consequences of deep flaws such as cronyism in the Asian economies.

Regardless of interpretations of the TFP debate, the difficulty is how to explain why adjustment was not smooth and slow in a normal, neo classical process. Krugman's Pangloss investment story may explain why investment boomed despite falling rates of return (although his explanation of the breaking of the cycle depends crucially on a dramatic change of regime as implicit guarantees are suddenly withdrawn) (Krugman 1998a). However, the theory underlying his account of the interaction between the short-term breaking of the bubble and a worsening of the long-term trend of diminishing returns (or that the breaking of the bubble 'revealed' the longer-term trend which had previously not been recognized), is not clear.

Worsening terms of trade   Another variety of 'supply-side' story is the China factor. Here the idea is that the other Asian economies have gradually lost competitiveness in important standardized export commodities but that China has had an overvalued exchange rate and internal difficulties that held back competition. The resolution of those difficulties and the devaluation of the yuan in 1994 were equivalent to a negative productivity shock to the other Asian Tigers (though the IMF in 1998 noted that appropriately trade-weighted the shock of the yen depreciation was much larger).[2] In a model incorporating expectations, the impact of this is immediate and severe as expectations of growth are rapidly revised downward with a predictable impact on asset values and stock markets. The result is that previously valid lending for investment projects is now invalidated.

Financial Structure

Immediately after the currency crisis began to build momentum, favored explanations used the well-developed currency crisis model. As the differences between the Asian experience and those in Europe and Latin America have become better appreciated, attention has shifted elsewhere.

Krugman vs. Radelet and Sachs An explanation by Krugman acknowledged in descriptive terms the role played by the collapse of asset prices in creating a solvency crisis but analytically still relied on the currency-crisis model. Krugman (1998b) argued that the Asian crisis had very little to do with currencies or even monetary issues per se, but rather was mainly about bad banking and its consequences. These explanations try to capture some observed facts, such as the build-up of private bank debt, the development of bad loans, different regulatory regimes, lack of transparency, and some government guarantees leading to moral hazard.

Krugman (1998d) emphasized moral hazard as the central motivating factor in the onset of the Asian crisis, although he agreed that it was essentially a symptom of a banking crisis, or more generally, of an internal financial crisis. Krugman modeled the crisis by assuming that domestic financial intermediaries enjoyed implicit government guarantees in case of default and therefore undertook excessively risky investment projects based primarily on highest possible return rather than expected value. This investment behavior would then lead to asset over-valuation, i.e. the resulting market prices in equity markets would not be sustainable in the absence of moral hazard if investors had to bear the full risk of their investment decisions.

In such a setting, a crisis would ensue as soon as investment risk materialized and economic agents ceased to expect government bailout in future cases. If the conditions for moral hazard are removed while equity prices are still over-valued, rapid asset price deflation is bound to follow. This will reduce financial intermediaries' debt-equity ratios in a constrained domestic scenario but even more so if the deflationary contraction is accompanied by a currency outflow and a devaluation in the presence of a significant foreign-denominated debut exposure.

This description appears to fit the South East Asian events up to a point, in particular so far as there was indeed an asset price bubble that burst prior to the onset of the adverse currency movements (Corsetti, Pesenti and Roubini 1998). However, Radelet and Sachs (1998) doubted the importance of moral hazard problems arising from implicit government guarantees. One should bear in mind that the affected South East Asian economies were relatively open to trade before they embarked on financial liberalization. If the domestic currency is not allowed to appreciate as capital flows in, it is likely to lead to a relative asset price increase in non-tradable sectors. This kind of development could also be in close correspondence to the developments observed in the region: while a peg against the US currency was maintained, asset prices in sectors such as real estate in particular rose dramatically.

Pangloss investment Krugman describes 'Pangloss investment' in both capital assets and land as a result of implicit or explicit guarantees. Guarantees mean that investment goes beyond the point where the expected return is equal to the borrowing cost because investors ignore the possibility of bad outcomes. The result is over-investment or rising prices in the case of assets in fixed supply (land). In this story, financial structure matters to the extent of providing guarantees. It is possible to think of a fixed exchange rate as a form of guarantee; and a regime of fixed price non-flexible interest rates likewise.

The critical element in the bursting of the bubble is a change of regime (Weber 1997). When guarantees are no longer available (either because one has been required and found too costly or because something else causes a reduction in returns, and guarantees are withdrawn precisely because they will be needed, i.e. 'endogenous' removal of guarantees), the Pangloss values collapse, banks become insolvent and this justifies and intensifies the drop in values. Although Krugman calls this a 'self-fulfilling' financial crisis, it is in fact close to an 'efficient' bank run liquidity. The *Economist* correctly points out that the policy conclusions in Krugman's case would be: the real problem lies with banks and their regulators. International capital mobility may not maximize economic efficiency if banks are guaranteed and under-regulated, and there should be no bailout since the collapse of these bubbles is inevitable *(Economist* 1998 Jan 10).

The IMF explanation   The IMF subscribes to the moral hazard story too. Its program for Korea insisted on major changes in conglomerate governance, and were intended to weaken the large, diversified, family-owned conglomerates. The changes include such things as consolidated balance sheets for the whole conglomerate (rather than for individual firms), disclosure requirements, abolition of cross-guarantees (whereby one affiliate guarantees the debt of another), and abolition of other dubious practices (such as when one affiliate borrows money and uses the borrowed money to buy equity in another affiliate, converting the debt into what appears to be equity, spuriously raising the 'equity' base of the second affiliate) (IMF 1998a). All these are justified partly by the argument that if lenders had had better knowledge of their borrowers' situations, and if there had been more 'transparency', they would have lent less, because of being less confident of implicit government guarantees.

Knock-on effect   Edison, Luangaram and Miller (1998) presented the familiar description of liquidity crisis leading to insolvency crisis, exacerbating the falls in asset prices and resulting in a credit crunch with serious real consequences. From the study of Bernanke and Gertler (1995), it is shown that once an asset price bubble has burst, credit constrained borrowers who had used the asset collateral for loans will be forced into sales of the assets which will further reduce their prices. The 'knock-on' effects of these forced sales create the conditions for a magnified financial crisis. The initial downturn may be triggered either by falls in domestic asset prices or by currency devaluation which causes liquidity problems for borrowers with unhedged foreign exchange positions. The ultimate cause of the collapse, however, is still unidentified.

Financial infrastructure in Asian countries   Domestic financial systems contributed heavily to weak balance sheets and financial vulnerability in Asia, not just through the excessive quantity but also through the low quality of foreign capital flows (Davies and Vines 1998). Table 7.5 presents the extent of risk exposure in Asian banking systems at the outbreak of the crisis. Non-performing loans were the highest in 1997 in Korea (16 per cent of total assets), Thailand (15 per cent) and Indonesia (11 per cent). This compares to a non-performing loan ratio of 9.3 per cent in Mexico in early 1995, where the cost of rescuing banks was estimated at some 15 per cent of GDP on a net present value basis (Carprio and Klingebeil 1996). As the banks, with the exception of the Philippines and possibly Malaysia, were severely under-capitalized in the Asian-crisis countries (with capital-to-asset ratios estimated at 6 to 10 per cent), non-performing loans had already wiped out the total capital of banks in Korea, Thailand and Indonesia at the end of 1997.

Table 7.5   Banking system risk exposure and financial infrastructure

	Indonesia	Malaysia	Philippines	Korea	Thailand
Banking system exposure to risk (as % of assets at the end of 1997)					
Non-performing loans	11	16	8	6	15
Capital ratio	8–10	6–10	8–14	15–18	6–10
Real estate exposure	25–30	15–25	30–40	15–20	30–40
Collateral valuation	80–100	80–100	80–100	70–80	80–100
Regulatory features during the 1990s					
Bank lending to connected firms	high	high			
Government directed bank lending	yes	yes	yes	yes	yes
Bank deposit insurance	none	none	none	yes	none
Importance of state-owned bank	high			high	
Accounting standards	weak	weak		weak	weak
Enforcement of existing regulations	weak	weak	weak	weak	weak
Incentive for capital flows					
Short-term inflows	L	L	L	F	P
Long-term inflows	L	L	P	P	P
Outflows	F	L	L	F	L

Source: Folkerts-Landau et al. (1995).

Notes: L, F and P represent 'limited', 'free' and 'promoted', respectively.

As previously in Latin America, excessive real estate exposure has been a prominent feature of lending and spending boom in Asia (Ferench-Davies and Reisen 1998). Real estate exposure was estimated at 30 to 40 per cent of bank assets in Indonesia, Malaysia and Thailand, while it was somewhat lower in the Philippines and in Korea (where the bad loans were concentrated with the chaebols). The high real-estate exposure of Asian banks indicated the extent to which loans were used to finance not productive investment, but speculative demand for existing assets in fixed supply. Thus, part of the foreign inflows went into feeding speculative asset price bubbles. The excessive real-estate exposure was related to excessive collateral valuation. As shown in Table 7.5, the Philippines had the lowest real-estate exposure and the lowest collateral valuation. As the asset bubble burst, the deflating values of real estate, equities and other assets, and the falling value of loan collateral determined the extent of the non-performing loans.

In Indonesia and Korea, balance-sheet weakness in the banking system was also related to credit exposures to borrowers connected to the lending bank (Folkerts-Landau et al. 1995). Regulatory restrictions on bank ownership did not prevent banks from becoming controlled by non-bank ownership. In Korea, where the use of dummy accounts was widespread, this prevented the enforcement of restrictions against concentrations of lending to the bank shareholders.

Slacker portfolio discipline and debt imbalances which were fuelled by heavy inflows can be partly traced to government intervention in bank lending and corporate finance. Folkerts-Landau et al. (1995) pointed out that many developing countries, including all the crisis economies, had regulatory requirements to allocate fixed proportions of bank loan portfolios to particular sectors. As mandated loans carry an implicit bailout guarantee and as they are usually refinanced by the central bank at below-market interest rates, banks have little incentive to limit their credit risk.

The pursuit of growing market share led to a neglect of the cost of capital, in particular where government allocation of credit played an important role in industrial policy. 'Picking the winners' may be fairly easy during the very early stage of development, but even then it invites moral hazard and rent-seeking behavior (Vitta and Wang 1991). Once countries have moved up the global product cycle, the chance that government-led credit allocation leads to capital waste, increases disproportionately. As problem loans develop as a result of mandated lending, the implicit guarantees given by governments to the banks often obviate the need to identify such problem loans properly and to build reserves against them.

Even more endemic are the poor accounting standards and limited disclosure requirements in the emerging markets, e.g. inconsistent financial reporting, the limited power of auditors (or tax collectors) to examine company records, the lack of sanctions or incorrect reporting of information, and the issue of reliability of reported information. [3] Poor accounting standards imply that even detailed examination by supervisors and regulators may not reveal much information.

Another shortcoming in the Asia countries is the lack of enforcement of existing regulations. In fact, the Asian crisis countries tried to strengthen their supervisory and regulatory systems during the 1980s and 1990s, partly in response to costly banking crises (such as in Indonesia and Malaysia) a decade ago (Fischer and Reisen 1993). Bank regulators also imposed limits on bank lending, including liquidity requirements and exposure limits. After the crisis, countries affected also introduced risk-based capital requirements.

However, capital requirements are ineffective as long as accounting standards are ineffective. Inaccurate reporting on non-performing loans, with interest recorded as accrued for bad loans rolled over, or unclear definitions of what can be included in capital, will show up in high capital-adequacy ratios but disguise the extent of non-performing loans. Fictitious names in bank accounts make it impossible to enforce restrictions on overexposure by banks to individual or corporate counterparts.

Macro-Mismanagement and Currency Crisis Models

As noted above, early explanations of the Asian crisis, and the fundamental thinking of the IMF, were based on currency crisis models. This resulted in some debate about whether first- or second-generation models were appropriate and whether the crisis had elements of the self-fulfilling, sunspot models of Obstfeld (1994b).

First-generation model It was quickly recognized that the first-generation crisis model, put forward by Krugman (1979b), failed to explain the Asian crisis. The main insight is that crisis arises as a result of an inconsistency between an excessive public sector deficit that becomes monetized and the exchange-rate system. In this sense, a crisis is both unavoidable and predictable in an economy with a constant deterioration of its fundamentals.

As can be seen from Table 7.6, government budgets were balanced or moving into surplus (partly in appropriate fiscal response to higher net private capital flows) in the crisis economies. Growth in monetary aggregates was fairly high in all crisis countries, but cannot be described as runaway monetary expansion. Except in Thailand, inflation rates were coming down, nominal GDP growth was largely at levels corresponding to money creation, and all countries were at a stage of development where money demand was still growing.

Second-generation model The logic of the second-generation crisis model, postulated by Obstfeld (1994b), does not apply to the Asian crisis either. This literature, developed in the aftermath of the European currency crises, stresses the trade-off between the benefits of a credible exchange rate peg and the costs in terms of higher interest rates, higher unemployment or lower growth of defending the peg. There was no such trade-off in the Asian crisis countries before the crisis. Past growth was high, interest rates and sovereign yield spreads were going down, not up, and unemployment was informal (as usual in developing countries) (Wade and Veneroso 1998). Traditional second-generation crisis models cannot explain the Asian crisis.

Table 7.6   Traditional crisis indicators

	Indonesia	Korea	Malaysia	Philippines	Thailand
Government budget (% of GDP)					
1990–94	0.4	–0.4	–0.7	–1.4	3.2
1995–96	1.7	0.1	0.8	0.4	2.6
M2 (annual growth, %)					
1990–94	19.4	18	21.4	20.6	16.7
1995–96	27.2	15	20.9	23.7	14.8
Inflation rate (CPI)					
1990–1994	8.8	5.3	4.1	11.1	4.6
1995–96	8.7	4.7	4.4	8.3	5.8
Change in foreign reserves (% of GDP)					
1990–94	1.8	0.9	6.2	1.8	3.4
1995–96	2.0	0.4	1.3	2.6	0.6
Real exchange–rate appreciation (%)					
1990–1994	8	9	14	38	11
1994–1997	18	2	16	15	16
1989–96 average GDP growth (%)					
Actual	6.9	8.3	8.5	3.7	9.5
EIU forecasts	7.8	6.3	7.6	n.a	6.8
Current account (% of GDP)					
1990–94	–2.7	–1.5	–7.4	–4.5	–7.5
1995–96	–3.8	–3.4	–9.7	–5.5	–9.1
Difference	–1.1	–1.9	–1.7	–1.0	–1.6

Sources: Davies and Vines (1998), Radelet and Sachs (1998).

Conventional flow explanation   The conventional flow theory which relies on current account sustainability or real over-valuation cannot explain the Asian crisis either. There has been considerable appreciation resulting largely from the rise in the US dollar to which the Asian currencies were effectively pegged, and from the depreciation of the yen, a key competitor currency. The inappropriateness of a dollar peg for the APEC currencies had long been recognized (although it had prevented beggar-thy-neighbor policies through competitive devaluation in the region), but in no way did the estimated over-valuation of the victim currencies reach Latin American or East European dimensions. Empirical evidence shows that the estimated overvaluation did not exceed 5 per cent by mid-1997. However, by early 1998, Asian currencies were undervalued by up to 70 per cent on these estimates (Davies and Vines 1998).

'Self-fulfilling' crisis A model by Wyplosz (1998), focuses on multiple equilibria. The EMS crisis of 1992–93 has been seen as an example of self-fulfilling crisis. It has been argued that attacks had been directed at countries such as France or Denmark because markets calculated that, given the current recession and rising unemployment, the authorities would not be willing to raise interest rates to deter capital outflows (Eichegreens, Rose et al. 1995). Similarly, once Mexico devalued its exchange rate in December 1994, the markets figured out that the new administration was not as committed as the previous one to the inherited exchange-rate system.

The self-fulfilling crisis is also applicable in the context of the present crisis. Sachs (1997b) states that investors and lenders panicked, ignoring persistently sound fundamentals. Wolf (1998) says that the inconsistencies in economic fundamentals were far too modest to justify the panic reaction that followed and that some developments, such as rising account deficit and repercussions on either the exchange rate or domestic relative asset prices are inevitable and foreseeable consequences of large capital inflows.

The discrepancy in the extent of changes in economic fundamentals and consecutive investor reactions should lead one to ask how exactly investment decisions are linked to economic fundamentals. In many cases, investor behavior is unlikely to be a strictly determined function of the economic conditions of the country in question but may be directly influenced by other investors' perceptions. The problem is that international investors act on the basis of expectations rather than on judgements of economic fundamentals. This analogy easily carries over to the East Asian case where a large number of countries were dependent on a continued supply of short-term capital. The availability of short-term finance in turn is closely linked to perceptions about the future development of the capital market, i.e. ultimately it depends on investors' expectations of what other investors' average expectations are.

This also implies that in a situation of possible multiple equilibria, crises can be contagious to countries that are not confronted by immediate fundamental problems. Specifically, an economy with limited structural problems in a process of consolidation can easily be affected by a sudden change in market sentiment. If the country in question is dependent on short-term external financing, then an expectation of generalized capital flight leading to liquidity constraints can easily prove self-fulfilling and disrupt the domestic financial system. This is applicable in the context of the Asian financial crisis. When the attacks occurred in Thailand, where fundamentals were wrong, foreign currency borrowings also became a source of acute financial distress in other East Asian countries (with sound fundamentals).

7.3 FURTHER EVIDENCE

Several conclusions can be drawn from the existing literature (eg. Wyplosz 1998). First, a currency crisis is typically preceded by overvalued exchange rates, fast growth in domestic credit and current account deficit. Second, there is no clear link between fiscal policy and crises. Third, crises are followed by exchange rate under-valuation, inflation, high interest rates and an improvement in the current account. Fourth, domestic asset prices do not fall ahead of the crisis: they are often high before, and quickly decline at the time of the crisis. Fifth, in the case of developing countries, crises tend to occur when interest rates in developed countries begin to rise. Although not yet hard evidence, these stylized facts lend themselves to a number of tentative but important implications. It seems that financial market liberalization is the best predictor of currency crisis. This was true in Latin America in the 1980s, in Europe in the early 1990s and in Asia in 1997. The channels are capital inflows (which pose delicate policy problems) exposure to currency risk, and heightened volatility.

The appendix to this chapter provides country-by-country evidence during the period leading up to the crisis. A number of observations are common to most of the countries, but there are several important country differences.

Domestic Macroeconomic Balance

Real GDP growth slowed down modestly before the crisis in all countries except the Philippines, where the rate of growth was still 4.3 per cent. Current account deficits were large in Malaysia and Thailand. Moreover, cyclically adjusted and corrected for underlying FDI cover, current account imbalances were not held to be excessive in the region, given the high past growth and expected growth potential. Rather than a crisis due to conventional current-account sustainability or real overvaluation problems, the Asian crisis seems primarily a capital-account crisis of stock.

It can also be seen that unemployment data, where available, did not show significant increases. There was no significant budget deficit being recorded in any country. Government budgets were balanced or moving into surplus partly due to the appropriate fiscal response to higher net private capital flows. There was no pattern of declining official reserves (in months of imports) in any country although there were significant cross-country differences in levels.

Broad aggregate efficiency numbers also failed to support the notion that capital flows reversed as investors perceived that they were not invested efficiently. While efficiency dropped somewhat in Korea, Malaysia and Thailand, that drop may at least partly be explained by a decline in marginal productivity of capital, as high net capital flows added to high domestic investment rates. In the two poorest countries (Indonesia and the Philippines), capital efficiency actually rose during 1995–96 relative to the 1990–94 period. Thus, there is no evidence of the government's over-expansion of fiscal and monetary policy, and the need to maintain the peg.

Monetary Policy and Credit Growth

Patterns of money and credit growth varied across the countries. Nominal GDP growth was largely at levels corresponding to money creation, and all countries were at a stage of development where money demand was still growing.

Korea, Hong Kong and Singapore showed money growth rates in line with the growth of nominal GDP (with moderate and falling inflation rates). Taiwan had brought growth down to a rate in line with nominal GDP by 1995. Growth of domestic credit was high in all countries and there was a rising trend in bank credit/GDP ratio (where data are available).

The Philippines, Malaysia and Indonesia had considerably higher rates of money growth than rates of nominal GDP growth, with relatively high levels of inflation in the Philippines and Indonesia. Domestic credit growth rates in the Philippines and Indonesia were also higher than in Korea and Singapore. Thailand was mid-way between, with nominal money growth in line with GDP growth but much higher growth of domestic credit until a slowdown in 1996 and onwards.

It seems that the crisis prediction literature can partially account for the Asian crisis. It rightly points to the strong nexus between banking and currency crises. Table 7.7 shows clearly that those currencies become vulnerable to speculative attacks because of rising imbalances between real cash balances, short-term debt and official reserves. In the crisis economies, particularly during 1995 and mid-1997, lending to the private sector clearly outpaced GDP growth. Malaysia and Thailand, the two countries that experienced the highest net capital inflows, also experienced the most rapid expansion in the commercial bank sectors.

Abundant foreign supply of capital (offered at rapid falling sovereign yield spreads) and the greater ability of Asian non-bank and bank borrowers to tap the international financial markets interacted to fuel a rise in non-bank and bank foreign liabilities. In terms of foreign assets, non-bank foreign liabilities exploded in Indonesia, Korea and Thailand, while bank foreign liabilities grew quickly in the Philippines and Thailand during 1995 and mid-1997.

Rapid bank and non-bank foreign borrowing finally made Asian currencies vulnerable to an attack. When short-term foreign debt exceeded official reserves (indicated by a ratio higher than one), each creditor knew that there were not enough liquid foreign-exchange reserves. Thus, there was a race to exit. Table 7.7 shows that such a situation clearly held for Indonesia and Korea by mid-1994 and for Thailand thereafter. While Malaysia and the Philippines displayed a short-term debt/reserves ratio lower than one, they were financially open. Openness implies that M2/reserves have become the relevant indicator for financial vulnerability, as residents may try to obtain foreign currency for their domestic currency holdings. The M2/reserves ratio exceeded one in all the crisis countries, even though it stopped growing during 1995–96, except in Indonesia and Malaysia.

Table 7.7 Indicators of financial vulnerability

	Indonesia	Korea	Malaysia	Philippines	Thailand
Lending to private sector (% of GDP)					
1993	49	54	74	26	84
1996	55	62	90	48	n.a.
Foreign liabilities/foreign assets (%)					
non–bank					
1994	9.9	5.9	1.9	0.9	5.3
1997	14.0	8.5	2.4	1.5	6.7
bank					
1994	2.2	2.6	1.3	1	8.6
1997	2.8	2.7	1.8	2.6	12.4
Short-term foreign debt/reserves (%)					
1994	1.7	1.6	0.3	0.4	1.0
1997	1.7	2.1	0.6	0.8	1.5
M2/reserves (%)					
1993	6.1	6.9	2.1	4.9	4.1
1996	6.5	6.5	3.3	4.5	3.9

Notes: The short-term foreign debt/reserves are mid-year figures. Other figures are recorded at the end of the year.

Source: Corsetti et al. (1998).

Competitiveness and Export Performance

There are some interesting consistencies across countries in terms of competitiveness and export performance. Current account balances had worsened in all the countries except Singapore. The only country with a really large deficit was Thailand with a current account balance of 8 per cent.

Malaysia had also reversed a worsening trend, with a current account balance of 6 per cent.

The deficits were related to the growth of private investment, not private consumption. Ostry (1997) estimated that for the Asian countries the actual current account deficits were fairly close to 'optimal consumption-smoothing current account deficits' consistent with an increase in expectations of future growth.

Competitiveness, measured by real exchange rates, had worsened in most countries. The countries where competitiveness had declined by more than 10 per cent since 1990 were Indonesia, the Philippines, and Hong Kong. Singapore, Malaysia and Thailand were close to 10 per cent. Korea and Taiwan had virtually no decline. Despite the varied competitiveness measures all countries had experienced declines in export revenues and in export market growth.

Table 7.8 shows that the export growth in Thailand and Korea experienced a collapse and that Malaysia and Indonesia also experienced slower export growth. The most extreme case was Thailand, where the dollar value of exports actually fell 1 per cent in 1996, after two years of growth above 20 per cent. Korea's exports grew by just 4 per cent (down from 30 per cent growth in 1995), and Malaysia's by only 6 per cent (down from 26 per cent growth in 1995). Indonesia's situation was a bit different, as it registered 10 per cent export growth, about the same as in the previous three years (but well below the 1990–92 average). Only the Philippines registered substantial export growth of 19 per cent in 1996.

Table 7.8 Changes in exports from selected countries (%)

Country	Value growth		Volume growth		Change in unit value	
	1995	1996	1995	1996	1995	1996
China	22.9	1.6	15.3	8.3	6.6	–6.2
India	22.7	7.4	22.4	16.9	0.2	–8.1
Hong Kong	14.8	4	1.9	–8.6	12.6	13.8
Korea	30.3	3.7	24	19.1	5	–12.9
Singapore	22.1	5.7	15.7	6.3	5.6	–0.6
Indonesia	13.4	9.7	10.3	4.8	2.8	4.7
Malaysia	26	5.8	15.6	16.3	9	–6.9
Philippines	31.6	16.7	17	18.8	12.4	–1.8
Thailand	25.1	–1.3	14	–0.7	9.5	–0.6

Source: Radelet and Sachs (1998).

Table 7.8 also shows that the fall in dollar export earning between volume and unit value differed widely across countries. In Korea and Malaysia, export volume appears to have grown rapidly and continuously (19 and 16 per cent respectively), but the unit values of exports fell sharply. In Thailand by contrast, the volume of exports stagnated in 1996, while unit values changed little. Indonesia is an intermediate case, with much slower growth in volumes than Korea and Malaysia but greater than Thailand. The rise of China might have dramatically shifted export-oriented production away from East Asia. From a mere $20 billion in exports 20 years ago, China's $150 billion in exports in 1996 made it the eleventh largest exporter in the world. China's manufactured exports grew by more than 22 per cent per year in nominal dollar terms between 1990 and 1995. Concerns about competition from China were heightened by its effective 40 per cent devaluation of the yuan in January 1994. As Liu et al. (1998) have pointed out, this competition could be expected to put downward pressure on both wages and export growth in the rest of the region. Indeed, some observers have directly linked the 1996 decline in East Asian exports to China's 1994 devaluation.

Chinese firms compete directly with other firms in the region in textiles, apparel, electronics and in certain other products. China has clearly gained market shares. Nevertheless, while China's emergence might have affected certain markets, its overall impact on the East Asian export slowdown in 1996 was probably modest at best. After all, China's export growth also plunged in 1996, registering a rather anemic growth rate of just 1.5 per cent. Its textile exports fell 12 per cent, and its garment exports grew by just 4 per cent. China's share of total manufactured exports from the six countries was 32 per cent in 1996, actually down 2 per cent from 1994 and exactly the same as in 1992. In other words, China's presence had little impact in displacing total manufactured exports from the rest of the region between 1992 and 1996. The 1994 devaluation of the yuan also probably had a relatively limited impact, since its real effects had substantially eroded by 1996 through a gradual nominal appreciation of the yuan and two years of inflation averaging 20 per cent.

Table 7.9 shows that between 1990 and 1996, China's share of exports from these countries grew slightly from 25.8 to 27.8 per cent, while Mexico's fell slightly from 11.3 to 10.9 per cent. Relative to 1992, China's share of the total was about the same, while Mexico's share increased. The Asian countries show a different pattern. Indonesia and Korea's share of total exports from the group fell, while Malaysia's and the Philippines' rose. Thailand's share rose from 9.6 per cent in 1990 to 11 per cent in 1994, and then fell to 10.2 per cent in 1996. As a whole, the East Asian countries were not losing major market shares to China and Mexico.

Perhaps each of these factors contributed to the export slowdown in 1996, which, in turn, probably raised concerns among East Asia's creditors about the ability of firms in these countries to repay their debts. However, the effect appears to be modest. Unlike the Latin American debt crises of the 1980s, it is difficult to attribute much weight to international shocks as a critical contributor to the East Asian financial crisis.

Table 7.9   Growth rates and shares of exports (based on nominal US$)

Year	China	Indonesia	Korea	Malaysia	Philippines	Thailand	Mexico
Annual growth rates (%)							
1990	18.2	15.9	4.2	17.4	4.0	14.9	17.7
1991	15.8	13.5	10.5	16.8	8.7	23.2	0.9
1992	18.1	16.6	6.6	18.5	11.2	14.2	1.4
1993	7.1	8.4	7.3	15.7	13.7	13.3	9.2
1994	33.1	8.8	16.8	24.7	20.0	22.7	14.2
1995	22.9	13.4	30.3	26.0	31.6	25.1	40.3
1996	1.6	9.7	3.7	5.8	16.7	−1.3	22.6
Shares of exports (as % of total exports)							
1990	25.8	10.7	27.0	12.2	3.4	9.6	11.3
1991	26.5	10.7	26.4	12.6	3.2	10.5	10.1
1992	27.7	11.1	25.0	13.3	3.2	10.6	9.0
1993	27.1	11.0	24.5	14.1	3.3	11.0	9.0
1994	29.6	9.8	23.5	14.4	3.3	11.0	8.4
1995	28.9	8.8	24.3	14.4	3.4	10.9	9.4
1996	27.8	9.1	23.8	14.4	3.7	10.2	10.9

Source: Radelet and Sachs (1998).

7.4   CONSEQUENCES OF THE CRISIS

The Depth of the Slowdown in Crisis Economies

A reduction in economic activity is the inevitable result of a sharp turnaround in a country's current account. Massive capital outflow requires an immediate shift from current account deficit to surplus: by definition this requires a reduction in expenditures relative to domestic income. This is accomplished through increases in interest rates, credit constraints that limit borrowing and investment, and negative terms-of-trade effects of devaluation that reduce real domestic purchasing power (Rodrik 1998).

Along with automatic market adjustments, macroeconomic policies were tightened in an effort to restore financial market stability. The three economies operating under IMF stabilization agreements agreed to restrain fiscal policy through combinations of spending cutbacks and revenue increases, and to maintain relatively tight monetary policy conditions with high interest rates to restore demand for domestic currencies. [4] IMF requirements to close insolvent banks and to end the practice of subsidizing favored projects and loans further restricted credit and repressed economic growth.

Economies not subject to IMF assistance also implemented contractionary macroeconomic policies. Monetary contraction was forced on these economies by their determination to avoid massive devaluation. Perhaps the clearest case of this was Hong Kong, where the currency board worked to raise three-month Hong Kong interbank offer rates (HIBOR) from 6 to 12 per cent between June and November 1997 (the three-month rate soared to 25 per cent at the height of the crisis on October 23, and overnight rates went to 100 per cent) (Reisen 1997). In Malaysia, the government postponed and cancelled public projects (Stiglitz 1996). The Philippines also introduced greater monetary and fiscal stringency and closer scrutiny of lending. Malaysia and the Philippines also encouraged financial sector consolidation and enhanced prudential regulations.

The result of these adjustments was a significantly slow growth in the following two years (Table 7.10). Negative growth was recorded in a few countries, in particular in the crisis-affected economies of Indonesia, the Philippines, Korea, Malaysia and Thailand in 1998. This was down from GDP growth rates of 6 to 8 per cent per year in the decade prior to the crisis. In Hong Kong, the monetary contraction necessary to maintain the dollar peg caused a marked slowdown in consumption and investment and subsequently a negative GDP growth in 1998. Behind the 1998 downturn in these economies was a sharp drop in investment spending and in consumer confidence and expenditure.

Table 7.10   GDP growth and inflation rates for selected economies (%)

	Growth				Inflation		
	1997	1998	1999	2000	1998	1999	2000
Indonesia	4.7	−13.1	0.8	4.8	58.5	20.5	3.7
Korea	5.0	−6.7	10.7	n.a.	7.5	0.8	2.3
Malaysia	7.3	−7.4	5.8	8.5	5.3	2.7	1.5
Philippines	5.2	−0.6	3.3	3.9	9.8	6.6	4.3
Thailand	−1.7	−10.3	4.2	n.a.	8.1	0.3	1.5
Hong Kong	5.0	−5.3	3.1	10.5	2.8	−4.0	−3.7
Taiwan	6.8	4.8	5.4	6.0	1.7	0.2	1.3
Singapore	8.4	0.4	5.4	9.9	−0.3	0.0	1.3
China	8.6	7.8	7.1	8.1	−2.6	−3.0	n.a.

Sources: World Bank (2000), ADB (2001), State Statistical Bureau (2000) and various government websites.

The large devaluation experienced by these countries sparked an increase in inflation in 1998. As can be seen from Table 7.10, inflation rates were generally higher in the crisis-affected economies, with Indonesia being the worst. In addition to directly raising import prices, devaluation has increased competition between exporters and the domestic market for some agricultural staples, further raising product prices. And because of heavy reliance of industry on imported inputs, devaluation creates a significant supply shock that contributes to output declines.

Within the Asian developing economies, the effects of recession and inflation are not uniformly distributed, but are likely to lead to changes in income distribution that may have profound social and political implications. The new poor are mainly the middle-income workers who were employed in export industries and buy substantial amounts of imports (Dornbusch 1998). Layoffs and devaluation have fallen much harder on this group than on poor rural residents. General austerity has also forced cutbacks of public services and, in some cases, created food shortages for the poorest residents, layoffs of guest workers, and (for example, in Indonesia) rekindling of social problems and ethnic frictions. In Indonesia, where the contagion hit a desperately weak financial system and where the policy response was seen as inadequate, the fall in economic activity continued (Radelet and Sachs 1998). This decline in business confidence was exacerbated by uncertainty and anxiety over political succession and by the realization that economic decline is associated with social unrest and the danger of political instability. The recession immediately after the crisis pushed millions of East Asians below the poverty line and reversed the decade-long trend of steady reduction in poverty. For example, poverty rose from 11.4 per cent in 1997 to 23.2 per cent in 1998 in Korea and from 25.7 per cent in 1997 to 37 per cent in 1999 in Indonesia according to the World Bank (2001).

Transmission to Other Developing Economies

The economic crisis in Asia was transmitted to other developing economies through fall in trade and financial market contagion. Among developing countries, China was among the most dependent on exports to these countries. In 1998, China's exports recorded a rate of growth of about 0.5 per cent only, as a result of weaker demand in the crisis economies and the loss of competitiveness from devaluation in these economies (State Statistical Bureau 2000).

Sharply lower export growth also brought Singapore's growth rate down from 8.4 per cent in 1997 to 0.4 per cent in 1998. However, Taiwan only experienced modest adverse economic effects of the crisis on exports and overall activity.

For developing countries outside of Asia the direct effect will be small, since there are generally only limited trade linkages to the region. The more direct effect on other developing countries is the pure contagion effect of the crisis on loan premiums for developing country debt. Interest rate spread on Latin America bonds rose about 250 basis points in fall 1997, but declined a little in 1998 (Radelet and Sachs 1998).

7.5   RECOVERY AND OUTLOOK

By late 2000, East Asia had recovered from the 1997 financial crisis impressively (Table 7.10). Both internal and external factors contributed to the faster than expected economic revival in the crisis-affected economies.

The crisis has dislocated the use of resources, but it has not negated the years of human and physical capital accumulation and institutional development. Many of the conditions that supported sustained rapid growth remain in place, for example high savings and investment, a skilled labour force and acceptance of international economic integration. Those factors together with pragmatic policies have determined the capacity of the affected economies for recovery.

Since late 1997, policy efforts throughout the region to provide stronger structural underpinnings to growth have paid dividends in the form of more rapid growth. In particular, after a painful period of austerity, moves to more expansionary monetary policies helped the recovery. For example, the deflationary threat since 1997 in China gradually disappeared in late 2000 and early 2001.

In general, net export growth led the economic recovery in a context of weak domestic demand. The US economy, which experienced continuous growth in the 1990s, played an important role in supporting global demand. In addition, intra-regional trade in East Asia also played a part in propelling regional growth.

Following the end of the El Nino and La Nina phenomena, more favourable weather conditions have raised agricultural output in the region, especially in Indonesia and the Philippines.

The consensus is that recovery and hence growth will continue in East Asia. High growth (6 to 7 per cent) is expected in some economies, for example Korea, Malaysia, Singapore and China. Modest growth (4 to 5 per cent) is predicted for countries such as Thailand, Indonesia and the Philippines (ADB 2001). Will the recovery signal the beginning of a new era of high growth in East Asia? The answer to this question varies for each individual country in the region. In general, growth in the short run will be affected by changes in world oil prices and performance of the major economies such as the US and Japan. Prolonged high oil prices will negatively affect some of the region's economies, for example Japan. The speculated hard landing of the US economy may also affect the region's growth as the US is the largest export market. In the long run, the growth prospect of East Asia is determined by sound economic fundamentals and pragmatic government policies in the region. In addition, the region's commitment to structural reform and increasing intra-regional trade will strengthen the region's internal dynamism and resilience to external shocks, and hence its self-propelling growth momentum.

APPENDIX TO CHAPTER 7

Table A7.1 Selected economic indicators of Thailand, 1991–1998

	1991	1992	1993	1994	1995	1996	1997	1998
Macroeconomics								
Inflation	5.7	4.1	3.4	5.1	5.8	5.9	5.6	8.1
Real GDP growth	8.6	8.2	8.6	8.9	8.7	5.5	-1.3	-9.4
Current account/GDP	-7.7	-5.7	-5.1	-5.6	-8.1	-8.1	-1.9	12.5
Budget surplus/GDP	4.2	2.6	2.1	2	2.6	1.6	-0.4	
Unemployment	3.5	3.6	2.6	2.6	1.7	1.5	0.9	4.4
Total international reserves (bil. US$) [a]	17.5	20.4	24.5	29.3	36.1	37.8	26.2	28.8
Official reserves/imports (in months)	5	5.2	5.5	5.5	5.3	5.4	n.a	
Monetary policy								
Nominal money growth [b]	19.8	15.6	18.4	12.9	17	12.6	16.5	9.7
Domestic credit growth [c]	n.a	18.7	21.2	27.6	23.7	13.8	28	
Growth of credit to the private sector	20.4	20.5	24	30.3	23.8	14.6	13.6	-11.3
Bank credit to private sector/GDP [d]	67.7	72.2	80	91	97.6	101.9	116.3	
Nominal deposit rate [e]	13.7	8.9	8.5	8.5	11.6	10.3	10.5	
Real deposit rate [f]	8	4.8	5.2	3.4	5.8	4.4	4.9	

Competitiveness

Nominal exchange rate (Baht/US$) [g]	25.3	25.5	25.5	25.1	25.2	25.6	31.4	41.4
Growth of nominal export values	21	16.1	14.5	17.5	24.2	3.3	25.7	
Growth of export volumes [h]	19.4	12.1	11.7	18.4	37.1	n.a	n.a	
Exports/GDP	36	37	37.8	38.8	41.7	39.3	47	
Growth in exports/GDP	5.6	2.8	2.3	2.6	7.6	-5.9	19.7	
Growth of nominal import values	17.2	8.9	13.6	19	28.3	3.2	7.9	
Growth of import volumes [h]	8.7	7.4	11.2	16.3	n.a	n.a	n.a	
Imports/GDP	42.5	41	41.6	43.2	48	45.1	46.4	
Growth in imports/GDP	1.9	-3.6	1.4	3.9	11.2	-6	2.7	

Notes: Unless stated, the figures are percentage points.

[a] Total reserves minus gold.

[b] Annual percentage change in M2.

[c] Bank credit to private sector is domestic banks' claims on the private sector. Domestic banks comprise resident domestic banks and branches of foreign banks (balances of branches abroad are excluded).

[d] 1991 figures are from the IMF (1997a). Others are from the Bank of Thailand.

[e] The maximum rate on 3 to 6 month saving deposits offered by commercial banks.

[f] Calculated as the nominal rate less inflation.

[g] Recorded at the end of the year.

[h] Derived from the indices of the volumes of exports and imports (IMF 1997a, lines 72 and 73).

Sources: IMF (1997a, 1997b), and the Bank of Thailand.

Table A7.2 Selected economic indicators of Indonesia, 1991–1998

	1991	1992	1993	1994	1995	1996	1997	1998
Macroeconomics								
Inflation	9.5	5	10.2	9.6	9	6.6	6.2	58.5
Real GDP growth	8.9	7.2	7.3	7.5	8.2	8	5.5	5.8
Current account/GDP	-3.4	-2.1	-1.5	-1.7	-3.3	-3.3	-2.2	4.2
Budget surplus/GDP	n.a	-1.2	-0.7	n.a	0.8	1.4	2	
Unemployment	2.6	2.7	2.8	4.4	7.2	4.9	4.7	5.5
Total international reserves (bil. US$) [a]	9.3	10.4	11.3	12.1	13.7	18.3	16.6	22.7
Official reserves/imports (in months)	5.7	6.6	7.5	6.2	5	5.5	n.a	
Monetary policy								
Nominal money growth [b]	17.5	19.8	20.2	20	27.2	27.2	25.2	63.5
Domestic credit growth	18.9	14.1	21	22.9	21.7	22.7	n.a	
Growth of credit to the private sector	16.7	11.4	25.5	23	22.6	21.4	17.2	25
Bank credit to private sector/GDP [c]	50.3	49.5	48.9	51.9	53.5	55.4	62	
Nominal deposit rates [d]	23.3	19.6	14.5	12.5	16.7	17.3	20	
Real deposit rates [e]	13.8	14.6	4.4	2.9	7.7	10.6	8.4	

Competitiveness

Nominal exchange rate (Rupiah/US$) [f]	1992	2062	2110	2200	2308	2383	2909	10013
Growth of nominal export values	19.85	22.7	15.5	14.8	18	15	n.a	
Exports/GDP	27.37	29.39	26.75	26.51	26.31	25.82	n.a	
Growth in exports/GDP	3.06	7.37	-8.97	-0.91	-0.75	-1.87	n.a	
Growth of nominal import values	20.47	14.6	11.44	23.69	29.61	13	n.a	
Imports/GDP	26.98	27.07	23.77	25.37	27.65	26.66	n.a	
Current account/GDP (%)	-3.4	-2.1	-1.5	-1.7	-3.3	-3.3	-2.2	4.2
Growth in current account/GDP	-21.43	35.29	31.82	-13.33	-94.12	n.a	12.12	

Notes: Unless stated, the figures are percentage points.

[a] Total reserves minus gold.

[b] Annual percentage change in M2. The figures up to 1996 are from the IMF (1997a). 1997 figures are from Bank Indonesia.

[c] Bank credit to private sector is domestic banks' claims on the private sector. The domestic banks include all commercial banks (private national, state, regional government, foreign-owned, and joint-venture banks).

[d] Weighted average rate paid on three-month deposits at commercial banks.

[e] Calculated as the nominal rate less inflation.

[f] Recorded at the end of the year.

Sources: IMF (1997a, 1997b), the United Nations (1997) and Bank Indonesia.

Table A7.3   Selected economic indicators of Malaysia, 1991–1998

	1991	1992	1993	1994	1995	1996	1997	1998
Macroeconomics								
Inflation	4.4	4.8	3.5	3.7	5.3	3.5	2.7	5.3
Real GDP growth	8.6	7.8	8.3	9.2	9.5	8.6	7.7	-6.7
Current account/GDP	-8.8	-3.8	-4.8	-7.8	-10	-4.9	-4.7	13
Budget surplus/GDP	0.1	-3.5	-2.6	2.5	3.8	4.2	1.6	
Unemployment	4.3	3.7	3	2.9	2.8	2.5	n.a	3.2
Total international reserves (bil. US$) [a]	10.9	17.2	27.2	25.4	23.8	27	20.8	25.6
Official reserves/imports (in months)	3.3	4.7	6.2	4.5	3.3	n.a	n.a	
Monetary policy								
Nominal money growth [b]	16.9	29.2	26.6	12.7	20	25.3	17.4	-1.4
Domestic credit growth	18.5	16.6	12.3	14.8	29.5	27.4	29.2	
Growth of credit to the private sector	20.6	11.2	11.6	15.3	30.5	25.7	19.9	-2.2
Bank credit to private sector/GDP [c]	77	75.2	75.6	76.5	86.8	93.4	n.a	
Nominal deposit rates [d]	7.2	n.a	n.a	n.a	5.9	7.1	n.a	
Real deposit rates [e]	4.6	n.a	n.a	n.a	2.5	3.6	n.a	

Competitiveness

Nominal exchange rate (Ringgit/US$) [f]	2.7	2.6	2.7	2.6	2.5	2.5	2.8	3.9
Growth of nominal export values	18.5	5.6	22.6	23.5	20.1	20.1	n.a	
Exports/GDP	84	78.2	87	93.6	97.7	92	n.a	
Growth in exports/GDP	6.1	-4.7	11.2	7.6	4.4	-5.8	n.a	
Growth of nominal import values	27.7	-7.2	33.4	18.6	22.9	4.5	n.a	
Imports/GDP	91	75.6	90.3	93	99.4	91	n.a	
Growth in imports/GDP	14.3	-16.9	19.4	3	6.9	-8.5	n.a	
Current account/GDP	-8.8	-3.8	-4.8	-7.8	-10	-4.9	-4.7	13
Growth in current account/GDP	-319	57.2	-27.6	-62.5	-28.2	51	-18.4	

Notes: Unless stated, the figures are percentage points.

[a] Total reserves minus gold.

[b] Annual percentage change in M2.

[c] Bank credit to private sector is domestic banks' claims on the private sector. Domestic banks consolidate accounts of 38 commercial banks.

[d] Rate quoted for 3-month deposits.

[e] Calculated as the nominal rate less inflation.

[f] Recorded at the end of the year.

Sources : IMF (1997a, 1997b) and the United Nations (1997).

Table A7.4   Selected economic indicators of the Philippines, 1991–1998

	1991	1992	1993	1994	1995	1996	1997	1998
Macroeconomics								
Inflation	18.7	8.9	7.6	9	8.1	8.4	5.9	9.8
Real GDP growth	-0.6	0.3	2.1	4.4	4.8	5.7	5.2	-0.5
Current account/GDP	-2.3	-1.6	-5.5	-4.6	-4.4	-4.7	-5.3	2.4
Budget surplus/GDP	-2.1	-1.2	-1.6	-1.6	-1.4	-0.4	-0.9	
Unemployment	9	9.8	9.3	9.5	9.5	7.4	7.9	9.6
Total international reserves (bil. US$) [a]	3.2	4.4	4.7	6	6.4	10	7.3	9.2
Official reserves/imports (in months)	2.8	3.1	2.7	2.8	2.3	n.a	n.a	
Monetary policy								
Nominal money growth [b]	17.3	13.6	27.1	24.4	24.2	23.2	25	8.1
Domestic credit growth	-2.6	17.6	131.2	19	31.3	40.3	30.82	
Growth of credit to the private sector	7.3	25.4	39.6	26.5	25.2	48.7	20.2	-15.5
Bank credit to private sector/GDP [c]	17.8	20.4	26.4	29.1	27.5	48.4	55.9	
Nominal deposit rates [d]	18.8	14.3	9.6	10.5	8.4	9.7	10.2	
Real deposit rates [e]	0.1	5.4	2	1.5	0.3	1.3	5.1	

Competitiveness

Nominal exchange rate (Pesos/US$) [f]	26.7	25.1	27.7	24.4	26.2	26.3	40.9	39.1
Growth of nominal export values	24.6	6.6	17.4	23.8	21	33	23.2	
Exports/GDP	29.6	34	31.4	33.8	42	42	46.3	
Growth in exports/GDP	7.6	4.4	7.7	7.9	15.4	15.4	10.4	
Growth of nominal import values	13.4	13.1	27.6	15.8	35	35	19.9	
Imports/ GDP	32.6	34	39.8	40.1	51.7	51.7	55.6	
Growth in imports/GDP	-2.1	4.4	17	0.8	17.2	17.2	7.4	
Current account/GDP	-2.3	-1.6	-5.5	-4.6	-4.4	-4.7	-5.3	2.4
Growth in current account/GDP	62.3	30.4	-243.8	16.4	-6.8	-6.8	4.3	

Notes: Unless stated, the figures are percentage points.

[a] Total reserves minus gold.

[b] Annual percentage change in M2.

[c] Bank credit is credit to the private sector from domestic banks.   Domestic banks comprise commercial banks including rural banks accepting demand depostis.

[d] Deposits of one year or more at domestic banks.

[e] Calculated as the nominal rate less inflation.

[f] Recorded at the end of the year.

Sources : IMF (1997a, 1997b) and the United Nations (1997).

Table A7.5 Selected economic indicators of Korea, 1991–1998

	1991	1992	1993	1994	1995	1996	1997	1998
Macroeconomics								
Inflation	9.3	6.2	4.8	6.3	4.5	4.9	4.4	7.5
Real GDP growth	9.1	5.1	5.8	8.6	8.9	7.1	5	-5.8
Budget surplus/GDP	-1.6	-2.6	-1	1	..	..	..	
Unemployment	2.3	2.4	2.8	2.4	2	1.9	2.6	6.8
Total international reserves (bil. US$) [a]	13.7	17.1	20.2	25.6	32.7	34	20.4	52
Official reserves/imports (in months)	1.8	2.2	2.5	2.6	2.5	2.3	n.a	
Monetary policy								
Nominal money growth [b]	21.9	14.9	16.6	18.7	15.6	15.8	14.1	27
Domestic credit growth	22.4	11.7	12.7	18.4	14.7	19.4	23.3	
Growth of credit to the private sector	20.1	11.5	13.3	19.5	15.6	19.8	14.4	4.3
Bank credit to private sector/GDP [c]	52.8	53.3	54.2	56.8	57	61.8	69.8	
Nominal deposit rates [d]	10	10	8.6	8.5	8.8	7.5	10.8	
Real deposit rates [e]	0.7	3.8	3.8	2.2	4.4	2.6	6.5	

Competitiveness

Nominal exchange rate (Won/US$) [f]	760.8	788.4	808.1	788.7	844.2	844.2	951.3	1401.4
Growth of nominal export values	13.6	14.3	12.6	17.9	26.3	8.5	27.6	
Growth of export volumes [g]	9.9	8.4	6.7	14.9	23.9	19.8	24.9	
Exports/GDP	28.2	28.9	29.2	30.1	33.1	32.4	38.1	
Growth in exports/GDP	-5.5	2.6	1.3	2.9	9.8	-2.1	17.8	
Growth of nominal import values	21.4	8.8	7.1	22.6	27.3	18.2	15.2	
Growth of import volumes [g]	16.7	2	6.4	21.6	21.2	12.6	1.5	
Imports/GDP	30.6	29.9	28.8	30.8	34.2	36.4	28.8	
Growth in imports/GDP	1	-2.4	-3.6	7	10.6	6.7	6.7	
Current account/GDP (%)	-3	-1.5	0.1	-1.2	-2	-4.9	-1.7	
Growth in current account/GDP	-233.3	50	106.7	-1300	-66.7	-145	40.8	12.6

Notes: Unless stated, the figures are percentage points.

[a] Total reserves minus gold. 1997 figure is as of end of November.

[b] Annual percentage change in M2.

[c] Bank credit of private sector is domestic banks' claims on the private sector, where domestic banks include commercial and specialized banks.

[d] Maximum rate for deposits of one year to less than two years at domestic banks.

[e] Calculated as nominal rate less inflation.

[f] Recorded at the end of year.

[g] Derived from the indices of the volumes of exports and imports (IMF 1997a, lines 72 and 73 respectively).

Sources: IMF (1997a, 1997b).

Table A7.6   Selected economic indicators of Singapore, 1991–1998

	1991	1992	1993	1994	1995	1996	1997	1998
Macroeconomics								
Inflation	3.4	2.3	2.3	3.1	1.7	1.4	2	-0.3
Real GDP growth	7.3	6.2	10.4	10.5	8.8	7	9	0.3
Current account/GDP	11.2	11.3	7.4	17.1	16.9	15	17.9	25.4
Budget surplus/GDP	10.3	11.3	14.3	13.7	12	8.4	8.3	
Unemployment	1.9	2.7	2.7	2.6	2.7	2	1.8	3.2
Total international reserves (bil. US$) [a]	34.1	39.9	48.4	58.2	68.7	76.8	74.4	74.9
Official reserves/imports (in months)	5.8	6.1	6.3	6.3	6.1	6.5	n.a	
Monetary policy								
Nominal money growth [b]	12.4	8.9	8.5	14.4	8.5	9.8	10.3	30.2
Domestic credit growth	13.9	5.5	12	12.8	17.4	17.3	19.6	
Growth of credit to the private sector	12.4	9.8	15.2	15.3	20.3	15.8	10.4	9.5
Bank credit to private sector/GDP [c]	83.3	85.1	84.1	84.2	90.8	96	n.a	
Nominal deposit rates [d]	4.6	2.9	2.3	3	3.5	3.4	3.5	
Real deposit rates [e]	1.2	0.6	0	-0.1	1.8	2	1.5	

Competitiveness

Nominal exchange rate (S$/US$) [f]	1.63	1.64	1.61	1.46	1.41	1.4	1.48	1.67
Growth of export volumes [g]	13	8.8	17.9	29	15.5	6	7	
Growth of nominal import values	55.2	-7.6	-0.4	16.7	15.9	-4.6	n.a	
Growth of import volumes [g]	7	6.5	20.2	n.a	12.7	6.2	8	
Imports/GDP	12.3	10.6	9.1	138.3	17.7	15.4	n.a	
Growth in imports/GDP	39.9	-14.1	-14.4	3.6	3.8	-12.9	n.a	
Current account/GDP	11.2	11.3	7.4	17.1	16.9	15	17.9	25.4
Growth in current account/GDP	34.9	1.3	-34.8	-78.4	-1.2	-11.2	-6.7	

Notes:　Unless stated, the figures are percentage points.

[a] Total reserves minus gold. 1997 figure is as of end November.

[b] Annual percentage change in M2.

[c] Nominal rate of interest on time deposits of 12 months (not exceeding S$10,000).

[d] Deposits of 3 months.

[e] Calculated as the nominal rate less inflation.

[f] Recorded at the end of the year.

[g] Derived from the indices of the volumes of exports and imports (IMF 1997a, lines 72 and 73 respectively).

Sources : IMF (1997a, 1997b), the United Nations (1997) and the Monetary Authority of Singapore.

Table A7.7 Selected economic indicators of Hong Kong, 1991–1998

	1991	1992	1993	1994	1995	1996	1997	1998
Macroeconomics								
Inflation	11.6	9.3	8.5	8.1	8.7	6	6.5	
Real GDP growth	5.1	6.3	6.1	5.4	3.9	4.9	5.3	-5.1
Current account/GDP	7.1	5.7	7.4	1.6	-3.9	-1.3	-1.5	
Budget surplus/GDP	3.2	2.5	2.3	1.3	-0.3	2.2	4.2	
Unemployment	1.8	2	2	1.9	3.2	2.8	2.2	4.7
Total international reserves (bil. US$) [a]	28.9	35.3	43	49.3	55.4	63.8	63.4	
Official reserves/imports (in months)	8.2	8.6	10.1	10	9.1	10.9	10.7	
Monetary policy								
Nominal money growth [b]	n.a.	8.5	14.5	11.7	10.6	12.5	n.a	
Domestic credit growth	n.a	9.6	21	25	8.6	18	n.a	
Growth of credit to the private sector	n.a	10.2	20.1	19.9	11	15.8	n.a	
Bank credit to private sector/GDP	n.a	n.a	n.a	n.a	n.a	n.a	n.a	
Nominal deposit rates [c]	n.a	n.a	n.a	n.a	n.a	n.a	8.5	
Real deposit rates [d]	n.a	n.a	n.a	n.a	n.a	n.a	2	

Competitiveness

Nominal exchange rate (HK$/US$) [e]	7.77	7.74	7.74	7.73	7.74	7.73	7.74	7.75
Growth of nominal export values	18.5	20.2	13.2	11.8	15.1	4.8	n.a	
Exports/GDP	138.7	143	140.6	139.5	149.7	142.6	n.a	
Growth in exports/GDP	3.3	3.1	-1.7	-0.7	7.3	-4.7	n.a	
Growth of nominal import values	20.5	21.5	11.7	16.7	18.8	3.1	n.a	
Imports/GDP	132.1	137.6	133.6	138.3	153.2	143.6	n.a	
Growth in imports/GDP	5	4.2	-3	3.6	10.7	-6.2	n.a	
Current account/GDP	7.1	5.7	7.4	1.6	-3.9	-1.3	-1.5	
Growth in current account/GDP	n.a	-19.7	29.8	-78.4	-343.8	66.7	-15.4	

Notes: Unless stated, the figures are percentage points.

[a] Figures for 1993 reflect accounting policies adopted in 1994. Figures for 1991 and 1992 have not been restated. 1993 figures are as of end March.

[b] Annual percentage change in M2.

[c] Nominal rate of interest on time deposits of 12 months (not exceeding HK $10,000).

[d] Calculated as the nominal rate less inflation.

[e] Recorded at the end of the year.

Sources: IMF (1997a, 1997b), the United Nations (1997) and Hong Kong Monetary Authority.

Table A7.8   Selected economic indicators of Taiwan, 1991–1998

	1991	1992	1993	1994	1995	1996	1997	1998
Macroeconomics								
Inflation (% per annum)	3.6	4.5	2.9	4.1	3.7	3.1	0.9	
Real GDP growth (% per annum)	7.6	6.8	6.3	6.5	6	5.7	6.8	4.9
Current account/GDP	6.7	3.8	3	2.6	1.9	5.2	4.2	
Budget surplus/GDP	0.5	0.3	0.6	0.2	0.4	0.2	0.2	
Unemployment	1.5	1.5	1.5	1.6	1.8	2.6	2.7	2.8
Total international reserves (bil. US$) [a]	82.4	82.3	83.6	92.5	90.3	88	83.5	
Monetary policy								
Nominal money growth [b]	19.4	19.1	15.4	15.1	9.4	9.1	8	
Domestic credit growth [c]	26.3	28.9	20.6	15.4	11.2	8.9	9.2	
Growth of credit to the private sector	21.2	28.7	19.3	16.2	10	6	8.9	
Bank credit to private sector/GDP	109.1	126.4	136.8	146.8	148.8	144.1	145.2	
Nominal deposit rates [d]	8.3	7.8	7.6	7.3	6.7	6	6	
Real deposit rates [e]	4.7	3.2	4.7	3.2	2.9	2.9	5.1	

Competitiveness

Nominal exchange rate (NT$/US$) [f]	25.7	25.4	26.6	26.2	27.3	27.5	28.7	33.46
Growth of nominal export values	13.2	1.5	12.2	8.2	19.5	8	10.7	
Growth of export volumes [g]	10.9	4	3.9	6.1	5.7	5.2	7.1	
Exports/GDP	47.4	43.4	44.2	44.1	48.8	48.6	49.4	
Growth in exports/GDP	1.4	-8.5	2	-0.3	10.6	-0.5	1.7	
Growth of nominal import values	14.6	6.9	12.9	8.2	19.9	3.6	13.7	
Growth of import volumes [g]	13.4	13.4	5.4	2.6	8.6	1.1	19.4	
Imports/GDP	42.9	41.3	42.4	42.2	46.8	44.7	46.7	
Growth in imports/GDP	2.6	-3.7	2.6	-0.3	10.9	-4.5	4.6	
Current account/GDP	6.7	3.8	3	2.6	1.9	5.2	4.2	
Growth in current account/GDP	0	-43.3	-21.1	-13.3	-26.9	173.7	-19.2	

Notes: Unless stated, the figures are percenatge points.

[a] Total reserves minus gold.

[b] Annual percentage change in M2.

[c] Domestic credit figures from the Centrl Bank of China (1992-Q1 1998 observations) consolidate the accounts of monetary institutions and the post saving system. 1991 figure is from the IMF (1997b).

[d] Rates paid on one-year deposits by the banks.

[e] Calcualted as the nominal rate less inflation.

[f] Recorded at the end of the year.

[g] Calculated from the indices of the volumes of exports and imports (IMF1997a, lines 72 and 73 respectively).

Sources: IMF (1997a, 1997b), the United Nations (1997) and the Central Bank of China.

NOTES

1. For example, see Corsetti, Pesenti and Roubini (1998).
2. Refer to IMF (1998b).
3. For Latin America, see Rojas-Suarez and Weisbrod (1996).
4. See IMF (1998b).

Bibliography

Abd-el-Rahman, K. (1991), 'Firms' competitive and national comparative advantages as joint determinants of trade composition', *Weltwirtschaftliches Archiv*, **127**(1), 83-97.

Abramovitz, Moses (1986), 'Catching up, forging ahead, and falling behind', *Journal of Economic History*, **46**(2), 385-406.

ADB (Asian Development Bank) (2001), 'Asian recovery report 2001', mimeo, Asian Recovery Information Centre, Asian Development Bank.

Aigner, D.J., Lovell, C.A.K. and Schmidt, P.J. (1977), 'Formulation and estimation of stochastic frontier models', *Journal of Econometrics*, **6**(1), 21-37.

Akdogan, H. (1996), 'A suggested approach to country selection in international portfolio diversification', *Journal of Portfolio Management*, **23**(1), 33-39.

Amsden, Alice H. (1985), 'The state and Taiwan's economic development', in Peter Evans, Dietrich Rueschemeyer and Theda Skocpol (eds), *Bringing the State Back*, Cambridge University Press, Cambridge.

Andersen, P. and Gruen, D. (1995), 'Macroeconomic policies and growth', in P. Andersen, J. Dwyer and D. Gruen (eds), *Productivity and Growth: Proceedings of a Conference Held at the H.C. Coombs Centre for Financial Studies*, Ambassador Press, 237-259.

Aquino, A. (1978), 'Intra-industry trade and inter-industry specialization as concurrent sources of international trade in manufacture', *Weltwirtschaftliches Archiv*, **114**, 756-762.

Arestis, P. and Demetriades, Panicos (1997), 'Financial development and economic growth: assessing the evidence', *Economic Journal*, **107**, 783-799.

Atje, R. and Jovanovic, Boyan (1993), 'Stock markets and development', *European Economic Review*, **37**, 632-640.

Azhar, A.K.M., Khalifah, N.A. and Elliott, R.J.R. (1998), 'Intra-industry trade and adjustment in ASEAN: revisiting the methodology', *Discussion Papers in Economics No. 9803*, Manchester Metropolitan University, Manchester.

Azhar, A.K.M., Khalifah, N.A. and Elliott, R.J.R. (1999), 'Analysing changes in trade patterns: the industry trade box', *Discussion Papers in Economics No. 9905*, Manchester Metropolitan University, Manchester.

Balassa, B. (1978), 'Exports and economic growth: further evidence', *Journal of Development Economics*, **5**, 181-189.

Balassa, B. (1989), 'Outward orientation', in H. Chenery and T.N. Srinivasan (eds), *Handbook of Development Economics*, vol. 2, North-Holland, Amsterdam.

Barro, R.J. (1990), 'Government spending in a simple model of endogenous growth', *Journal of Political Economy*, **98**(5), S103-126.

Barro, R.J. (1991), 'Economic growth in a cross section of countries', *Quarterly Journal of Economics*, **106**, 407-43.

Barro, R.J. (1997), *Determinants of Economic Growth: A Cross-country Empirical Study*, M.I.T. Press, Cambridge, MA.

Barro, R.J. and Lee, Jong-Wha (1993), 'International comparisons of education attainment', *Journal of Monetary Economics*, **32**(3), 363-94.

Barro, R.J. and Sala-i-Martin, Xavier (1995), *Economic Growth*, McGraw Hill, New York.

Battese, George and Coelli, Tim (1995), 'A model for technical inefficiency effects in a stochastic frontier production function', *Empirical Economics*, **20**, 325-32.

Bekaert, G. and Harvey, C.R. (1997), 'Emerging equity market volatility', *Journal of Financial Economics*, **43**, 29-77.

Bello, W. and Rosenfeld, S. (1990), *Dragons in Distress: Asia's Miracle Economies in Crisis*, Penguin Books, London.

Bencivenga, V.R., Smith, Bruce D. and Starr, Ross M. (1996), 'Equity markets transactions costs and capital accumulation: an illustration', *World Bank Economic Review*, **10**(2), 241-265.

Bernanke, B. and Gertler, M. (1995), 'Inside of black box – the credit channel of monetary policy transmission', *Journal of Economic Perspectives*, **9**(4), 257-276.

Bhide, A. (1993), 'The hidden costs of stock market liquidity', *Journal of Financial Economics*, **34**, 31-51.

Birdsall, N., Ross, D. and Sabot, R. (1995), 'Inequality and growth reconsidered: lessons from East Asia', *World Bank Economic Review*, **9**(3), 477-508.

Bollerslev, T. (1986), 'Generalised autoregressive conditional heteroscedasticity', *Journal of Econometrics*, **31**, 307-328.

Bradshaw, Y.W. and Tshandu, Z. (1990), 'Foreign capital penetration, state intervention and development in sub-Saharan Africa', *International Studies Quarterly*, **34**, 229-251.

Brulhart, M. (1994), 'Marginal intra-industry trade: measurement and the relevance for the pattern of industrial adjustment', *Weltwirtschaftliches Archiv*, **130**(3), 600-613.

Brulhart, M., Murphy, A. and Strobl, E. (1998), 'Intra-industry trade and job turnover', *GLM Research Paper No.98/4*, Centre for Research on Globalisation and Labour Markets, University of Nottingham, Nottingham.

Brulhart, M. and Thorpe, M. (1999), 'East-Asian export growth, intra-industry trade and adjustment', mimeo, University of Manchester.

Burrowes, R. (1970), 'Multiple time-series analysis of national-level data', *Comparative Political Studies*, **2**, 465-480.

Cameron, Gavin, Proudman, James and Redding, Stephen (1999), 'Openness and its association with productivity growth in UK manufacturing industry', mimeo, Bank of England.

Carprio, G. and Klingebeil, D. (1996), 'Bank insolvency: bad luck, bad policy or bad banking?', mimeo, the World Bank, Washington D.C.

Caudill, Steven B. and Ford, Jon M. (1993), 'Biases in frontier estimation due to heteroscedasticity', *Economics Letter*, **41**, 17-20.

Chalmers, I. (1991), 'International and regional integration', *ASEAN Economic Bulletin*, **12**(1), 194-209.

Chase-Dunn, C. (1975), 'The effects of international economic dependence on development and inequality', *American Sociological Review*, **40**, 720-739.

Chen, Edward K.Y. (1979), *Hyper-growth in Asian Economies*, Macmillan Press, London.

Cheung, Y.W. and Lai, K.S. (1993), 'Finite sample sizes of Johansen's likelihood ratio tests for cointegration', *Oxford Bulletin of Economics and Statistics*, **55**, 3131-328.

Choi, E.K. and Beladi, H. (1996), 'Why East Asian countries grow faster than others: a recipe for economic growth', *Journal of International Trade and Economic Development*, 5(2), 207-237.

Chou, Ji (1995), 'Old and new development models: the Taiwanese experience', in Takatoshi Ito and Anne O. Krueger (ed.), *Growth Theories in Light of the East Asian Experience*, University of Chicago Press, Chicago.

Clemente, L. (1994), 'Investing in Asia's emerging equity market', *Columbia Journal of World Business*, 29(2), 92-111.

Coe, D.T., Helpman, E. and Hoffmaister, A.W. (1997), 'North-South R&D spillovers', *Economic Journal*, 107(440), 134-149.

Coelli, Tim J. (1992), 'A computer program for frontier production function estimation: FRONTIER, version 2.0', *Economics Letters*, 39, 29-32.

Corden, W.M. (1984), 'Macroeconomic targets and instruments for a small open economy', *Singapore Economic Review*, 29(2), 27-37.

Corsetti, G., Pesenti, P. and Roubini, N. (1998), '*What caused the Asian currency and financial crisis?*', mimeo (*www.stern.nyu.edu/~nroubini/asia/AsaiHomepage.html*).

Council for Economic Planning and Development (1996), *Taiwan Statistical Data Book 1996*, Republic of China.

Davies, G. and Vines, D. (1998), 'Currency crises: multiple equilibria and the evolution of the expectations', mimeo, Institute of Economics and Statistics, Oxford University.

De Long, Bradford, J. and Summers, Lawrence H. (1991), 'Equipment investment and economic growth', *Quarterly Journal of Economics*, 106(2), 445-502.

Demirguc, A. and Levine, Ross (1996), 'Stock markets, corporate finance and economic growth: an overview', *World Bank Economic Review*, 10(2), 223-239.

DeRosa, D.A. (1995), 'Regional trading agreements among developing countries: the ASEAN example', *Research Reports*, 103, International Food Policy Research Institute, Washington DC.

Devereux, M.B. and Smith, G.W. (1994), 'International risk sharing and economic growth', *International Economic Review*, 35(3), 535-550.

DGBAS (Directorate General of Budget, Accounting and Statistics) (1998), *Statistical Yearbook of the Republic of China*, Executive Yuan, Taipei Republic of China.

Dornbusch, Rudiger (1998), 'Asian crisis themes', mimeo, M.I.T. (*http://web.mit.edu/rudi/www/asianc.html*).

Dowrick, S. (1995), 'The determinants of long-run growth', in P. Andersen, J. Dwyer, and D. Gruen (eds), *Productivity and Growth: Proceedings of a Conference Held at the H.C. Coombs Centre for Financial Studies*, Ambassador Press, 7-47.

Drake, P.J. (1977), 'Securities markets in less-developed countries', *Journal of Development Studies*, 13, 73-91.

Dufey, G. (1999), 'Asia financial markets: A pedagogic note', *Journal of Asian Business*, 15(1), 65-71.

Easterly, William and Yu, Hairong (2000), 'Global development network growth database', unpublished, the World Bank, Washington D.C.

Economist (1997), 'The Asian miracle: is it over?', March 1, 23-25.

Economic Survey of Singapore (various issues), Department of Statistics, Singapore.

Edison, H.J., Luangaram, P. and Miller, M. (1998), 'Asset bubbles, domino effects and "lifeboats"': elements of the East Asian crisis', mimeo (*http://www.stern.nyu.edu/globalmacro*).

Edwards, S. (1992), 'Trade orientation, distortions and growth in developing countries', *Journal of Development Economics*, 39, 31-57.

Edwards, S. (1998), 'Openness, productivity, growth: what do we really know', *Economic Journal*, **108**, 383-398.

Eichengrees, B., Rose, A.K., et al. (1995), 'Exchange market mayhem: The antecedents and aftermath of speculative attacks', *Economic Policy*, **21**, 249-313.

Engel, R.F. (1982), 'Autoregressive conditional heteroscedasticity with estimates of the variance of United Kingdom inflation', *Econometrica*, **50**, 987-1007.

Engle, R.F. and Granger, C.W.J. (1987), 'Co-integration and error correction: representation, estimation and testing', *Econometrica*, **55**(2), 251-276.

Falvey, R. (1981), 'Commercial policy and intra-industry trade', *Journal of International Economics*, **11**(4), 495-511.

Farrell, Michael J. (1957), 'The measurement of productive efficiency', *Journal of the Royal Statistical Society*, Series A, General, **120**, 253-82.

Feldman, R.A. and Kumar, Manmohan S. (1995), 'Emerging equity markets: growth, benefits and policy concerns', *World Bank Research Observer*, **10**(2), 181-200.

Ferench-Davis, R. and Reisen, H. (1998), *Capital Flows and Investment Performance: Lessons from the Latin American Experience*, OECD Development Centre Studies, Paris.

Finger, J.M. (1975), 'Trade overlap and intra-industry trade', *Economic Inquiry*, **13**(4), 581-589.

Finger, J.M. and De Roosa, D.A. (1979), 'Trade overlap, comparative advantage and protection', in Herbert Giersch (ed.), *On the Economics of Intra-Industry Trade Symposium*, Mohr, Tubingen.

Fischer, B. and Reisen, H. (1993), *Liberalizing Capital Flows in Developing Countries: Pitfalls, Prerequisites and Perceptivities*, OECD Development Center Studies, Paris.

Fischer, S. (1991), 'Growth, macroeconomics, and development', *NBER Macroeconomics Annual*, 329-364.

Fischer, S. (1993), 'The role of macroeconomic factors in growth', *Journal of Monetary Economics*, **32**, 485-512.

Fischer, S. (1998), 'The Asian crisis: a view from the IMF', mimeo (*http://www.imf. org/external/np/speeches/1998/012298.htm*).

Folkerts-Landau, D., Schinasi, G.J., Cassard, M., Ng, V., Reinhart, C.M. and Spencer, M.G. (1995), 'Effect of capital flows on the domestic financial sectors in APEC developing countries', *IMF Occasional Paper*, **122**, 31-57.

Franses, P.H. (1996), 'Recent advances in modelling seasonality', *Journal of Economic Surveys*, **10**(3), 299-345.

Fukasaku, K. (1992), 'Economic regionalization and intra-industry trade: Pacific-Asian perspectives', *OECD Technical Paper*, **53**, OECD, Paris.

Galenson, W. (1979), *Economic Growth and Structural Change in Taiwan: The Postwar Experience of Republic of China*, Cornell University Press, Ithaca.

George, R.L. (1989), *A Guide to Asian Stock Markets*, Longman Group (Far East) Ltd, Hong Kong.

Gersovitz, M. (1988), 'Saving and development', in H. Chenery and T.N. Srinvasan, (eds), *Handbook of Development Economics*, vol. 1, North-Holland, Amsterdam.

Geyer, Alois L.J. (1994), 'Volatility estimates of the Vienna stock market', *Applied Financial Economics*, **4**, 449-455.

Goh, K.S. (1977), *The Practice of Economic Growth*, Federal Publications, Singapore.

Goh, K.S. and Low, L. (1996), 'Beyond "miracles" and total factor productivity: the Singapore experience', *ASEAN Economic Bulletin*, **13**(1), 1-13.

Goldsmith, Raymond W. (1969), *Financial Structure and Development*, Yale University Press, New Haven.

Gray, H.P. (1983), 'Intra-industry trade: the effects of different levels of data aggregation', in P.K.M. Tharakan (ed.), *Intra-industry Trade: Empirical and Methodological Aspects*, Elsevier Science, New York.

Greenaway, D., Hine, R.C. and Milner, C. (1995), 'Vertical and horizontal intra-industry trade: a cross industry analysis for the United Kingdom', *Economic Journal*, **105**, 1505-1518.

Greenaway, D., Hine, R.C., Milner, C. and Elliott, R. (1994), 'Adjustment and the measurement of marginal intra-industry trade', *Weltwirtschaftliches Archiv*, **130**(2), 418-427.

Greenaway, D. and Milner, C. (1986), *The Economics of Intra-Industry Trade*, Basil Blackwell, Oxford.

Greenaway, D. and Milner, C. (1987), 'Intra-industry trade: current perspectives and unresolved Issues', *Weltwirtschaftliches Archiv*, **123**(1), 39-57.

Greenaway, D. and Torstensson, J. (1997), 'Back to the future: taking stock on intra-industry trade', *Weltwirtschaftliches Archiv*, **127**(3), 356-367.

Greene, W.H. (1997a), 'Frontier production functions', in M.H. Pesaran and P. Schmidt (eds.), *Handbook of Applied Econometrics II: Microeconomics*, 81-166, Blackwell, Oxford.

Greene, W.H. (1997b), *Econometric Analysis*, 3rd edition, Prentice Hall International Inc, New York.

Greenwood, J. and Jovanovic, Boyan (1990), 'Financial development, growth, and the distribution of income', *Journal of Political Economy*, **98**(5), 1076-107.

Grossman, G. and Helpman, E. (1990), 'Comparative advantage and long-run growth', *American Economic Review*, **80**(4), 796-815.

Grossman, S.J. and Stiglitz, Joseph E. (1980), 'On the impossibility of informational efficient markets', *American Economic Review*, **70**(3), 393-408.

Grubel, H. and Lloyd, P.J. (1975), *Intra-Industry Trade*, Macmillan, London.

Hale, D. (1994), 'Stock markets in the new world order', *Columbia Journal of World Business*, **29**(2), 14-28.

Hamilton, C. and Kniest, P. (1991), 'Trade liberalisation, structural adjustment and intra-industry trade', *Weltwirtschaftliches Archiv*, **127**(2), 356-367.

Hargis, H. and Maloney, Willam F. (1997), 'Emerging equity markets: are they for real?', *Journal of Financial Research*, **20**(2), 243-263.

Harris, R.D.F. (1997), 'Stock markets and development: a re-assessment', *European Economic Review*, **41**, 139-146.

Harrison, Ann (1996), 'Openness and growth: A time-series, cross-country analysis for developing countries', *Journal of Development Economics*, **48**, 419-447.

Harvey, C.R. (1989), 'Forecasts of economic growth from the bond and stock markets', *Financial Analysts Journal*, **55**(5), 38-45.

Hausman, J.A. and Taylor, W.E. (1981), 'Panel data and unobservable individual effects', *Econometrica*, **49**, 1377-1398.

Havrylyshyn, O. and Civan, E. (1983), 'Intra-industry trade among advanced developing countries', mimeo, Economic Analysis and Projection Department, International Trade and Capital Flows Division, the World Bank, Washington, DC.

Havrylyshyn, O. and Civan, E. (1985), 'Intra-industry trade among developing countries', *Journal of Development Economics*, **18**, 253-271.

Hazari, B.R. and Sgro, P.M. (1995), 'Tourism and growth in a dynamic model of trade', *Journal of International Trade and Economic Development*, **4**(2), 243-252.

Helpman, E. (1981), 'International trade in the presence of product differentiation, economies of scale and monopolistic competition: a Chamberlin-Heckscher-Ohlin approach', *Journal of International Economics*, **11**(3), 305-340.

Henriques, I. and Sadorsky, P. (1996), 'Export-led growth or growth-driven exports? The Canadian case', *Canadian Journal of Economics*, **29**(3), 540-555.

Hill, H. (1989), *Unity and Diversity: Regional Economic Development in Indonesia since 1970*, Oxford University Press, Singapore.

Hirata, A. (1988), 'Promotion of manufactured exports in developing countries', *Developing Economies*, **26**(4), 412-437.

Ho, Samuel P.S. (1978), *Economic Development of Taiwan 1860-1970*, Yale University Press, New Haven and London.

Holmstrom, B. and Tirole, Jean (1993), 'Market liquidity and performance monitoring', *Journal of Political Economy*, **101**(4), 678-709.

Hsiao, C. (1986), *Analysis of Panel Data*, Cambridge University Press, New York.

Huang, C.J. and Liu, J.T. (1994), 'Estimation of a non-neutral stochastic frontier production function', *Journal of Productivity Analysis*, **5**, 171-180.

Huff, W.G. (1995), 'What is the Singapore model of economic development', *Cambridge Journal of Economics*, **19**, 735-759.

Hughes, H. (1995), 'Why have East Asian countries led economic development?', *Economic Record*, **71**(212), 88-104.

Hylleberg, S., Engle, R.F., Granger, C.W.J. and Yoo, B.S. (1990), 'Seasonal integration and cointegration', *Journal of Econometrics*, **44**, 215-238.

IFC (various issues), *Emerging Market Database Factbook*, International Finance Corporation, Washington, DC.

IIF (Institute of International Finance) (1998), 'Capital flows to emerging market economies', mimeo (*http://www.iif.com/PublicPFD/CF-0198pde*).

IMF (1997a), *International Financial Statistics (Yearbook 1997)*, International Monetary Fund, Washington, DC.

IMF (1997b), *World Economic Outlook 1997*, International Monetary Fund, Washington, DC.

IMF (1998a), *International Capital Markets*, Annual Report, International Monetary Fund, Washington, DC.

IMF (1998b), *World Economic Outlook-Interim Assessment*, International Monetary Fund, Washington, DC.

IMF (2000), *International Financial Statistics (Yearbook 2000)*, International Monetary Fund, Washington, DC.

IMF (2001), 'World economic outlook 2001 database', International Monetary Fund (*http://www.imf.org/external/pubs/ft/weo/2001/01/data/index.htm*).

IMF (various issues), *International Financial Statistics*, International Monetary Fund, Washington DC.

Isimbabi, M.J. (1997), 'Stock markets, foreign investment and economic growth in Africa', *SAIS Review*, **17**(2), 141-152.

Ito, Takatoshi (1995), 'Comment', in Takatoshi Ito and Anne O. Krueger (eds), *Growth Theories in Light of the East Asian Experience*, University of Chicago Press, Chicago.

Jefferis, K. (1995), 'The Botswana share market and its role in financial and economic development', *World Development*, **23**(4), 663-678.

Jensen, M.C. and Murphy, Kevin J. (1990), 'Performance pay and top-management incentives', *Journal of Political Economy*, **98**(2), 225-264.

230   *The Macroeconomics of East Asian Growth*

Johansen, S. (1988), 'Statistical analysis of cointegration vectors', *Journal of Economic Dynamics and Control*, **12**, 231-254.

Jorgenson, W. Dale and Fraumeni, Barbara M. (1981), 'Relative prices and technical change', in Ernst R. Berndt and Barry C. Field (eds.), *Modeling and Measuring National Resource Substitution*, M.I.T. Press, Cambridge, MA.

Keynes, J.M. (1936), *The General Theory of Employment, Interest and Money*, Macmillan, London.

Khalifah, N.A. (1996), 'AFTA and intra-industry trade', *ASEAN Economic Bulletin*, **12**(3), 351-368.

Kim, J. and Lau, L. (1994), 'The sources of economic growth of the East Asia newly industrialised countries', *Journal of the Japanese and International Economies*, **8**, 235-271.

Klevmarken, N.A. (1989), 'Panel studies: what can we learn from them?' *European Economic Review*, **33**, 523-529.

Kol, J. and Mennes, L.B.M. (1989), 'Corrections for trade imbalance: a survey', *Weltwirtschaftliches Archiv*, **125**, 703-717.

Korajczyk, Robert A. (1996), 'A measure of stock market integration for developed and emerging markets', *World Bank Economic Review*, **19**(2), 276-289.

Kormendi, R.C. and Meguire, P.G. (1985), 'Macroeconomic determinants of growth: cross-country evidence', *Journal of Monetary Economics*, **16**, 141-163.

Kritzman, M. (1991a), 'What practitioners need to know about estimating volatility', part 1, *Financial Analysts Journal*, **47**(4), 22-25.

Kritzman, M. (1991b), 'What practitioners need to know about estimating volatility', part 2, *Financial Analysts Journal*, **47**(5), 10-11.

Krueger, A. (1995), 'East Asian experience and endogenous growth theory', in Takatoshi Ito and Anne O. Krueger (eds.), *Growth Theories in Light of the East Asian Experience*, University of Chicago Press, Chicago.

Krugman, P. (1979a), 'Increasing returns, monopolistic competition and international trade', *Journal of International Economics*, **70**, 469-479.

Krugman, P. (1979b), 'A model of balance of payments crises', *Journal of Money, Credit and Banking*, **11**, 311-325.

Krugman, P. (1981), 'Intra-industry specialization and the gains from trade', *Journal of Political Economy*, **89**(5), 959-973.

Krugman, P. (1991a), 'Increasing returns and economic geography', *Journal of Political Economy*, **99**(3), 483-499.

Krugman, P. (1991b), *Geography and Trade*, M.I.T. Press, Cambridge, Mass.

Krugman, P. (1994), 'The myth of Asia's miracle', *Foreign Affairs*, **73**, 62-78.

Krugman, P. (1995), 'The miracle of the sausage-makers', *The Economist*, 9 December, 25-26.

Krugman, P. (1998a), 'Fire sale FDI', mimeo (*http://web.mit.edu/krugman/www.FIRESALE.html*).

Krugman, P. (1998b), 'Asia: what went wrong', *Fortune*, March 2.

Krugman, P. (1998c), 'What happened to Asia?', mimeo (*http://www.mit.edu/krugman/www.DISINTER.html*).

Krugman, P. (1998d), 'I told you so', mimeo (*http://web.mit.edu/krugman/www.I-told-you-so-html*).

Kumbhakar, S., Ghosh, S. and McGuckin, J. (1991), 'A generalised production frontier approach for estimating determinants of inefficiency in US dairy farms', *Journal of Business and Economic Statistics*, **9**(3), 279-286.

Kunst, R.M. (1993), 'Seasonal cointegration in macroeconomic systems: case studies for small and large European countries', *Review of Economics and Statistics*, **75**(2), 325-330.

Kuo, S., Ranis, G. and Fei, J. (1981), *The Taiwan Success Story: Rapid Growth with Improved Distribution of Income in the Republic of China, 1952-1979*, Westview Press, Boulder.

Kuznets, Simon (1974), 'Modern economic growth: findings and reflections', in Simon Kuznets, *Population, Capital, and Growth: Selected Essays*, Heinemann Educational Books, London, 165-184.

Kuznets, Simon (1989), 'A note on production structure and aggregate growth', in Simon Kuznets, *Economic Development, the Family, and Income Distribution: Selected Essays*, Cambridge University Press, Cambridge, Chapter 2, 30-46.

Kyle, A.S. (1984), 'Market structure, information, futures markets and price formation', in Gary G. Storey, Andrew Schmitz and Alexander H. Sarris (eds.), *International Agricultural Trade: Advanced Readings in Price Formation, Markets Structure and Price Instability*, Westview Press, Boulder, Colorado.

Lafay, G. (1992), 'The measurement of revealed comparative advantages', in M. Dagenais and P.A. Muet (eds), *International Trade Modelling*, Chapman and Hall, New York.

Laffont, J.J. and Tirole, Jean (1988), 'Repeated auctions of incentive contracts, investment, and bidding parity with an application to takeovers', *RAND Journal of Economics*, **19**(4), 516-537.

Lancaster, K. (1980), 'Intra-industry trade under perfect monopolistic competition', *Journal of International Economics*, **10**(2), 151-175.

Leong, K. (1997), 'Seasonal integration in economic time series', *Mathematics and Computers in Simulation*, **43**(3-6), 413-419.

Levine, R. (1991a), 'Stock markets, growth and tax policy', *Journal of Finance*, **46**(4), 1445-1465.

Levine, R. (1991b), 'Financial development and economic growth: views and agenda', *Journal of Economic Literature*, **35**(2), 688-726.

Levine, R. (1996), 'Stock markets: a spur to economic growth', *Finance and Development*, **33**(1), 7-10.

Levine, R. and Renelt, D. (1992), 'A sensitivity analysis of cross-country growth regressions', *American Economic Review*, **82**(4), 942-963.

Levine, R. and Zervos, Sara (1996), 'Stock market development and long-run growth', *World Bank Economic Review*, **10**(2), 323-339.

Levine, R. and Zervos, Sara (1998a), 'Stock markets, banks and economic growth', *American Economic Review*, **88**(3), 537-558.

Levine, R. and Zervos, Sara (1998b), 'Capital control liberalisation and stock market development', *World Development*, **26**(7), 1169-1183.

Lim, D. (1996), *Explaining Economic Growth: A New Analytical Framework*, Edward Elgar, Cheltenham.

Lipsey, R.E. (1976), 'Review of Herbert G. Grubel and P.J Lloyd (eds), Intra-Industry Trade', *Journal of International Economics*, **6**, 312-314.

Liu, Li-gang, Noland, M., Robinson, S. and Wang, Zhi (1998), 'Asian competitive devaluation', *Working Paper* 98-2, institute for international economics (*http://www.iie.com/98-2.htm*).

Lovell, C.A. Knox (1996), 'Applying efficiency measurement techniques to the measurement of productivity change', *Journal of Productivity Analysis*, **7**, 329-40.

Low, S.K. and Mitra, D. (1998), 'A study of risk and return in developed and emerging markets from a Canadian perspective', Mid-Atlantic Journal of Business, 34(1), 75-91.

Lucas, R. (1988), 'On the mechanics of economic development', Journal of Monetary Economics, 22(1), 3-42.

Lucas, R. (1993), 'Making a miracle', Econometrica, 61(2), 251-272.

Maddison, Angus (1998), Chinese Economic Performance in the Long Run, OECD Development Centre, Paris.

Mankiw, N.G. (1995), 'The growth of nations', Brookings Papers on Economic Activity, part 1, 275-326.

Mankiw, N.G., Romer, D. and Weil, David N. (1992), 'A contribution to the empirics of economic growth', Quarterly Journal of Economics, 107(2), 407-38.

Markusen, J.R. and Venables, A.J. (1996), 'The theory of endowment, intra-industry and multinational trade', CEPR Discussion Paper No.1341, London.

Mbaku, J.M. (1994), 'The political economy of development: An empirical analysis of the effects of the institutional framework on economic development studies', Comparative International Development, 29(2), 3-22.

McAleer, M. (1995), 'The significance of testing empirical non-nested models', Journal of Econometrics, 67, 149-171.

McAleer, M. and Pesaran, M.H. (1986), 'Statistical inference in non-nested econometric models', Applied Mathematics and Computation, 20, 271-311.

McCombie, J.S.L. and Thirlwall, A.P. (1994), Economic Growth and the Balance of Payment Constraint, St. Martin's Press, New York.

Meeusen, W. and van den Broeck, J. (1977), 'Efficiency estimation from Cobb-Douglas production functions with composed error', International Economic Review, 18(2), 435-44.

Monthly Bulletin of Statistics (various issues), Statistical Office of the United Nations, New York.

Monthly Digest of Statistics Singapore (various issues), Department of Statistics, Singapore.

Morishima, M. (1982), Why Has Japan Succeeded?, Cambridge University Press, Cambridge.

Myers, Raymon H. (1984), 'The economic transformation of the Republic of China on Taiwan', China Quarterly, 99, 500-28.

Neary, J.P. (1985), 'Theory and policy of adjustment in an open economy', in D. Greenaway (ed), Current Issues in International Trade, Macmillan, London.

Nelson, D.B. (1991), 'Conditional heteroscedasticity in asset returns: a new approach', Econometrica, 59, 347-370.

Nelson, Richard R. (1990), 'Acquiring technology', in Hadi Soesastro and Mari Pangesto (eds), Technological Challenge in the Asia-Pacific Economy, Allen & Unwin, Sydney.

Nishimizu, M. and Page, J.M. (1982), 'Total factor productivity growth, technological progress and technical efficiency change: dimensions of productivity change in Yugoslavia, 1965–78', Economic Journal, 92, 920-36.

Obstfeld, M. (1994a), 'Risk-taking, global diversification and growth', American Economic Review, 84(5), 1310-1329.

Obstfeld, M. (1994b), 'The logic of currency crises', Cahiers Economiques et Banque de France, 43, 189-213.

Oliveras, J. and Terra, I. (1997), 'Marginal intra-industry trade index: the period and aggregation choice', Weltwirtschaftliches Archiv, 133(1), 170-178.

Ostry, J.D. (1997), 'Current account imbalances in ASEAN countries: are they a problem?', *IMF Working Papers*, WP/97/51, Asia and Pacific Department, IMF.

Pack, H. (1994), 'Endogenous growth theory: intellectual appeal and empirical shortcoming', *Journal of Economic Perspectives*, **8**(1), 55-72.

Pagan, A.R. and Schwert, G.W. (1990), 'Alternative models for conditional stock volatility', *Journal of Econometrics*, **45**, 267-290.

Park, B.U., Sickles, R.C. and Simar, L. (1998), 'Stochastic panel frontiers: a semiparametric approach', *Journal of Econometrics*, **84**, 273-301.

Perron, P. (1989), 'The great crash, the oil price shock, and the unit root hypothesis', *Econometrica*, **57**(6), 1361-1401.

Pindyck, R.S. and Rubinfeld, D.L. (1991), *Econometric Models and Economic Forecasts*, 3th edition, McGraw-Hill, New York.

Psacharopoulos, George (1973), *Returns to Education: An International Comparison*, Josey Boss, San Francisco.

Quah, D.T. (1996), 'Empirics for economic growth and convergence', *European Economic Journal*, **94**, 56-73.

Radelet, S. and Sachs, J. (1997), 'Asia's re-emergence', *Foreign Affairs*, **76**(6), 44-59.

Radelet, S. and Sachs, J. (1998), 'The onset of the East Asia financial crisis', mimeo (http://www.stern.nyu.edu/globalmacro/).

Radelet, S., Sachs, J. and Lee, J. W. (1997), 'Economic growth in Asia', *Development Discussion Paper, No.89*, Harvard Institute for International Development, Harvard University.

Ray, E.J. (1991), 'Protection and intra-industry trade: the message to developing countries', *Economic Development and Cultural Change*, **40**(1), 169-87.

Reifschneider, D. and Stevenson, R. (1991), 'Systematic departures from the frontier: a framework for the analysis of firm inefficiency', *International Economic Review*, **32**, 715-23.

Reisen, H. (1997), 'The limits of foreign savings', in R. Hausmann and H. Reisen (eds.), *Promoting Savings in Latin America*, IDB/OECD, Washington, 233-264.

Riedel, J. (1984), 'Trade as an engine of growth in developing countries: revisited', *Economic Journal*, **94**, 56-73.

Rivera-Batiz, L.A. and Romer, P.M. (1991), 'International trade with endogenous technological change', *European Economic Review*, **35**(4), 971-1004.

Rodrik, Dani (1998), 'Who needs capital account convertibility', mimeo, University of Harvard (*http://www.nber.org/~drodrik/essay.PDF*).

Rojas-Suarez, L. and Weisbrod, S. (1996), 'Building stability in Latin America financial markets', in R. Hausmann and H. Reisen (eds), *Securing Stability and Growth in Latin America*, OCED, Paris.

Romer, Paul M. (1986), 'Increasing returns and long-run growth', *Journal of Political Economy*, **94**(5), 1002-37.

Romer, Paul M. (1994), 'The origins of endogenous growth', *Journal of Economic Perspectives,* **8**(1), 3-22.

Rostow, W.W. (1960), *The Stages of Economic Growth*, 2nd edition, Cambridge University Press.

Sachs, J. (1997a), 'The limits of convergence: nature, nurture and growth', *The Economist*, June 14, 19-22.

Sachs, J.D. (1997b), 'The wrong medicine for Asia', *The New York Times*, November 3.

Sachs, J.D. and Warner, A. (1995), 'Economic reform and the process of global integration', *Brookings Papers on Economic Activities*, **1**, 1-118.

Sala-i-Martin, Xavier (1997), 'I just ran two million regressions', *American Economic Review (Papers and Proceedings)*, **87**, 178-83.

Sanjaya, Lall (1996), *Learning from the Asian Tigers: Studies in Technology and Industrial Policy*, St. Martin's Press, New York.

Sarel, M. (1995), 'Growth in East Asia: what we can and what we cannot infer from it', in P. Andersen, J. Dwyer and D. Gruen (eds), *Productivity and Growth: Proceedings of a Conference Held at the H.C. Coombs Centre for Financial Studies*, Ambassador Press, 237-259.

Sarel, Michael (1996), 'Growth and productivity in ASEAN economies', paper prepared for the *Conference on Macroeconomic Issues Facing ASEAN Countries*, November, 7-8, Jakarta.

Schwert, G.W. (1989), 'Why does stock market volatility change over time?', *Journal of Finance*, **44**, 1115-1153.

Shaked, A. and Sutton, J. (1984), 'Natural oligopolies and international trade', in H. Kierzkowski (ed.), *Monopolistic Competition and International Trade*, Oxford University Press, Oxford.

Shleifer, A. and Vishny, Robert W. (1986), 'Large shareholders and corporate control', *Journal of Political Economy*, **94**(3), 461-488.

Simon, Denis Fred (1992), 'Taiwan's emerging technological trajectory: creating new forms of comparative advantage', in Denis Fred Simon and Michael Y.M. Kau (eds), *Taiwan: Beyond the Economic Miracle*, M.E Sharpe, New York.

Singh, A. (1993), 'The stock market and economic development: should developing countries encourage stock markets?', *UNCTAD Review*, **4**, 1-28.

Singh, A. (1997), 'Financial liberalisation, stock markets and economic development', *Economic Journal*, **107**, 771-782.

Singh, A. and Weisse, Bruce A. (1998), 'Emerging stock markets, portfolio capital flows and long-term economic growth: micro and macroeconomic perspectives', *World Development*, **26**(4), 607-622.

Smith, Ben and Jordan, James (1990), 'Trade transformation and technology transfer', in Hadi Soesastro and Mari Pangesto (eds), *Technological Challenge in the Asia-Pacific Economy*, Allen & Unwin, Sydney.

So, M.K.P., Lam, K. and Li, W.K. (1997), 'An empirical study of volatility in seven southeast Asia stock markets using ARV models', *Journal of Business Finance and Accounting*, **24**(2), 261-275.

Solow, R.M. (1956), 'A contribution to the theory of economic growth', *Quarterly Journal of Economics*, **70**, 65-94.

Solow, R.M. (1957), 'Technical change and the aggregate production function', *Review of Economics and Statistics*, **39**(3), 312-20.

Solow, R.M. (1994), 'Perspectives on growth theory', *Journal of Economic Perspectives*, **8**(1), 45-54.

State Statistical Bureau (2000), *China's Statistical Yearbook 2000*, China's Statistical Publishing House, Beijing.

Stiglitz, J.E. (1985), 'Credit markets and the control of capital', *Journal of Money, Credit and Banking*, **17**(2), 133-152.

Stiglitz, J.E. (1993), 'The role of the state in financial markets', *Proceedings of the World Bank Annual Conference on Development Economics*, 19-52.

Stiglitz, Joseph (1996), 'Some lessons from the East Asia miracle', *World Bank Research Observer*, **11** (2), 151-177.

Sudweeks, B.L. (1989), *Equity Market Development in Developing Countries*, Prager Publishers, New York.

Summers, Robert and Heston, Alan (1991), 'The Penn World table (mark 5): an expanded set of international comparisons, 1950–1988', *Quarterly Journal of Economics*, **106**(2), 327-68.

Syrquin, Moshe (1988), 'Patterns of structural change', in H. Chenery and T.N. Srinivasan (eds), *Handbook of Development Economics*, vol 1, North Holland, Amsterdam.

Taylor, S.J. (1994), 'Modeling stochastic volatility', *Mathematical Finance*, **4**, 183-204.

Thirlwall, A.P. (1994), *Growth and Development*, 5th edition, Macmillan, London.

Thom, R. and McDowell, M. (1999), 'Measuring marginal intra-industry trade', *Weltwirtschaftliches Archiv*, **135**(2), 48-61.

Todaro, M.P. (1994), *Economic Development*, 5th edition, Longman, New York.

Toh, Mun-Heng and Low, Linda (1996), 'Differential total factor productivity in the four dragons: the Singapore case', *Journal of International Trade and Economic Development*, **5**(2), 161-81.

Tsao, Y. (1985), 'Growth without productivity: Singapore manufacturing in the 1970s', *Journal of Development Economics*, **18**, 25-38.

United Nations (1989), 'Classification by broad economic categories', *Statistical Papers, Series M No. 53*, United Nations Publications, New York.

United Nations (1997), *Statistical Yearbook for Asia and the Pacific 1997*, Economic and Social Commission for Asia and the Pacific, Bangkok.

United Nations (various issues), *Statistical Yearbook for Asia and the Pacific*, Economic and Social Commission for Asia and the Pacific, Bangkok.

United Nations (various years), *International Trade Statistics Yearbook*, vol. I, United Nations Publications, New York.

USAID (1992), *Philippines: Barriers to Entry Study – Final report (Vol. I and II)*, United States Agency for International Development, Washington DC.

van Elkan, Rachael (1995), 'Accounting for growth in Singapore', in K. Bercusson (ed.), *Singapore: A Case Study in Rapid Development*, IMF Occasional Paper 119, 4-10.

Velloor, R. (1999), 'Call to speed up trade pacts', *The Straits Times*, October 1, Singapore.

Vitta, D. and Wang, B. (1991), 'Credit policy in Japan and Korea: a review of the literature', *World Bank Working Paper Series*, **747**, Washington, DC.

Vona, S. (1991), 'On the measurement of intra-industry trade: some further thoughts', *Weltwirtschaftliches Archiv*, **127**, 678-700.

Wade, Robers and Veneroso, Frank (1998), 'The Asian crisis: high debt model vs the Wall-Street-Treasury-IMF complex', Russell Sage Foundation, March 2 (*http://www.epn.org/stage/imf24.html*).

Warr, P. (1993), *The Thai Economy in Transition*, Cambridge University Press, Cambridge.

Warr, P. (1997), *Asia Pacific Profiles*, FT Newsletter and Management Reports, Hong Kong.

Weber, A. (1997), 'Sources of currency crises: an empirical analysis', University of Bonn *Discussion Paper*, no. B-418, University of Bonn.

Wolf, Martin (1998), 'Flows and blows', *Financial Times*, March 3.

Woo, Wing Thye (1998), 'Chinese economic growth: sources and prospects', in M. Fouquin and F. Lemoine (eds), *The Chinese Economy*, Economica Ltd, Paris.

World Bank (1993), *The East Asian Miracle: Economic Growth and Public Policy*, Oxford University Press, New York.

World Bank (1995), *World Development Report*, Oxford University Press, New York.

World Bank (1997a), *China 2020: Development Challenges in the New Century*, Washington DC.

World Bank (1997b), *World Development Report 1997*, Oxford University Press, New York.

World Bank (1998), *World Development Indicators*, World Bank, Washington, DC.

World Bank (2000), '*East Asia brief*', mimeo, East Asia and Pacific Region, World Bank, Washington, DC.

World Bank (2001), '*World savings database*', mimeo (*http://www.worldbank.org/ research/projects/savings/data.htm*).

Wyplosz, C. (1998), 'Globalised financial markets and financial crises', Geneva, internet.

Young, Alwyn (1992), 'A tale of two cities: factor accumulation and technical change in Hong Kong and Singapore', *NBER Macroeconomics Annual*, 13-54.

Young, Alwyn (1994), 'Lessons from the East Asian NICs: a contrarian view', *European Economic Review*, **38**(3/4), 964-73.

Young, Alwyn (1995), 'The tyranny of numbers: confronting the statistical realities of the East Asian growth experience', *Quarterly Journal of Economics*, **110**(3), 641-80.

Young, Alwyn (2000), 'The razor's edge: distortions and incremental reform in the People's Republic of China', *Quarterly Journal of Economics*, **115**(4), 1091-1136.

Index

correlation matrix 48
creation of liquidity 6, 31
crisis-affected economies 204, 206
cross-country
    analysis 150
    regressions 6, 25, 35, 138, 171
cross-section
    approaches 25
    regression 39
currency devaluation 192

deflationary contraction 191
depreciation 14
    rates 135
deterministic
    seasonality 173
    time trend 174
devaluation 202
diagnostic test statistics 180
differencing filter 173
diminishing returns 189
    to factors 131
disaggregation 60
    statistical 64
distortionary tax effect 166
diversification opportunities 25
dividends 206
dollar peg 197
domestic savings 3
dummy
    accounts 194
    variable 13

efficiency changes 18
emerging markets 40
endogenous technological change 149
engines of growth 3
    alternative 176
    competing 182
equity
    financing 30
    markets 26, 30
estimation results 15
export
    earning 201
    promotion schemes 141
        strategies 168
    value of 60
extent of state intervention 162

factor
    accumulation 130, 133
    endowments 59
    reallocation 89
    shares 138
financial
    crisis 1, 185, 191
    market liberalization 198
fixed-effect approach 39
flow theory 196
frontier 13
    curve 13
    framework 12
    production level 11

government
    intervention 151
    recurrent expenditure 172
Greene, W. 24, 39
growth
    determinants of 6
    factor-biased 148
    momentum 206
    regression method 6

Heckscher-Ohlin theory 59
heteroscedasticity 180
hosting economies 3
Hughes, H. 6, 132, 169
human capital 135, 151, 161
    accumulation of 163
    development of 142
    improvements in 169
    indicator of 4
    investment in 3, 180

IFC 26, 33, 39, 45, 56
IMF 14, 24, 40, 192, 195
    assistance 204
    stabilization agreements 203
imperfect
    competition 65, 133
    substitutes 59
import substitution 141
    strategy 164
incentives to save 163
income distribution 205
indicator for
    financial vulnerability 200